Justin McCarthy

A Short History of the United States

Justin McCarthy

A Short History of the United States

ISBN/EAN: 9783744748056

Printed in Europe, USA, Canada, Australia, Japan

Cover: Foto ©ninafisch / pixelio.de

More available books at **www.hansebooks.com**

A SHORT HISTORY

OF THE

UNITED STATES

BY

JUSTIN HUNTLY M'CARTHY

AUTHOR OF 'THE FRENCH REVOLUTION,' 'ENGLAND UNDER GLADSTONE,'
'AN OUTLINE OF IRISH HISTORY,' 'IRELAND SINCE THE UNION,' ETC.

LONDON
HODDER AND STOUGHTON
27 PATERNOSTER ROW
1898

TO
CECIL CLARK

PREFACE

I HAVE tried to tell in a few pages the tale of a nation. The history of the United States covers little more than a hundred years. The history of the American colonies from the hour of the earliest English settlement adds not quite two centuries more to the record. Yet another hundred years backward and the New World was unknown. Only four hundred years lie between the first voyage of Columbus and the second Presidency of Grover Cleveland. There are gaps in our knowledge of the history of Egypt greater than this, ruined spaces in the table of its lines of kings, beads dropped unheeded from its chaplet of wars and conquests and wonders. Yet no four centuries in the world's story are more momentous than America's; no single century can surpass the century of the United States. The history of the United States, of the American Colonies cannot be too well known, too deeply studied. It is the history of the growth of civilisation under conditions new to humanity, of the greatest effort for freedom, the greatest experiment in democracy ever made by men. If it taught nothing—and it can teach the historical student almost everything—it still would charm with the fascination of romance. The pages of America's chronicle are adventurous as an epic, splendid with heroic deeds, crowded with heroic figures. The Human Comedy, the Human Tragedy find a great stage and great players. This small book is no more than the key to the noble picture, the outline map to the vast continent. It directs attention to some famous names and some famous places in the hope of quickening interest towards a wider knowledge. If it does so much it will serve an honourable end.

CONTENTS

CHAPTER I

THE OLD WORLD AND THE NEW . . . . PAGE 1

CHAPTER II

PILGRIM FATHERS 25

CHAPTER III

THE OLD THIRTEEN 55

CHAPTER IV

THE INDIAN WARS 68

CHAPTER V

HOW NOT TO GOVERN 80

CHAPTER VI

THE BOSTON TEA-PARTY 95

CHAPTER VII

THE EMBATTLED FARMER . . . 111

CHAPTER VIII

BUNKER HILL . . 128

CHAPTER IX

INDEPENDENCE 145

CHAPTER X

SARATOGA AND YORKTOWN 156

CHAPTER XI

THE CRITICAL PERIOD 169

CHAPTER XII

THE SUCCESSORS OF WASHINGTON . . 181

CONTENTS

CHAPTER XIII

WAR WITH ENGLAND NUMBER TWO 192

CHAPTER XIV

FROM PRESIDENT TO PRESIDENT . . 201

CHAPTER XV

NEGRO SLAVERY 214

CHAPTER XVI

SUMTER 231

CHAPTER XVII

BULL RUN 245

CHAPTER XVIII

ARMS AND THE MEN . . 260

CHAPTER XIX

THE WAR AT SEA 278

CHAPTER XX

APPOMATTOX 292

CHAPTER XXI

AMERICA VICTRIX 303

FOOTNOTE 321

CHAPTER I

THE OLD WORLD AND THE NEW

ABOUT the year one thousand of the Christian era, the civilisation of the Eastern Hemisphere was troubled with a superstitious fear. Men believed that the end of the world was at hand, believed that the span of the earth's career was ten centuries; and, believing this, all Christendom went in fear and trembling. Yet it seems certain that in this very season of agony, a handful of European adventurers, with no thought for the threatened doom of the old world, set sail upon an unknown sea to find a new world. The story of this adventure lives in the Saga of the Red Erik, and the Saga of the Red Erik survives in the Flateyar-bók and the Hauks-bók, two precious possessions of Icelandic literature. Over the story told in the Saga of the Red Erik, scholars disputed and scholars will dispute. But it seems easy to believe, and hard to disbelieve, that sailors from Iceland found their way to the shores of Greenland before the modern world was a thousand years old, and that the modern world had not long outgrown its tenth century when other sailors from Iceland made their way farther south. Leif Erikson, the son of the Red Erik, found a land which he called Wineland the Good, and some of the wisest of modern historians believe, with show of reason, that Wineland the Good was situated on the shore of Rhode Island. Leif and his companions fought with strange natives whom they called Skraelings, and who correspond in important and curious particulars with North American Indians. Leif and his companions found many things in Wineland the Good which were to be found in New England long afterwards—foxes and bears, salmon and halibut, abundance of eider ducks, and abundance of wild grapes. It seems difficult to doubt that Leif Erikson found his way to the coast of North America, probably to that part of the coast which is now called Massachusetts Bay, and possibly to that part of the coast which lies between Cape Cod and Cape Ann.

Among the many legends of the Iroquois nation there is one which is known as the legend of the Stonish Giants. The origin of the story is unknown, but it tells of mighty men whom the Indians encountered at a remote period of their history. These giants were fabled to be clothed in a clothing that was impenetrable to the Indian spears and the Indian arrows. There is an extant Iroquois drawing which represents three savage chiefs running desperately for their lives from two pursuing giants many times larger than the flying Indians. The course of the giants is in no way checked by the showers of arrows which the Indians are directing against them. The giants appear to be enveloped in some singular kind of panoply which covers every part of them, save, apparently, their faces. Students of this picture ask if these seemingly mail-clad men could have been the Vikings who are said to have discovered America many centuries before Cabot.

THE OLD WORLD AND THE NEW 3

If the story of Wineland the Good is to be accepted, it need scarcely be surprising that the memory of the Northmen should persist as long within the memory of the Red Men as the memory of the Skraelings persisted in the memory of the descendants of the Red Erik and of Leif. At least we learn from the Sagas that the Northmen came again and again, fierce men and fiercer women who first traded with the natives and then quarrelled with them, and gave and took blows bloodily, and carried back a strange and undying story to the halls and the hearths of Iceland. Lovers of the Wineland story have striven time and again to discover definite proofs of the residence of the Northmen on the continent. There was a mill at Newport long cherished by the romantic as a Viking fortress, until it was proved to be a last century reproduction of a mill near Leamington, in England, a reproduction erected by Governor Arnold late in the seventeenth century. There was a painted stone at Dighton which was fondly supposed to be a faithful presentation of a Norse expedition, but which is now accepted as a Red Indian painting of a Red Indian hunting-expedition. The 'Skeleton in Armour' of Longfellow's poem, found at Fall River, Massachusetts, was certainly no Norse Viking, but probably a Red Indian.

We cannot know what the Skraelings were; or whether, indeed, they were the same as that copper-coloured race whom later white sailors found on the continent, and whom these sailors called Indians, because they assumed that America was a part of India. The history of the Red Indian is lost in darkness, in which science gropes helplessly, and speculation entertains itself in vain. According to Agassiz, America, as far as her physical history is concerned, has been falsely denominated the New World. 'Hers was the first dry land lifted out of the waters, hers the first shore washed by the ocean that enveloped all the earth beside; and while Europe was represented only by islands rising here and there above the sea, America already stretched an unbroken line of land from Nova Scotia to the far West.' There is no certain proof of the existence of man in the days when the mammoth and the mastodon roved over the American continent. No sign of him remains as signs remain in prehistoric Europe. If he existed, he passed away with the strange beasts and birds of that dawn of time. People have imagined that in the infinite azure of antiquity the continent was populated with races akin to those of the South, people who built splendid cities, who honoured with gorgeous temples the fantastic gods they worshipped, who commanded a rude sculpture and some skill in metal-working, who were wealthy and learned in an amazing degree for the age in which they lived, an age in which the inhabitants of Europe dwelt in caves, and fought as the wild beasts fight, and scratched strange effigies of prehistoric beasts on fragments of bone for the benefit of latter-day museums. The mysterious pyramids that are found in North America have suggested racial associations with Egypt, with India, with Central America. The mound-builders whose remains have long been the puzzle and passion of American archæologists were once thought to represent a different race from the Red Indian, though recent research has tended to lessen this belief. But all these speculations are mere conjecture. There is no positive historical evidence as to the origin of the native races of America. All we know is that through dim and lonely centuries the great processes of Nature went on ; that the seasons followed their ordained course, and that for long before the White Man came, the Red Man fished the streams and hunted the forests, and wandered over the plains, and fought and was cruel to his enemies and content with his clan, and loved and died, and began the game of life all over again. The Red Man thought himself the lord of creation until his title was disputed by the strange creatures with pale faces who took him unawares, coming up stealthily out of the sunrise and the sea, to pen him in little corners of what had once been his illimitable kingdom.

These Indians, in the period in which they are known to the rest of the world, differ greatly in degree of savagery. Professor Fiske divides them into three principal divisions, as savage Indians, barbarous Indians, and half-civilised Indians. In the uncounted hundreds of years in which the Red Men had dwelt upon the American continent, differences of race had grown up. All the Red Men had in common the same copper-coloured skins, the same black eyes, the lank, black hair, the same almost hairless faces, and the same high cheek-bones. It would seem as if their languages were formed upon the same model and subjected to the same grammatical rules, and came therefore from the same stock. But the long lapses of time and the conditions incidental to life on a vast continent brought about marked differences of size, appearance, customs, manners, and dialects. The savage Indians, such as the Athabaskans, Bannocks, and Apaches, were a nomad race, fishers and game-hunters and basket-weavers, careless of agriculture. They ranged to the west of Hudson Bay, and to the south between the Pacific and the Rocky Mountains to the north of Mexico. The barbarous Indians inhabited the regions east of the Rocky Mountains. They were fishers and hunters, too, but they had some rudimentary knowledge of agriculture, could raise maize or Indian corn, pumpkins, squashes, beans, tomatoes, sunflowers, and tobacco. They could make pottery, and instead of wandering about the world carrying wigwams with them, they lived in villages and made themselves large houses, lasting for several years. They had dogs of an inferior kind, but no cattle or domesticated animals. They had strange social customs and strange religious beliefs. All families descended from the same female ancestor formed a clan. The clan lived together in the same house, or group of houses and held all property in common, except weapons and personal ornaments. Each clan had a name, generally the name of an animal. That animal was sacred to that clan, and its image was the clan's totem, a kind of sanctified heraldic bearing.

So many clans formed a tribe. All members of the tribe were equal and free in the most democratic sense. Each clan chose its own chief or sachem, and could depose him if he failed to give satisfaction. Each clan chose a certain number of war chiefs or generals. Questions affecting the clan were settled by the clan; questions affecting the tribe in the council of the tribe composed of the sachems of the clans. These Indians had a fantastic religion, composed of a mixture of ancestor-worship, with worship of the powers of Nature. They were very brave, very hospitable in peace, and very merciless in war. They regarded fighting as the main reason for life, and no young man could hope to be married until he had killed many enemies and carried away their scalps. They put captives to death with cruel tortures. It was a point of honour with them to face torture with immovable composure, and to defy their tormentors to the last with taunts and insults. They were hospitable to those who needed hospitality; they had almost a Greek sense of the rights and privileges of a guest; their cruelty and ferocity were tempered by much that was admirable if not even amiable.

These barbarous Indians were divided into three distinct races with distinct languages: the Maskoki, who spread over a vast field of territory in the South; the Iroquois, of whom a few were in the South but the most in the North, in and about what is now New York state; and lastly, the Algonquins, who covered the most country of all, as the remainder of the Continent east of the Mississippi formed their hunting-ground. As for the half-civilised Indians, the third in Professor Fiske's division, they have almost nothing to do with the story of the United States. They are the Pueblo Indians, so called from the Pueblos or strongholds they build and dwell in. They dwelt in the mountainous country from New Mexico southward to Chili, and theirs was the vanished splendour of Aztec civilisation.

After the Vikings abandoned their short-lived hold upon Wineland the Good, the Skraelings were left in undisputed lordship of the land. It is possible that, as the centuries waxed and waned, other mariners from Europe made their way—desperate fishermen from France, desperate fishermen from England—to catch cod off Newfoundland, off Labrador. We know little of these shadowy adventurers, less real and less interesting than the Vikings. It is probable that they did not dream that they had looked upon the shores of a new world.

Nearly five hundred years had come and gone since the comrades of Erik had descended on Wineland, when a Genoese seaman wrote a letter to an Italian sage. Since the days of Aristotle, even before the days of Aristotle, men of learning had busied themselves with speculations upon the formation of the earth on which they found themselves. Aristotle believed that it was globular; so did the Arabs who studied Aristotle and his philosophy; so did many of their philosophical successors in Europe. The Genoese sailor, merchant, adventurer, mapmaker, Christopher Columbus, lapped in the tranquillity of a happy married life upon a peaceful island, conceived the idea, based upon the globular shape of the earth, of sailing westward to the Indies. One of the greatest of geographers then living was Paolo Toscanelli, the Florentine. Columbus wrote to him for his advice and counsel. Toscanelli sent him a long letter applauding his 'great and noble desire to go to the place where the spices grow,' and sending him a sailing chart of that part of the world as it existed in Toscanelli's knowledge, tempered by Toscanelli's imagination. The map has long been lost, but it has been restored easily and more than once from its description. It is, of course, a blank where the great continent, the unknown continent, lay. With the aid of this map, the ruddy, blue-eyed, white-

THE OLD WORLD AND THE NEW

haired adventurer set out in 1492 on his first voyage towards immortality.

It is scarcely a paradox to say that Columbus did not discover America. It is almost a paradox to assert that he did discover America. Columbus never dreamed of discovering a new world. He went to his death without any idea that he had discovered a new world. When he set out on what Humboldt called his conquest of reflection, his hope was to find a new way from Europe towards the wealth of Asia. When in his first voyage he sighted the Bahama Islands, and made slight examination of Cuba and Hayti, he believed that he was in some part of Asia. When in his third voyage he sighted the coast of South America, near the mouth of the Orinoco, he still believed that he beheld an Asiatic shore. On his last voyage, made in desperate rivalry to Vasco da Gama's successful expedition to Hindostan, Columbus followed the coasts of Honduras and Veragua in the vain hope of finding a strait from the Indian Ocean to the Caribbean Sea. The country which is sometimes called after him, Columbia, he never heard of, never dreamed of, never saw. The two Cabots, John and Sebastian, father and son, Genoese in the service of Henry the Seventh of England, were the first navigators since the Northmen to be directly associated with North America. In 1497 and 1498 they came upon and explored parts of the American north coast. It is not quite certain that Sebastian Cabot deserves to share his father's glory. Indeed it does not matter. Henry Stevens's formula holds good: 'Sebastian Cabot minus John Cabot equals 0.' At least John Cabot's work is unquestioned and unquestionable.

In the same years Vincent Pinzon, one of Columbus's lieutenants, accompanied by a Florentine, named Amerigo Vespucci, led an expedition from Cadiz, reached and followed the Atlantic coast of North America, as far, probably, as Chesapeake Bay. Amerigo Vespucci afterwards entered the service of Portugal, and in 1501 he piloted an expedition of three ships which explored the Brazilian coast, and afterwards sailed south-east, until driven back by Antarctic cold and ice. It was this voyage which revealed to astonished Europe the existence of the New World.

Learned geographers proposed and agreed to give the new-found world the name of America, in honour of Amerigo, according Columbus's name to the islands which the Genoese had discovered. The name of America soon appeared on what is now known as South America in the maps of the time. When it became known that the American continents were one, the name America was given to both of them, Northern and Southern alike. Vasco Nuñez de Balboa was the next of the famous adventurers in the New World. Spurred by desire for gold, and the fabled tales of Indian chiefs, he climbed the Cordillera Mountains, and beheld the waters of an unknown sea. Balboa named this sea the South Sea. A few years later it was reached by water from the Atlantic for the first time by the Portuguese Fernão da Magalhães who gave his name to the straits by which he reached the sea, which we call in his honour the Straits of Magellan. Magellan called this new sea the Pacific, and sailed boldly across its waters to his death by savage hands on the Philippine Islands. In the year of Balboa's dis-

THE OLD WORLD AND THE NEW 11

covery of the Pacific, the Spaniard, Juan Ponce de Leon, made the first attempt to found a colony within the present limits of the United States. Seeking for a kind of earthly paradise he found and named Florida. But his attempted settlement failed. He, too, a victim of savage hostility, died of his wounds in Cuba. The discovery that Cuba was an island, and its conquest, were the next steps in the story. They led in turn to the discovery and conquest of Mexico by Fernando Cortez and his companions. The brave, cruel story of adventure and exploration runs on, glittering with fairy gold. In 1526 Lucas Vasquez d'Ayllon attempted to found a settlement on Chesapeake Bay, only to perish of fever with most of those who were with him. The names of Pánfilo de Narvaez, of Francisco de Coronado belong to the search for treasure beyond Mexico. The name of Hernando de Soto is associated for ever with the Mississippi, by whose shores he died, and in whose waters his body was buried, that the Indians might not learn the folly of his assurances that the White Man was immortal.

Our concern is not close with all this pompous pageant of adventurers. Bearded Vikings with winged helmets, misty yellow-faced Mongolians, Arabian sailors on the Sea of Darkness, possible or impossible Welsh princes, who may or may not leave descendants speaking a kind of Cymric speech, astounding Venetian brethren of magnificent imagination, white-haired, ruddy-faced Genoese pioneers, English Tudor mariners, gold-hunting hidalgos, polite pirates who may have known Gil Polo, amiable freebooters with the Diana of Montemayor in their sea-chests, eager, patient, strenuous Jesuits accepting the martyr's crown of Indian apostleship for the glory of the Lord, all this procession hurries by, a masque of splendid shadows, over the rough, raw continents, through the horrid woods, by the shores of undreamed-of, unbaptized seas, on the scarps of undreamed-of, undefeated mountains. They pour from the East, along the pathway of the sun, into the new, the wonderful West, and so they vanish. Our concern is not with them. They seldom came to colonise, they seldom came to stay. They were, for the most part, but birds of passage. They came in search of wealth, in the service of great sovereigns, in the service of the church to save alive the souls of naked savages. For their own ends or the ends of others they risked their lives, buffeted the buffeting seas, tramped the trackless desert, risked the arrow and the tomahawk and the stake, like the brave, needy, reckless, earnest adventurers that they were. Those who came for gold had no nobler motive than gain. Those who came in the name of the Cross had no dream of building up a Commonwealth in the waste places of the heathen. That antique spirit of colonisation, which sent argosy after argosy of the children of Hellas to create a greater Greece upon another soil, was denied to and was not desired by those who first furrowed the strange seas and trampled the strange soil of the New World. It is not amongst them or theirs that we must look for the men whose names stand at the beginning of the story of the United States.

Before Soto fell asleep, or Coronado's enterprise came to nothing, the Spaniards had found European rivals in America. The French had made their appearance in the northern part of the country. In

1534 and 1535 the Frenchman, Jacques Cartier, explored the St. Lawrence. The ambition of Henry IV. of France to found a French Colonial Empire sent de Monts to make a settlement on the Bay of Fundy, and prompted Samuel de Champlain to found the town of Quebec and to discover Lakes Champlain and Huron. These experiments were followed by frequent, and for the most part disastrous, attempts to found colonies on the Florida and Carolina coasts. Privations, native wars, mutiny, and the merciless hostility of the Spaniards destroyed these colonies. But by this time a third race of colonists had made their appearance upon the scene of the New World. The English gentlemen adventurers of the Elizabethan age were slave-dealers, privateers, almost pirates, always splendid fighters. Hawkins, Drake, Gilbert, and Raleigh busied themselves in harassing the Spaniards, planning colonies, eager to make the most of the New World and the new opportunities. From the dawn of the seventeenth century adventurers of all kinds were hot to follow in the wake of the vessels of Drake. The voyages of Bartholomew Gosnold, of Martin Pring, and of George Weymouth to the New World, and their return with valuable cargoes and glowing tales, prepared the way for the formation of the first permanent English colony in the New World. The early English colonies were no better successes than the early Spanish or the early French. The story of Roanoke Island is one of the saddest and the strangest in the history of colonisation. But with the defeat of the Spanish Armada and the ruin of Spain's power at sea, Englishmen found themselves free to found colonies in America in comparative peace.

When Raleigh fell under King James's displeasure, his charter to colonise in America was taken away from him and conferred instead upon an association known to history and to the world as the Virginia Company. It was so called because the name 'Virginia,' from the virgin queen, had been given in courtier spirit to all the territory in America which was claimed by England. The members of the company fell into two divisions—members who resided in or near London, and members who resided in or near Plymouth. Virginia, from the Cape Fear River to the Bay of Fundy, was divided between them, with the exception of an intervening belt of territory from the thirty-eighth to the forty-first degree of latitude. This was to be left open to whichever of the two sub-companies of London or Plymouth should be quickest to colonise it. The Plymouth sub-company fitted out an expedition to the coast of Maine in 1607, but the severity of the winter, the hostility of the natives, and the absence of gold discouraged the would-be colonists, and they made haste to return home in the spring of 1608, leaving no permanent trace of their experiment behind them.

On the 19th of December 1606 three ships, the *Good Speed*, the *Discovery*, and the *Susan Constant*, sailed for the Thames, Westward Ho. The three ships carried an odd mixture of men who were sailing for Virginia with dreams of gold and glory humming in their heated brains. They represented the London Company. They were the first to turn to the New World under the authority of the New Charter. The New Charter laid down certain very definite rules and regulations for the governing of any colony established by the company. The

THE OLD WORLD AND THE NEW 15

supremacy of the Church of England and of the King of England were to be maintained. Equity and land tenure were to be the same as in England. Any laws passed by the colonists were subject to the approval of the monarch. On paper in fact the colonists had little or no power to administer their own affairs; these were to be administered according to the wisdom of the English Solomon. It is probable that the men who made up the ships' companies of the *Susan Constant,* the *Discovery,* and the *Good Speed* cared extremely little for the conditions under which they might be permitted to found a colony. The fact that they carried with them no women and no children, and that out of their number of one hundred and forty-three only twelve were labourers, proves that they had no serious, at least no immediate, thoughts of colonisation. Most of the voyagers were of the kind known as gentlemen adventurers, men always eager to get money, men always ready to fight, courageous, greedy, scorning to work with their hands, and wholly inexperienced in the rude business of building up a settlement. Such artisans as went with the expedition were rather of a kind suited to conditions of ease and even of luxury than to the encampment of the explorer and the trials of the pioneer. We read of jewellers, of gold refiners, and of a perfumer. Altogether they were a queer set. With the exception of the commander of the little fleet, Christopher Newport, a sailor of repute, there was only one man worth naming in the whole expedition, Captain John Smith.

Captain John Smith had lived a wild, adventurous life. He had served in the Dutch wars. He had fought for Hungary against the Turks. He had been captured and sold as a slave in Constantinople. He had killed his taskmaster and made his escape. He had fought the Moors in Morocco. He was the sort of man made for a rough country and a rough life, an adventurer, a fighter, a toiler, a man with kindness in his heart, and much of honour in his tough composition. He was much too good for the gang he was thrown with, men who did not understand him, who were jealous of him. When they landed in Chesapeake Bay in April 1607, they were at first for giving Smith no share in the government of the new colony. But by the time that they had named the James River after their king, and chosen a foolish site for their town, Jamestown, on its shores, they began to find that the aid of Smith was essential to their enterprise. He did help them stoutly and steadfastly, and it was while working in their service that he met the strangest and most famous of all his adventures. While he was exploring the river Chickahominy he was captured by Indians, who were about to put him to death when he was rescued by the sudden intervention of Pocahontas, the daughter of the chief Powhatan. Pocahontas was a child of twelve. Smith it seems had won her heart during his captivity by making toys for her, and she returned his kindness by begging Powhatan to spare his life. The chief relented; Smith was set at liberty and allowed to return to the English settlement. Years after Pocahontas was captured by the English and taken to Jamestown, where a young Englishman, John Rolfe, fell in love with her, married her, and took her to England. She was made much of in England. She was about to return with Rolfe to Jamestown when she was seized with a fatal disease, and died and was buried far from James River and old Powhatan and the people of her tribe.

The Virginian colonists knew very bitter fortunes. Disaster after disaster beat them to the dust. Instead of gold and glory they had only famine and fever. They had none of the arts of colonisation. Helpless at first, they soon became hopeless. Their only good man, John Smith, did all he could for them, but in the end he returned to England, disabled by a severe accident. Then the despairing adventurers were about to give up the settlement altogether, and were only prevented by the opportune arrival of Lord Delaware with three ships of provisions and supplies. Delaware was the newly appointed governor, and his first act was to kneel on Jamestown beach and thank God that he had come in time to save Virginia. He made a good governor, but he soon fell ill, and had to return to England. He was succeeded by Sir Thomas Dale, a sturdy, strenuous old soldier who did as much to pull the colony together and get it into working order as John Smith had done in his day. Up to this time the colonists had accepted a social system in which everything was common property. The scheme resulted in a general idleness that was drifting towards starvation when Dale arrived. He kept order with a firm hand, sent mutineers and robbers swiftly to the gallows, and altered the system which was ruining the colony. Every man was compelled to pay a tax of two barrels and a half of corn for the support of the colony. Whatever he made beyond this was to be his own private property. This restored to the industrious the lost incentive to labour, and even persuaded the idle that it was

worth their while to work. Dale was succeeded by
Sir Thomas Gates, under whom the prosperity of the
colony continued.

To the Jamestown settlement Europe owes tobacco
and America owes negro slavery. Raleigh had introduced tobacco to England in the reign of Elizabeth,
and James had fulminated against it in his famous
Counterblast to Tobacco. But nobody heeded James.
People found that it was pleasant to 'drink smoke,'
as the phrase then went. The demand for tobacco
grew, and the soil of Virginia was the best soil in
the world to meet the demand. So the colonists
who had helped to build up Jamestown soon found
that there were fortunes to be made by the cultivation of tobacco. It became yearly an article
of increasing importation to England. More and
more people came out from England for the sole
purpose of cultivating it. After a while most of the
settlers were devoted to the industry. To keep the
industry going much labour was needed, and cheap
labour, as the work did not call for any special gifts.
In the August of 1619 a Dutch man-of-war sold
twenty negroes to the settlers. That was the small
beginning of the great curse of negro slavery. But in
those days there were white slaves as well as black
slaves. When the prisons in England were overcrowded, the government would relieve the pressure
by shipping a certain number of them off to Virginia,
to be sold there into what was practically slavery for
a term of years. As slaves were always in demand,
their exportation became a source of profit. Kidnapping people for exportation to Virginia became
quite common. Many a detested enemy, many an
unwelcome relative, went his reluctant way to the

THE OLD WORLD AND THE NEW

plantations. In some cases poor persons sailed of their own accord to Virginia to serve on the plantations and so get a new start in the New World. The settlers always preferred white labour to black, and for a time that initial Dutch sale of twenty negroes did not lead to any marked results. But gradually as the white men served their time of indenture they drifted away from service to seek their fortunes elsewhere. White labour became more difficult to command. People bought more and more negroes. By the end of the seventeenth century there were enough black slaves in America to do all the work on the plantations.

Twelve years after the foundation of Jamestown, there were some four thousand white colonists in Virginia. They were governed by a governor appointed by the London Company. But they were not content with such a form of government. They came from a land of free institutions, and free institutions they would have too. The four thousand settlers were living in eleven little settlements which were called boroughs. The four thousand settlers set about forming for themselves a representative government such as they had been familiar with at home. Each of the eleven boroughs elected two representatives who were styled burgesses. The first representative assembly ever held in America met in the choir of the church at Jamestown on the 30th July 1619. 'The most convenient place we could finde to sitt in,' writes John Twine, who was clerk of the Assembly, 'was the Quire of the Churche . . . forasmuche as men's affairs doe little prosper where God's service is neglected, all the burgesses tooke their places in the Quire till a prayer was said by

Mr. Bucks, the Minister, that it would please God to guide and sanctifie all our proceedings to his owne glory and the good of this Plantation. Prayer being ended, to the intente that as we had begun at God Almighty, so we might proceed with awful and due respecte towards the Lieutenant, our most gracious and dread Soveraigne, all the Burgesses were intreatted to retyre themselves into the body of the Churche, which being done, before they were fully admitted, they were called in order and by name, and so every man (none staggering at it) took the oathe of Supremacy, and then entred the Assembly.' In such a spirit of piety and loyalty the Virginian Assembly began its labours. It called itself the House of Burgesses; it acted for Virginia as if it were a House of Commons; it took to itself the power of taxation. It is interesting to be reminded that one of the burgesses in the first assembly was named Jefferson, and to think that more than a century and a half later one of his blood, who bore his name, signed the Declaration of Independence. Three generations of English monarchs frowned disapproval upon the colonists for asserting over seas a liberty which they could not be denied at home. King James by strain and pressure of the law succeeded in annulling the London Company's charter. He then set about drafting a brand new set of laws for Virginia, but while he was about the business he died, and his son Charles reigned in his stead. His son Charles sent over a governor of his own, Sir John Harvey, who was extremely unpopular. After six years' trial the Colonists took the bold step of deposing the governor, and Charles very reluctantly gave way to the colonial wish.

THE OLD WORLD AND THE NEW 21

During the Commonwealth the little colony breathed a freer air. Its governor from 1642 had been Sir William Berkeley. Sir William Berkeley was an interesting, even a fascinating, figure. He was almost an ideal kingsman and cavalier, a soldier and a man of fashion, a dramatist and a man of the world, a firm believer in the creed that what the king did was right, and that what he, William Berkeley, did under the king's good will was right also. In adherence to which creed he acted doggedly, devotedly, during the five and thirty years in which he was associated with Virginia. He had the old scornful high caste disdain for the education of the people. He thanked God that there were no free schools in Virginia; he thanked God that they had no printing-press. 'And I hope we shall not have these hundred years, for learning has brought disobedience and heresy and sects into the world, and printing has divulged them, and libels against the best government. God keep us from both!' These were Berkeley's very words. These things seemed to his stiff and stubborn spirit to create disloyalty to the king. Nobody now reads Berkeley's plays: on no stage now do his puppets jerk at their strings. But he earned his immortality as one of the worst colonial governors that ever lived.

During the Commonwealth, Cromwell had allowed Virginia to elect her own governors, a privilege of which the colonists had taken advantage to shunt Berkeley from the office. After the Restoration, however, the House of Burgesses, in a somewhat unfortunate spirit of loyalty, elected Berkeley again to please the new king, and found his rule more oppressive than ever. A House that had elected him suited Berkeley's temperament so well, that he very composedly kept it in existence for fourteen years, by the simple expedient of adjourning it from year to year. At the end of these fourteen years, events compelled Berkeley to summon a new House of Burgesses. The Indians in the colony became very troublesome, burning and killing without restraint, as Berkeley was so unpopular that he did not dare to call out the military force of the colony, lest, instead of dealing with the red enemy, it should turn and rend him. Once again the independent spirit of the colonists manifested itself. If the governor would not act, they would act for him. They hastily organised a little force of volunteers, and sent them against the Indians, under the command of a young man newly from England, named Nathaniel Bacon. Berkeley in a rage proclaimed Bacon a rebel. This raised such indignation in the colony, that Berkeley could only make the storm abate by summoning a new House of Burgesses. To this House Nathaniel Bacon was elected, and in it he played a prominent part in attacking Berkeley, and denouncing him to the home government. But in the very heat of the struggle Bacon died, and Berkeley suppressed the opposition with so much cruelty and illegality, that even Charles had to disavow his conduct, and recall him to England. In England Berkeley died of a broken heart at being reprimanded by a prince for conduct to the mere people. There were many like him while colonial history endured, men as headstrong, as bloody, as intemperate, as rash. He and they were the main cause that colonial history ceased to endure.

In spite of Berkeley, and of those who thought

with Berkeley that education and printing-presses were instruments of the Devil, forged for use against God and the king, the Virginian colonists played their part, and a proud one in the advancement of education. William and Mary College, in Virginia, was founded in 1692. It was not the oldest college in America, but the second oldest. Like its predecessor, and like most of those that followed, it owed its establishment to the desire of the colonists for a ministry of some particular faith. The faith that Virginia professed was that of the Established Church, and William and Mary College was founded to provide the colony with clergy of that faith. The king and queen, from whom the college was named, gave it twenty thousand acres of land, and duties were levied for its support. These duties were not always paid in the beginning with the regularity desired by those who struggled to make their college a successful 'seminary for the breeding of good ministers, with which they were but very indifferently supplied from abroad,' as James Blair wrote, who was the first president of the college. But they wrestled manfully with their difficulties, and made Virginia a centre of education in spite of Berkeley's memory.

Yet Virginia, as has been said, was not the first to set the splendid example of founding a college in the New World. A colony younger than the Virginia colony had come into existence that had been the pattern to Virginia in this regard. The new colony was widely different from the old; its destinies were to be widely different; there was a time to come in their histories when they should stand arrayed against each other as representatives of absolutely opposing principles. For the present, the new colony differed from the older in its purposes, its principles, and its aims, as much as it differed in its climate and its geographical conditions. The Jamestown colonists had come for material advantages. The men of the new colony, so many hundreds of miles to the north, had come for spiritual freedom.

CHAPTER II

PILGRIM FATHERS

THE story of New England begins with the voyage of the *Mayflower*. The perilous seas of faery lands forlorn are ridden by the ghosts of famous ships, *Argo* and the *Long Serpent* and the *White Ship*, and the *Revenge* and the *Victory* and the *Vengeur*, but no one of them is more famous than the *Mayflower*. It carried a little company of English 'Separatists' in search of a new life. They had come with their pastor, John Robinson, to Leyden, some dozen years earlier, to escape from the harsh authority of the English Established Church, sternly intolerant of dissent. They had dwelt in Leyden during the long truce between the Dutch and the Spaniards, but they were not content with their halting-place. The wealthy, worldly, commercial burgesses of Holland did not seem admirable to them in the clear, cold light of their simple faith. They were afraid, too, of the effect of evil influences which they themselves could disdain upon the younger generation growing up among them. 'Many of their children,' writes Governor William Bradford, 'by these occasions, and the great licentiousness of youth in that country, and the manifold temptations of the place, were drawn away by evil examples into extravagant and dangerous courses, getting the reins off their necks, and departing from their parents. Some became soldiers, others took upon them far voyages by sea; and others some worse courses, tending to dissoluteness and the danger of their souls, to the great grief of their parents and dishonour of God. So that they saw their posterity would be in danger to degenerate and be corrupted.' They resolved therefore once more to wander, and they turned their gaze towards the Atlantic. 'The place they had thoughts on, was some of those vast and unpeopled countries of America, which are fruitful and fit for habitation; being devoid of all civil inhabitants; where there are only savage and brutish men, which range up, and down, little otherwise than the wild beasts of the same.'

The matter was argued over long and carefully. All that could be said in opposition was eloquently urged; the dangers, the privations, the difficulties, the possibility of miscarriage, the probability of utter disaster. 'It was answered, that all great and honourable actions are accompanied with great difficulties; and must be both enterprised and overcome with answerable courages. It was granted the dangers were great, but not desperate; the difficulties were many, but not invincible. Their ends were good and honourable, their calling lawful and urgent, and therefore they might expect the blessing of God in their proceeding. Yea, though they should lose their lives in this action, yet might they have comfort in the same, and their endeavour would be honourable. They lived here but as men in exile and in a poor condition; and as great miseries might possibly befall them in this place; for the twelve years of truce were now out, and there was nothing but beating of drums and preparing for war; the events of which are always uncertain; the Spaniard might prove as cruel as the savages of America; and the famine and pestilence as sore here as there; and their liberty less to look out for remedy.' So they resolved to go. Their fatherland could never be a home for them; they would find and found a new England on the far edge of the Atlantic. They applied to the Virginia Company, and obtained permission to settle within the limits of the Virginia Charter. They were very anxious for formal assurance from the king that they should not be interfered with on account of their religion. The most, however, that the king would accord, was that he would connive at their going, and not molest them if they behaved peaceably. Their greatest difficulty was to get the funds necessary for their enterprise. Those who had any goods to sell, sold them; money was borrowed on very hard terms from some English merchants. At last all the preliminary difficulties were overcome, all the necessary arrangements made; the exodus might begin.

The departure of the Pilgrim Fathers on their great pilgrimage seems to live for ever in the simple eloquence of Nathaniel Morton, the historian of the settlement. It is not to be bettered; it is always good to read. It preserves for us a clear image of the men and of the hour. The windy Dutch quay and the rocking ship, straining at its hawsers with the rising tide, the group of pale-faced women, and no less pale-faced men, in their sad-coloured garments, the kneeling pastor, the tears in the eyes of friends, in the eyes of strangers; all the pain, the pity, and the hope of that parting persist here, a possession for ever. 'So they left that goodly and pleasant city of Leyden, which had been their resting place for above eleven years; but they knew that they were pilgrims and strangers here below, and looked not much on these things, but lifted up their eyes to Heaven, their dearest country, where God had prepared for them a city, and therein quieted their spirits. When they came to Delfshaven, they found the ship and all things ready; and such of their friends as could not come with them followed after them, and sundry came from Amsterdam to see them ship and to take their leave of them. One night was spent with little sleep with the most, but with friendly entertainment and Christian discourse and other real expressions of true Christian love. The next day they went on board, and their friends with them, where truly doleful was the sight of that sad and mournful parting, to hear what sighs and sobs and prayers did sound amongst them, what tears did gush from every eye, and pithy speeches pierced each other's heart, that sundry of the Dutch strangers that stood on the Key as spectators could not refrain from tears. But the tide (which stays for no man) calling them away, that were thus loth to depart, their Reverend Pastor falling down on his knees, and they all with him, with watery cheeks, commended them with most fervent prayers unto the Lord and his blessing; and then with mutual embraces and many tears, they took their leaves one of another, which proved to be the last leave to many of them.'

The little band of brothers came to Southampton in the *Speedwell*. At Southampton the *Mayflower* was waiting for them. Both ships started, but the *Speedwell* leaked badly, and they had to put back twice to repair her. At last they were obliged to leave the *Speedwell* in England with such of the company as were now unwilling to pursue the voyage, and the *Mayflower* sailed alone on the 16th of September with exactly one hundred men, women, and children on board. More than three months later they came to the wild and stormy coast, and after escapes from shipwreck and the arrows of hostile Indians, they landed at last on the spot known as Plymouth Rock. 'Here,' says de Tocqueville, 'is a stone which the feet of a few outcasts pressed for an instant, and this stone becomes famous; it is treasured by a great nation; its very dust is shared as a relic: and what is become of the gateways of a thousand palaces?'

As the Pilgrim Fathers—for so they abide in history—had made their landing outside the limits of the Virginia Company, they were obliged to make new rules for the government of their colony, a course they were further impelled to by the fact that the brotherhood contained some members 'not well affected to unity and concord,' who 'gave some appearance of faction.' Accordingly they drew up a formal compact, in which they recorded themselves as the loyal subjects of King James, who had undertaken for the glory of God and the advancement of the Christian faith to plant the first colony in the Northern parts of Virginia. The compact set forth that those signing it, as almost all the men of the band did sign it, did solemnly and mutually, in the presence of God and one another, covenant and combine themselves together into a civil body politic, to enact, constitute, and frame such just and equal laws, ordinances, acts, constitutions, and offices, from time to time, as shall be thought most meet and convenient for the general good of the colony. 'Unto which we promise all due submission and obedience.'

The little colony suffered terribly in that first fierce winter. William Bradford tells the story in a strong and simple English that needs but a change of spelling to touch with an immediate pathos, to cheer with an immediate courage. 'In these hard and difficult beginnings they found some discontents and murmurings arise amongst some, and mutinous speech and carriage in others, but they were soon quelled and overcome by the wisdom, patience, and just and equal carriage of things, by the governor and the better part which clave faithfully together in the main. But that which was most sad and lamentable was, that, in two or three months time, half of their company died, especially in January and February, being the depth of winter, and wanting houses and other comforts; being infected with the scurvy and other diseases, which this long voyage and their inaccommodate condition had brought upon them, so that there died, sometimes two or three of a day in the aforesaid time; that of one hundred and odd persons scarce fifty remained, and of these, in the time of most distress, there were but six or seven sound persons, who, to their great commendation be it spoken, spared no pains, night or day, but with abundance of toil and hazard of their own health, fetched them wood, made them fires, dressed their meat, made their beds, washed their loathsome clothes, clothed and unclothed them, and, in a word, did all the homely and necessary offices for them which dainty and queasy stomachs cannot endure to hear named, and all this willingly and cheerfully, without any grudging in the least, showing herein their true love unto their friends and brethren.' All this is good and gallant reading of a good and gallant fellowship. 'A rare example and worthy to be remembered.' In suffering all, they suffered nothing. Their first governor, John Carver, died. They chose William Bradford, the writer of those brave words, for their next governor, and their governor he remained, as he deserved to remain, for many a long year.

The colonists were content, even happy. For all their trials, they were free. They had come prepared to endure privations cheerfully. They had come to stay, and they stayed. When the *Mayflower* returned to England in the spring of 1621, it carried back with it no single one of all those who survived of its shipload. They starved in patience. In patience they built themselves houses of logs, built themselves a church for their stout souls, and a hospital for their sick bodies. They fished and hunted and strove to make the earth fruitful. They lived in daily fear of the wolves, whom they called lions; they lived in daily fear of the Indians. As their dead were laid in earth the survivors planted corn over them to hide their graves, that the Indians might not learn how fast their numbers were dwindling. Sometimes the Indians were friendly; sometimes they were not. But against their unfriendliness the colonists could pit the strong hand of Miles Standish, the good soldier, and the strong heart of William Bradford, the good governor. Once an Indian chief sent Bradford a bundle of arrows wrapped in a rattlesnake's skin. This was a menace of war. Bradford put the arrows on one side, filled the snakeskin with black powder and bright bullets, and sent it back to the Indian chief. The Indian chief was keen-witted enough to appreciate the meaning of the message, and he left Bradford and his people alone. At another time a friendly Indian named Massasoit warned the Plymouth people of an Indian plot to massacre some later settlers at a place called Weymouth. At once Miles Standish and a handful of armed pilgrims hastened to the rescue. The Indians were met in a conference that turned to a brawl. There was a brisk fight in a small room; the Indians were defeated; Miles Standish slew the chief with his own hand, and carried his head back to Plymouth. The Indians began to appreciate that William Bradford and Miles Standish were bad men to pick a quarrel with. It is, however, characteristic of the spirit of the pilgrims that when news of victories over Indians reached old John Robinson at Leyden, his first words were words of sorrow that no Indians should have been converted before any had been killed.

At first the colonists had attempted to manage their small commonwealth on the communal system. 'Probably,' says Channing, 'the communal idea never has had, or never will have, a fairer trial than it had at the hands of the Pilgrims at Plymouth.' But the communal system failed them, and prosperity only came with its abandonment. 'The experience,' wrote Governor Bradford, 'that was had in this common course and condition, tried sundry years, and that amongst godly and sober men, may well evince the vanity of that conceit of Plato's and other ancients applauded by some of later times. That the taking away of property and bringing in community into a commonwealth would make them happy and flourishing, as if they were wiser than God, for this community, so far as it was, was found to breed much confusion and discontent, and retard much employment that would have been to their benefit and comfort.'

Gradually the little colony began to flourish as it deserved to flourish. More houses sprang up. A fort was built for defence against the Indians. The cleared fields grew more fruitful. Cattle were imported to be guarded watchfully from the wolves. Friends from Leyden came over seas to join the pioneers. A small beginning was made in trade with the Indians, the settlers giving corn to the Indians in exchange for furs. By the success of the fur-trade they were enabled to pay off the debt they owed to the London merchants. The prospering Pilgrims wrote many letters back to the mother-country, and in these letters they painted cheerily and faithfully enough their pleasant position, their freedom, their right to worship Heaven in their own way. The men at home to whom these letters went were chafing bitterly under the religious persecutions they had to endure. The words from New England came to the Puritans at home like messages of life, of hope. The paradise the pioneers wrote about seemed even more enchanting to the weary eyes of those who lingered at home. Year after year more Englishmen crossed the Atlantic: many in those early years in the hope of trade and gain. Trading-posts and fishing-villages began to grow up along the coast. The hour had come for the Puritan emigration.

Once again the *Mayflower* sailed the seas; once

C

again she carried brave hearts, strong brains, and willing hands to build up the New England of the New World. With four fellow vessels she sailed, in the June of 1629, into the harbour which is now called Salem, from the Hebrew word, which being interpreted means 'Peace.' The five ships bore the beginnings of a new colony that came under very different conditions from those that had governed the advent of the Pilgrim Fathers. The Pilgrims came as pioneers, pious adventurers drifting towards they knew not what; they came in winter to a forbidding coast; they landed on a shore savage with wild beasts, savage with yet wilder men; with only their trust in Heaven to sustain them, where all things earthly seemed so hostile. The new comers, these five shiploads of men, women, and children, came over a smiling sea that often during the voyage had 'appeared as a most plain and even meadow.' They sailed along a summer-coloured coast, coated with woods that the voyage's early chronicler calls 'gay woods' in the fulness of his heart, and the mirthfulness of his mind. An abundance of bright flowers carpeted the waters about the prows of the little fleet, brought from the low meadows by the tide to salute the strangers with cheerful salutation. These 'yellow flowers painting the sea' may well have seemed fair omens to those wanderers approaching in hope and joy to their 'new paradise of New England.' Where the Pilgrim Fathers came unheralded, these colonists came to find friends awaiting them, and the rudiments of a civil state. The year before a strong man had come from England, a strong man whom a writer of the time calls Mr. John Indicat, but who lives in history as John

Endicott. He was 'of courage bold undaunted, yet sociable, and of a cheerful spirit, loving and austere, applying himself to either as occasion served,' in the words of his friend, Captain Edward Johnson. At this time he was forty years of age, strong, stern, self-reliant, dominant, a born leader of men, and nation-maker, a man with the spirit of the Covenanter and the energy of the Ironside.

The new comers, with the Rev. Francis Higginson at their head, found Endicott, and a small nucleus of other colonists, ready to make them welcome. It may be that some of those earliest colonists of Endicott's were not unlike those who haunted the cave of Adullam because they were discontented and in distress and in debt. In any case John Endicott had made himself a captain over them. He was appointed governor of the colony, and a very good governor he made from the Puritan point of view. The year after the arrival of Higginson and his companions, some eight hundred more colonists came out under the leadership of John Winthrop. These men of the Massachusetts Bay Colony began their career under far kindlier auspices than their predecessors, the Pilgrim Fathers. They had friends of power and influence in England; they had men of wealth and education in their own midst; they were backed by a charter which they prized very highly. It gave them the right to govern themselves so long as they did nothing contrary to the law of England. Under this charter they now elected John Winthrop governor, and set to work busily at their business of colonisation. Salem was settled. Boston began to crown its triple hill. Roxbury, Charlestown, Dorchester, and Watertown came into being. But if the men of Massachusetts Bay started under fairer auspices than the men of Plymouth Rock, they too had to pass through their period of probation, their time of trial; and the period was long, and the time bitter. Winter was to them as cruel as it had been to the pioneers. Bad water brought disease with it. Death thinned their ranks. Two hundred of their number were buried in five months. Hunger gnawed them. Meat of any kind was a luxury not to be dreamed of. The colonists had come to their last handful of meal, when history repeated the salvation of Jamestown. A ship from England laden with provisions entered the harbour and rescued Boston.

Through all their tribulations, these brave men so bore themselves as indeed to deserve that title which their first pastor, Mr. Higginson, gave them, 'these Soldiers of Christ.' With a Spartan endurance, with a Roman dignity, with a Christian faith, they faced their trials, and smiled them down. Governor Winthrop wrote a letter to his wife, at a time when the suffering of the colony and his own sorrows were at their keenest, which deserves to be remembered for ever with all utterances that breathe an antique, heroic patience. 'We here enjoy God and Jesus Christ, and is not that enough? I thank God, I like so well to be here that I do not repent my coming. I would not have altered my course though I had foreseen all these afflictions. I had never more content of mind.' Men who could write with such proud fortitude, who could move with such a noble joy in the midst of adversities, were the men, the elect, appointed to make a great nation, to call a New England into being, to create the New World.

The New World began to increase with great rapidity. Fifty years after the coming of the *Mayflower*, the New England colonies had increased from but a poor hundred souls to no less than eight thousand, distributed amongst twenty thriving towns. Each of these towns was, as it were, a little centre of local government. Thus began that township independence which, as de Tocqueville says, is the life and mainspring of American liberty. It is interesting to note how the representative institutions of the old country were perpetuated in the new, but perpetuated with a difference rendered essential by the conditions of their transplantation. The English system was based, roughly speaking, upon the township or parish, and then upon the county. In America some colonies organised themselves in accordance with the township, others with the county system, according to the needs of their circumstances. In the southern colonies, as they came into existence, the large plantations, the vast estates, led to the establishment of an authority resembling the English county government, with its lieutenants, its militia, and its county courts. In the New England colonies, the closer conditions of life led to the establishment and to the retention of the parish or township plan of government. The result of the county system, accepted by the South, was to place authority in the hands of a few men; of the township method, accepted by the North, to leave the authority in the hands of the many, of the people themselves. In the beginning, each town had but one church, and the population of the town, and the congregation of the church, were equivalent. In England, the parish, the small piece of country which gives a congregation to a single church, is often called by the older name of township. It was this older name which persisted in New England. Massachusetts gradually became dotted with little centres of self-government called townships. Of course the county also existed in New England, but chiefly for judicial and military purposes, and it did not long concern itself with local administration. 'The township,' says de Tocqueville, 'was organised before the county, the county before the state, and the state before the union.' When the inhabitants of these little townships met to discuss the affairs of the church, they called their assemblage a parish meeting; when they met for civil concerns, they called it a town meeting. In the beginning, the village church was used as the building in which both religious and civil matters were discussed and transacted, and was generally known as the meeting-house. Later on, the church was reserved solely for church business, and a special building, called the town house or town hall, was built and set apart for civil business.

The characteristics of the occupants of these townships were their sincere piety, their intolerance of all opinions save their own, and their ceaseless activity as settlers and traders. Before their busy hands the wilderness withered. Roads and bridges, houses and fences, transformed the pathless desolation dear to the Red Man. There was a brisk trade with the mother-country in fur, lumber, and salt fish. European grains were planted and throve. Pigs and cattle were plentiful. The colonies were well to do.

With material prosperity came intellectual advance. Before ever a stone was laid of William and Mary College, down South at Jamestown in Virginia, the people of Massachusetts were proud of their college of Harvard. 'After God had carried us safe to New England,' says an anonymous writer of that time, 'and we had builded our houses, provided necessaries for our livelihood, rear'd convenient places for God's worship, and settled the Civil Government: one of the next things we longed for, and looked after was to advance learning and perpetuate it to Posterity; dreading to leave an illiterate Ministry to the Churches when our present Ministers shall lie in the dust. And as we were thinking and consulting how to effect this great work it pleased God to stir up the heart of one, Mr. Harvard (a godly gentleman and a lover of learning, there living amongst us) to give the one half of his Estate (it being in all about £1700) towards the erecting of a Colledge, and all his Library.' Others followed John Harvard's example. The college was set up at Newtown, three miles from Boston, and the name of Newtown, in honour of the mother-university of which so many of the settlers were graduates, was changed to Cambridge. The college itself was called after the godly gentleman and lover of learning who endowed it. There is no earthly immortality, says Wentworth Higginson, more secure than to have stamped one's name on the map. It is surely no less secure to confer it on some great centre of learning. Childless John Harvard remains immortal. Every man who carries from Cambridge the love of knowledge gained, and the desire for knowledge yet to gain, is one of John Harvard's spiritual children, and wears the dead scholar's name as well as the name of his own people. A little while after the fortunes of the college were ensured, the first printing-press of this

New World was set up in Cambridge, and the first book printed by it was the *Bay Psalm Book* in 1640. Once again New England anticipated the culture of the older colony of Virginia. The first newspaper printed in the colonies was the *Boston Newsletter*, which appeared in 1704.

Almost the only troubles that vexed the prosperous peace of the New England colonies came from over seas, with the occasional interference of the mother-country ; from without, from the Indian tribes who still persisted in regarding the country as their own, and the strangers as interlopers; and from within, from the daring persons, men and women, who ventured to entertain and to express opinions that were not in keeping with the tenor of colonial thought. The first attempt at interference from over seas began in 1636, when King Charles thought fit to feel and to express a disapproval of the way in which Massachusetts was carving out its own fortunes, and building up its own future. The king went so far as to talk of taking back the charter he had granted to Massachusetts, and of which Massachusetts had been so extremely proud. He was for dividing the colonists' land among some enemies of theirs in England, who had long cast an affectionate eye upon the New England coast and its possibilities of colonisation. When the news of the king's intentions was carried to Massachusetts, Massachusetts lost no time in making plain its intentions. Boston Harbour bristled with forts, and grinned with cannon. The militia of every village— for every village had its militia—went into training for active service. On the highest hill in Boston a great beacon was built, and stacked ready to be fired to give the alarm to all the country round at the first sign of an invader. King Charles did not carry out his intentions. Other troubles nearer home occupied him more closely and more fatally, and for the time the gallant people of Massachusetts were left alone. It would have been well for a later king of England if he had remembered or been told of the daring and the zeal shown by the infant colony in their determination to resist royal aggression. If that lesson had been rightly learnt, the course of history might have been very different. The stout stand made by the colonists is commemorated in the name of Beacon Hill.

There was graver trouble still in 1686, when James the Second made a desperate attempt to crush the growing power and freedom of the colonies and to annul their charters. He sent over a favourite officer, Sir Edmund Andros, to govern all New England, with New York and New Jersey as well, as his viceroy. This time, unfortunately, the colonists did not make ready to resist. Sir Edmund landed, an imposing presence, splendid in scarlet and gold, and promptly proceeded to make it plain to the colonists that they had met with their master. He would have no nonsense about printing-presses and popular taxation and popular education and nonconformity to the Church of England. He would have no nonsense neither about charters; and he strayed over New England destroying such papers with a light heart, till he came to Connecticut. When he demanded the charter there, a resolute man named William Wadsworth took the document away and hid it in a hollow oak tree, which is revered to this day as the Charter Oak. The loss of the charter made Andros very angry, but he consoled himself to some degree by taking the book of records of the colony and writing the word 'Finis' at the end, in sign that there was an end to the colony of Connecticut. In fact, there was soon to be an end of the rule of Andros. For when the news came of the revolution in England which sent James into exile and placed William of Orange on the throne, the colonists rose in arms and made Andros a prisoner. Andros came to no harm; the new king did not cause him to be punished; later on he was made Governor of Virginia, and he died in England in the early part of the eighteenth century. But his experiment in despotism left a bad feeling behind it, though the bad feeling was not to have any serious effect until nearly a century had passed away.

The troubles with the Indians began early, and lasted long. At first the colonists and the red men got on fairly well together, but in the end the inevitable dislike of the original occupier to the stranger grew and grew until it flamed into active hate. All the tribes in New England belonged to the Algonquin family. Of these the fiercest and most powerful were the Pequots or Pequods, who lived on the banks of the river now called the Thames. These Indians murdered a sailor named Stone; they murdered a sailor named Oldham. John Endicott and the New Englanders resolved to avenge these murders. Endicott assailed the Indians vigorously, burning and devastating their country. The red men in reprisal lurked in ambushes, killing or capturing stray colonists, and cruelly torturing those they captured. The colonists resolved to end the quarrel for good and all. A small force of under two hundred men attacked and surprised the

Pequots in a circular fort by the Mystic river. The Indians were taken by surprise. Of four hundred Indians who were in the fort only five escaped. John Underhill, one of the leaders of the colonists, said that outside the fort the dead bodies of Indians lay so thick upon the ground that he could not move without treading upon them. The remainder of the tribe took to flight, but they were mercilessly hunted down and exterminated. Soon there was not a Pequot left in the country, and their terrible fate so alarmed all the other Indian tribes that for nearly forty years no red men dared to molest one of the New England colonists.

But, when the forty years had nearly passed away, a very bitter and bloody war broke out between the Indians and the settlers—the war known as King Philip's war. Philip was the name the settlers gave to the son of the Indian chief, Massasoit, who had always been very friendly to the whites. Philip was not friendly to the whites. He was a brave man and a cunning man. Under other conditions, with a wider field to work in, with mightier forces to wield, he would have made a great conqueror and a great statesman. As it was, he dreamed a great dream, and very nearly made it a reality. It was his dream to sweep the white men out into the sea from which they came, to wrest back the land they were winning from the wilderness, and to turn the thriving towns and the fruitful fields once again into Indian camping-places and Indian hunting-grounds. He seems to have set about his scheme with great diplomatic skill. Secretly, stealthily, he went in turn to every tribe in New England, until by his arguments and his eloquence he had united them all in one common league against the white men. He meant to take these unawares, but something of his purpose was revealed by an Indian to the Plymouth magistrate. Three other Indians killed the tale-teller for his treachery; they, in their turn, were captured by the settlers and hanged. Then the war began. Thanks to King Philip's care it extended along a line of country two hundred miles long, and it was carried on by almost every tribe in the country, including some that the whites had always looked upon as friendly. Under King Philip the war lasted more than a year, the most terrible year that the colonists had ever known. Life was one long fear in Massachusetts in those dreadful days. No man ever lay down to sleep without fearing to be awakened by the hideous Indian war-whoop ringing in his ears; by the blaze of burning houses shining in his eyes. No man left his home in the firm hope that he would return to it alive, or, so returning, would find alive those whom he had left behind. Day and night, through summer and autumn and winter and spring, the desperate struggle went on. Band after band of brave white fighting men were taken by surprise and killed to the last man. Village after village was surprised, its people killed or taken captive, while its houses withered in a roar of flame. From villages yet unassailed the inhabitants began to throng in crowds to Boston and the other cities, crying out for protection against the savages. The ever-present physical fear brought with it strange mental perturbations. Such portents as the Romans read in the skies a little ere the mighty Julius fell, the Puritan farmers found in the New England heavens during the agony of King Philip's war. The stars at night took strange shapes to superstitious eyes, shapes of red men riding furiously, of drawn swords and bent bows, and even of bloody scalps. For all their fear, the settlers fought strenuously. In the wild winter, Josiah Winslow, Governor of Plymouth, led a little army of a thousand men against the Narragansett Indians, who were gathered together in a fort in the midst of swamps. At a great cost in killed and wounded Winslow won the day; the fort was carried by storm and burnt, and a large number of the Indians killed. Still the war went on. One village, Hadley, was assailed by the Indians on a Sunday morning when all the people were at church. Men hurried from the House of God to arm and fight, but the Indians were too numerous and were carrying all before them. Suddenly an elderly, grey-haired man who carried himself like a soldier appeared in the street, assumed command of the scattering disheartened whites, gave stern swift military orders that men naturally obeyed, and rallied the settlers so well that they drove the Indians headlong into the woods. Then this strange grey man disappeared as mysteriously as he had appeared. He had come like 'the true-hearted Greek God on the noon of that undying day of Marathon'; he had come like St. James in the Spanish battle; had done his great deed and disappeared. But he was neither a god nor a saint. He was the king-killer, William Goffe, the Cromwellian general who had fled to America when Charles the Second was restored, and long lay hiding in the New England woods.

Still the war went on. King Philip went north to the Great Lakes and to Canada, trying to persuade the

Indians of these parts to join him. He pleaded in vain. Then he came back to pit his own strength and courage and daring against his enemies. It is said that he slew with his own hand one of his warriors for venturing to talk of peace. But Philip's end was approaching. Captain Church, with a great force of Puritan fighting men, besieged Philip's camp, defeated his braves and captured his wife and child. It is not pleasant to read that the grandchild of Massasoit was sold into slavery in Bermuda, after due consultation of clergy and due reference to the authority of the Old Testament. 'Now I am ready to die,' said King Philip, and death was close at hand. He was hunted down, his hiding-place betrayed by one of his own braves, and killed. It is not pleasant to read that his dead body was beheaded and quartered as that of a rebel against his gracious majesty King Charles the Second; it is not pleasant to read that the dead head grinned on a pole at Plymouth for a quarter of a century to come. Yet there is no need to be too angry with the settlers for this barbarism. Nearly a century later the heads of other dead rebels grinned on Temple Bar, in the Strand, in London town, when Johnson lived, and Burke and Garrick and Goldsmith and Reynolds. The death of King Philip did not quite end King Philip's war. It lingered for some two years of desultory fighting before it came to an end. It cost the colonists some dozen villages, some six hundred men and one hundred thousand pounds; it burdened the colony with a heavy debt which was fully paid. But it taught the New England colonies the value of union against a common foe, and the lesson, dearly bought, was of great value.

The colonists' third trouble was the trouble that rose on them from within. They had come from the other side of the world to secure for themselves the blessings of religious liberty, but they proved in their new home as intolerant to the religious opinions of others as ever Laud had been to theirs. Stern almost to savageness in the laws which they passed to govern themselves—laws in which the death penalty made its appearance again and again with a hideous persistence—they were yet sterner to the men and women who dared to profess any other form of faith than that permitted by Puritan authority. The zealous Puritan visited with severe punishment and even with death the Christian who dared to worship God according to a ritual differing from his own. Massachusetts banished Anabaptists; chastened 'an accursed race of heretics called Quakers' with stripes, imprisonment, and hard labour; drove Catholic priests out of the colony, and doomed to death any who should return after having been expelled. Undoubtedly the Quakers were in the beginning extremely trying to the colonial temper. They defied the authority of the church; their protests were not passive but active; they used to invade places of worship and interrupt the services with unseemly brawling; they had queer ways, women and men, of going about naked as a proof of return to primal innocence. They were very hard to subjugate, though the Puritans did their best: banishing them, flogging them, imprisoning them, piercing their tongues with hot irons, clipping their ears—even, at a push, hanging four of them on Boston Common. No persecutions could completely quell the wild fanaticism of the early Quakers, or convert them into more agreeable neighbours and orderly citizens.

If the Puritans were harsh, it is hardly fair to reproach them for wanting a toleration which they never professed to extend. They left England in order to live their own life, and they did not wish their ideal community to be disturbed by the presence of others who did not think their thoughts. The Puritan had none of the spirit which was quickened a century and a half later—the spirit of the French Revolutionary, the spirit that desired to present liberty to others, that yearned and throbbed and panted to set men free in spite of themselves, and even against their wills. All the Puritans asked was liberty for themselves to live by their own light and worship in their own way. In their little commonwealths there must be no differences of opinion, no brawling about belief. They compelled no man to enter; they wooed no man to enter; but the man who did enter must conform, or it would go hard with him. That they were practising upon others the selfsame oppression against which of old their own minds had mutinied, did not ruffle their stern consciences. Authority in England would not suffer nonconformity to the Established Church. Therefore they had risen up and come together to this far corner of God's earth and made themselves their own spiritual republic, wherein they in their turn would tolerate no nonconformity. But the way of the world was not their way. Other men and other women with other beliefs would force their way into the guarded garden, would disturb with their jarring protests the peace of New England Puritanism, would assert noisily their right to say their say in the tents and the temples of supremacy.

One man and one woman stand out especially conspicuous in the army of anti-Puritan malcontents. The man was Roger Williams; the woman Anne Hutchinson. Roger Williams was a young Welsh clergyman of twenty-five who came to Salem seeking religious liberty. He sought and found not, and he lifted up his voice in eloquent indignation. What he said was amazing enough to his hearers. His religious opinions, his political opinions, sounded alike shocking in their ears. He declared that it was God's law that man's conscience should be free. He advocated the absolute separation of church from state. He insisted that law should deal only with man's social relations; that it had nothing to say to his religious beliefs. A man had a right to believe as his conscience guided him, to go to church, or not to go, as he chose. If his religious freedom annoyed, his political audacity alarmed. He said that the King of England had no right to dispose of the broad lands of America; that these were Heaven's gifts to the Red Man, and only to be obtained from the Red Man by fair and honourable purchase. The Puritans who were not prepared to tolerate Williams's free theology were determined to deal sharply with his subversive social theories. They had made up their minds to ship this troublesome person back to England whether he would or no. But he got wind of their design, and fled for his freedom to the free woods. There is a letter of his, written when he was an old man, more than a generation later, from which we learn that when he was, unkindly and unchristianly, as he believed, driven from his house and land and wife and children—this is the order in which he sets his belongings—the good-hearted governor Winthrop wrote to him privately to steer his course for Narragansett Bay and its Indians, 'for many high and heavenly and public ends, encouraging me from the freeness of the place from any English claims or patents. I took his prudent motion as an hint and voice from God, and waving all other thoughts and notions, I steered my course from Salem (though in winter snow which I feel yet) unto these parts, wherein I may say Peniel, that is, I have seen the face of God.' From the Indians he got land on Narragansett Bay, in what is now Rhode Island. He and five companions landed from a canoe at the point which he called 'Providence' in his gratitude to God. Here Williams set about to establish his ideal commonwealth. He gave away his lands freely to all who wanted them. It was to be a shelter for all persons distressed for conscience. Liberty of conscience was the law of the land. After a while it seemed to Williams that liberty was degenerating into licence, and he was at some pains to explain with the aid of an allegory what he understood by liberty, and what, in consequence, he wished the colonists to understand. He likened the leaders of a commonwealth to the captain of a ship among whose passengers are persons of many religions. Every passenger should be free to hold his own service; no passenger should be compelled to attend the service of the ship. It was, however, the duty of the captain of the vessel to direct its course, keep order on board, and punish any kind of mutiny.

Anne Hutchinson was as remarkable a woman as

Williams was a remarkable man. She was a religious enthusiast from Lincolnshire, who came to Boston in her thirty-sixth year to set dominant Puritanism by the ears. She insisted upon the right of freedom of conscience as vehemently as Williams had done. Her arguments had so much effect upon some of her hearers that they went so far as to refuse to serve in the militia because they did not approve of their pastor's Sunday sermon. At last offended authority could endure her no longer. She was brought before a court at Newtown and solemnly accused of having troubled the peace of the commonwealth and the churches. She defended herself with great dexterity and ability, but her cleverness could not save her from the fate of Roger Williams, and she in her turn was banished from Massachusetts. In their difficulty she and her friends naturally turned as a matter of course to Williams. With his aid they bought Aquidneck, which was afterwards called Rhode Island, from the Indians, and here they founded the town of Portsmouth. Another enthusiast, William Coddington, founded the town of Newport, and a third, named Samuel Gorton, helped to establish the town of Warwick. Rhode Island became the natural refuge for persons whose religious opinions brought them into spiritual conflict with authority. Even as according to Ariosto all lost objects are certainly carried to the moon, so it was said that any man who had lost his religion would be sure to find it again in some one or other of the villages of Rhode Island.

The vexations of the Puritans were not limited to those caused by the actions of misdirected godly. The ungodly were a thorn. There were the fishing folk of the scattered sea settlements that later grew into New Hampshire. These, on one occasion, rebuked with irreverence a wandering pastor, who bade them be religious, as that was their object in coming to those shores. They did not exactly tell him to mind his own business, but they assured him that he had mistaken his business. Such words might be sweet in the ears of the people of Massachusetts Bay, whose purpose in life was religion, but for themselves their purpose in life was to catch fish. They felt no call to be fishers of men. More active and flagrant in ungodliness was Thomas Morton of Merry Mount. Morton was of the very clan of those that are proclaimed in 'The Wisdom of Solomon.' It was his belief, as displayed in the practice of his life, that it was well to enjoy the good things that are present, and speedily use the creatures like as in youth. He counselled those about him to let no flower of the spring go by them, and to let no man go without his part of voluptuousness, seeing that his time was a very shadow that passeth away. Fired by this philosophy, Morton became the ringleader of a group of colonists at a place called Mare Mount, some five miles from Boston, which name the Puritans in irony, or in simplicity, perverted into Merry Mount. Here Morton and his fellow-roisterers gloried and drank deep, danced and dwelt with the comeliest of the Indian women, and set up a huge maypole with a pair of buck horns at the top, and a merry, mad poem of Morton's 'sung with a corus' nailed to it. The setting up of this maypole, says Morton himself, in his *New English Canaan*, 'was a lamentable spectacle to the precise separatists that lived at New Plymouth. They termed it an idol; yea, they called it the Calfe of Horeb; and stood at defiance with the place, naming it Mount Dagon; threatening to make it a woefull mount and not a merry mount.' Indeed, they kept their word. Morton was a humorist, but his humour was no match for the steely austerity of John Endicott, the steel sword of Miles Standish. The man who later cut the cross from the banner of St. George, because it seemed to him an idolatrous emblem, the man who, shut in a little room, killed the most dangerous of the Indian chiefs, were scarcely to be bested by a witty, drinking, rhyming rascal like Merry Morton. It is to be remembered, too, that if the Puritans resented Morton's riotous revels, they had other and graver causes for offence. Morton and his people, in the zeal of their beaver trade, taught the Indians how to shoot with the musket, and sold them arms and ammunition. This was a more serious piece of folly than mumming round a maypole. The Red Men were dangerous enemies enough without putting into their hands the weapons of precision which alone preserved the White Men from destruction. Morton was reasoned with. Morton refused to listen to reason. Puritan patience, never very long suffering, was overtaxed. Something had to be done. Something was done swiftly. Miles Standish marched against him, overawed his poor show of resistance, and had him shipped off to England. He came back again, but this time he fell into the hands of Endicott. Endicott, who had cut down the maypole, and burnt down Morton's house, now confiscated all his goods, clapped him in the stocks, and sent him back a second time to England. Morton had his revenge of a kind. He wrote a book. *The New English Canaan* is a witty, scurrilous, diverting attack upon Puritanism, as it appeared to Merry Morton's semi-pagan eyes. He tasted the pains of a year's imprisonment for it which did not heighten his love for the 'precise Separatists,' nor for 'Captain Littleworth,' as he nicknamed Endicott. He devoted the rest of his life to battling with Puritanism. He might as well have battled with the elements. The Pilgrim Fathers were too much for him.

Later on, towards the end of the seventeenth century, New England was vexed by a stranger trouble than the Paganism of Merry Mount or the distractions of the Quakers. A great wave of superstitious fear and superstitious cruelty swept over the country. A series of epidemics, a succession of misfortunes to the colony, were attributed to the influence of witchcraft. Two famous New England clergymen, Cotton Mather and Samuel Parris, instigated a fierce attack upon the witches who were supposed to be working havoc upon the people by their spells and incantations. A grotesquely credulous court was formed for the trial of persons accused of witchcraft, and on evidence that was always childish, and often from the mouths of children, a number of persons were found guilty and hanged. The shameful fear abated after a while, the hideous delusion dissipated. Samuel Parris solemnly and publicly repented for his grievous error in the Old South Church in Boston. Cotton Mather stuck more stubbornly to his belief in witchcraft. Indeed, people still believed in witchcraft long after Mather's day. But the feeling never again rose to the pitch of the witchcraft fear of Salem, the ugliest stain on the story of New England.

CHAPTER III

THE OLD THIRTEEN

IN the years that followed the coming of the *Mayflower*, New England expanded into four distinct colonies that claimed separate existence as States at a later day. The settlers of Plymouth Rock and the settlers of Massachusetts Bay had come together under the common name of Massachusetts. New Hampshire, where those fishermen lived whose business in life was not religion but the catching of fish, was long linked with Massachusetts, and only obtained the glory of a separate existence as a royal province towards the end of the seventeenth century. Rhode Island, not altogether loved by the other New England colonies, obtained its charter in 1662. Connecticut had been wrested by New England explorers from the Dutch in spite of their teeth. These were the New England colonies which joined in the great union of thirteen, of which the tale has yet to be told. There were three other New England settlements which afterwards played their part in history. The first was Maine, which had been experimented upon as a field for colonisation by Sir Ferdinand Gorges in the days of Charles the First, and was named by him Maine, after the French province, for some dubious reason. After his death, it was always more or less under the thumb of

Massachusetts, though it made its own laws, and made them much milder than those of the other New England colonies. It did not succeed in getting recognition for many a long day as an independent state. Vermont was in like case being regarded only as portion and parcel then of New Hampshire, and, later, of New York. The third, New Haven, founded in 1638, was at first associated with, and later for a time absorbed in, the Connecticut colony. At first it knew no laws but the text of the Bible, and it shared with Connecticut the misfortunes that came from the neighbourhood of the Dutch. The neighbourhood of the Dutch was a great trial to the enterprising New Englanders for long enough.

It is recorded by the fabulist, that on a memorable occasion when two lions were disputing the possession of a slaughtered deer, an enterprising and observant jackal sneaked up and secured the meal for which the royal beasts were warring. The settlement of the New Netherlands was effected something in this jackal fashion. Those two English companies to whom King James had granted charters had, it will be remembered, a debateable or No-Man's-Land between their two territories a hundred miles wide. This was to be the reward of whichever made such progress in colonisation as to justify advance upon the neutral zone. But before either of the chartered companies could do anything of the kind, the Dutch stepped in. There was a daring English sailor, named Henry Hudson, who had entered the service of the Dutch East India Company, and who was employed by them to try and find the long-dreamed-of passage to India. In pursuit of this purpose,

Hudson, in his ship the *Half Moon*, came upon the mouth of the great river which now bears his name. He sailed up it as far as he could till he could sail no farther. Then he put back, bitterly disappointed, and returned to Holland, and died a dismal death, in his next voyage, sailing the Northern seas. His men mutinied and put him adrift in an open boat, and that was the last of him in history. He still persists in legend. Lovers of Rip Van Winkle will remember how he and his spectral crew still drink and play at ninepins in the hollows of the Catskill mountains. On the strength of Hudson's discovery of the river which now flows under his name the Dutch claimed all the land along its course, and named it with the name of the New Netherlands. In pursuit of this policy came Adrien Block, who passed the winter of 1614 on Manhattan Island, and made the beginnings of a settlement called New Amsterdam. A settlement on the opposite shore was the beginning of what is now New Jersey. This was the modest beginning of half a century of Dutch dominion in America.

Fifty years the Dutch had of it; fifty years of great landed proprietors called Patroons; fifty years of a life as closely like the life they had left behind in Holland as possible. It was a blue-tiled, big-piped, well-fed, comfortable life, on the good side. On the bad side, it was a life of quarrels with restless New Englanders, of quarrels with murderous Red Indians. In one of these Indian wars in which the colonists suffered heavily, massacre found a noble victim. Mrs. Anne Hutchinson had left Rhode Island, and settled near the Dutch Colony, to perish miserably by savage hands. On the whole the

Dutch flourished, and on the whole they enjoyed themselves; but fifty years was their allotted span. In 1664 an English fleet appeared before New Amsterdam. The fleet had been sent by the Duke of York, to whom his brother King Charles the Second had, with careless ease, made a present of New Netherland. It was a mere piece of buccaneering, but it was successful. New Amsterdam was under the governorship of Peter Stuyvesant, a stout-hearted man with a wooden leg, who was known to his friends and his enemies as Hard-headed Pete. Stuyvesant was all for fighting the Duke of York's buccaneers. He tore in bits the letter of the English commander calling upon him to surrender. The burgesses of New Amsterdam were not so stout-hearted as their Governor, and they insisted on yielding, while old warlike Peter Stuyvesant hung his head and asked what would be thought of it all in the Fatherland. New Amsterdam became an English possession, and its name was changed to New York. Nine years later, during the English war with Holland, it surrendered anew to a Dutch fleet, but it was only New Amsterdam again for a few poor months, and when peace was concluded, it was given back to England as one of the conditions of the treaty. Then it became New York for good and all, and that was the last of the Dutch dominion in America. It had been a jealous, greedy, aggressive dominion while it lasted, as one of its neighbours found to its cost. A scheme of colonisation, dreamed of by Gustavus Adolphus of Sweden, was carried out by his minister Oxenstiern after the death of Gustavus. In 1638 a Swedish settlement called New Sweden was established on the Delaware River. The Dutch resented its presence and its prosperity, and made their resentment felt. After seventeen years, New Sweden was overcome and absorbed by New Netherland. It passed in time into the power of England.

A plan of colonisation, different from any other that had been tried on the American continent, called Pennsylvania into existence. William Penn, a wealthy, educated English quaker, who had suffered imprisonment for his belief, made up his mind to found a colony in America for the relief of those who suffered persecution for conscience sake. It happened that King Charles the Second owed him a large sum of money. Penn said that he was willing to take land in America instead of the money. As the king very much preferred to part with land in America for which he cared very little, and of which he had very much, to parting with money for which he cared very much, and of which he had very little, he cheerfully agreed. Penn got his land, which was as large as some European kingdoms, and he set up a little colony, the basis of which was absolute freedom, freedom of speech, freedom of thought, freedom of action. Although the plan as devised by Penn and executed by his people did not always work very smoothly, the colony throve rapidly, soon becoming, and long remaining, the most prosperous of all the colonies. It was great in trade, great in shipbuilding, great in farming. Its national tone was Quakerish as the national tone of New England was Puritan, but a steady stream of foreign immigration, largely German, soon set in and continued.

Down in the South colonisation was expanding. Virginia, the first of all the colonies, the 'Old Dominion' as it came to be called lovingly, was not to be the only settlement in those pleasant places. First Maryland came into being. It was opened by settlers from Virginia, under a Virginian adventurer named William Clayborne, in 1631. It soon passed into the hands of Lord Baltimore, to whom the king gave a charter, which allowed him to govern his colony very much in his own way without interference from England. Like Pennsylvania, like the New England colonies, Maryland was destined as a refuge for religion. The first Lord Baltimore was a Roman Catholic; it was his honourable ambition to found a colony where the Roman Catholics of England might profess their faith in peace. Such a spot he seemed to find in the north of Virginia. He died before he could carry out his enterprise, but his son Cecil, the second Lord Baltimore, and his younger son Leonard Calvert, took up their father's scheme. The second Lord Baltimore obtained the charter that had been prepared for his father, and his brother Leonard Calvert sailed for the New World with some two hundred English Catholics, in two vessels named the *Ark* and the *Dove*. The new province was called Terra Mariae in honour of Queen Henrietta Maria, wife of King Charles the First. The first settlement was called St. Mary's, in dutiful tribute to the faith, and the new comers often called themselves 'Pilgrims of St Mary's.' The new colony, although Catholic from its dawn, offered absolute religious equality to all who professed any Christian faith. It did not go so far as Rhode Island, which offered shelter to men of any creed or of no creed. But for its time and hour it was amazingly liberal and enlightened. It was an exceedingly prosperous little settlement. It suffered no initial agonies of cold or hunger or sickness. Its only early difficulties were with the man who had made a settlement before the coming of the *Ark* and the *Dove*, William Clayborne. Clayborne tried to fight with the new comers, but they were too much for him. They defeated him, dispersed his followers, and sent Clayborne himself as a prisoner to England. He came back again during the Commonwealth, and ravaged the province with religious war.

The power of Lord Baltimore over the new colony was little less than regal, at least in theory. His governorship was hereditary in his family. He could confer titles of nobility. He created the law courts; he created their judges; he had the royal right to pardon criminals. He coined his own money, and he made his own laws. In practice, however, the absoluteness of this authority was considerably minimised. The colonists insisted on having a voice in the government of their affairs, and in the end they got what they wanted, and the royal rule of the Baltimores was royal more in name than in fact. There came a time when their authority fell from them altogether. Though Maryland had been founded as a Roman Catholic colony, with religious freedom for all other sects, the other religious sects did not show themselves very grateful for toleration. First the Puritans and then the Episcopalians plotted against the Catholics. Their desires were gratified on the accession of William and Mary, when strong anti-catholic laws came into force in England. The charter of the Baltimores was taken away from them, and the profession of the Catholic faith, the exercise of Catholic rites, was made penal in Maryland. Early in the eighteenth century the Baltimores re-

sumed their sway over the colony as the fourth Lord
Baltimore became a Protestant, and it remained in
the hands of the family so long as a royal governor
was left in America. A quarrel between Maryland
and Pennsylvania as to their boundaries was settled
in 1767, when two London Mathematicians, Charles
Mason and Jeremiah Dixon, drew the division destined
to become famous as 'Mason and Dixon's line.'

King Charles the Second was always ready to
show his gratitude to the friends who had helped
him to enjoy his own again. The broad acres of
distant America offered as economic a form of paying
these debts of gratitude as, in the case of William
Penn, they had offered for the payment of a debt
of money. Charles now made a present of territory
lying between Virginia and the Spanish colony of
Florida to some eight noblemen of his court, of
whom George Monk, Duke of Albemarle, and Edward
Hyde, Earl of Clarendon, were the most conspicuous.
The territory was not exactly virgin soil. Early in
the second half of the sixteenth century an unsuccessful attempt at colonisation had been made by
a little brotherhood of French Protestants flying from
oppression. Refugees, they were still loyal, for they
named their new home Carolina, after their King
Charles the Ninth. The colony failed; the colonists
drifted away; and for about a century Carolina was
left alone, until Charles made his gracious gift to
his eight noblemen. The eight noblemen had some
very wonderful ideas about the colony they were
going to found. One thing they were resolved upon:
it was to be very different indeed from the existing
colonies with their eccentric theories of liberty and
equality. Carolina—they kept the name, for it fitted

Charles the Second of England as well as Charles the Ninth of France—was to be essentially an aristocratic colony. The plan of its constitution was made by the great philosopher, John Locke, with the assistance of one of the eight noblemen, Lord Ashley, who afterwards became Lord Shaftesbury. It was a very amazing constitution. By its provisions the people were to have very little power, and were indeed to be in scarcely better case than slaves. The authority was in the hands of an order of nobility, whose members were to carry sonorous titles and were to govern with no regard whatever for the wishes of those governed. The absurd scheme was never put seriously into practice. The colonists declined to be governed by so whimsical a constitution, and it ceased to be. The colony soon became populous. English, Irish, Scotch, Dutch, French, poured into it. It soon became prosperous. Different conditions of life in time divided it into North and South Carolina. In South Carolina rice was at first, and cotton much later, the chief product. The Lords Proprietary ruled the colonies with a very unpopular rule for more than half a century. Then they transferred the government to the crown, and the two Carolinas became separate royal provinces with governors appointed by the king.

Colonies had been founded for the relief of Separatists, for the relief of Puritans, for the relief of Quakers, for the relief of Roman Catholics. It remained, after the consolation of these spiritual sufferings, to found a colony for the solace of a present, practical, physical grievance, the grievance of being desperately in debt. In the third decade of the eighteenth century, a very high-minded and honourable English gentleman enter-

tained a very high-minded and honourable desire.
James Edward Oglethorpe was one of those rare
spirits whose blood and judgment are so well com-
mingled that they can be at once soldier and courtier,
and statesman and man of the world, and carry into
each and all of these callings a serene dignity of
carriage and a sweet purity of soul which fuses all
their parts into the best kind of gentlehood. Pope
commended his 'strong benevolence of soul,' and this
'strong benevolence' directed itself towards its own
Utopia. As a soldier he had served for a season
under Marlborough and Prince Eugène in Germany.
On his return he entered Parliament, and all
members of Parliament are presumed to be philanthropists. It was as a soldier, no less than as a
philanthropist, that he now schemed the scheme that
makes him famous. He noted the curious folly of
the English law relating to debt, which flung debtors
into prison where they could do nothing to redeem
themselves, and where, for the most part, they
languished till they died. He conceived a plan of
setting these poor people at liberty, and at the same
time of making them serviceable to the state. He
would free them, and found through them a colony
in America, and that colony should be where it
might serve as a barrier between the rapacity of the
Florida Spaniards and the colonists of the Carolinas.
He told his tale to King George the Second. King
George gave him a large tract of land between
Carolina and Florida. Oglethorpe took possession
of this land with his colony of rescued debtors and
others, and called it Georgia, in compliment to his
royal patron. Oglethorpe proved an admirable
governor. He was on excellent terms with the

Indians; he was tolerant of all religions; he was valorous to rashness in fighting with the Florida Spaniards who raided the new colony furiously; he was strenuously opposed to negro slavery. So long as Oglethorpe remained in Georgia, so long negro slavery remained out of it. In his colonial work he had the immediate aid of two great divines—of Wesley and of Whitefield. It is good to remember that Wesley was heart and soul with Oglethorpe in his opposition to slavery. It is bad to remember that Whitefield was opposed to Oglethorpe, and that when Oglethorpe left the colony, Whitefield helped to make slavery an abiding institution in Georgia. Oglethorpe went back to England and Parliament, and Dr. Johnson and Boswell, and to a long and beautiful old age. We know that he had the spirit of a boy when he was a very old man, and that he was ready to fight a duel for some affront put upon him when he was not far from ninety years of age. He carried back to England the first silk that was made in his dear colony, and it was fashioned into a dress for the English Queen. He never went back to Georgia, but his love for it was always warm; and if it had thriven as his affection would have had it thrive, it would have been the strongest and not the weakest of all the colonies at a time which was close at hand when he died. In all the early history of colonial America, there is no nobler name than Oglethorpe's. His were the virtues of the antique world, courage and courtesy, an unfailing spirit, a chivalrous temper, a gracious vitality that was buoyant in the season of senility, an eloquent tongue that only obeyed the promptings of an honourable heart. He was not faultless: there are things to regret in the record of James Oglethorpe. But he was a gentleman and a soldier, who was a Christian gentleman and a Christian soldier, and his is the sweetest and the noblest figure in American history until one came whose virtues dwarfed those of all who preceded as of all who followed him.

These thirteen colonies—the 'Old Thirteen,' as they are often affectionately called—formed in the beginning that union for a common purpose, which has grown into the great commonwealth, known by the world as the United States. Many of these colonies were almost as different from each other in climate, in soil, in population, in laws, in customs, in beliefs, as if they had been so many nations of the European continent. But they all had certain things in common. They were naturally all Christians. They all spoke the same speech, for, in spite of the flood of Dutch, Germans, Swedes, French, and other foreigners who poured into certain of the colonies, the English language dominated all these other tongues, and absorbed them all. Roosevelt has appreciated very happily, in his *Winning of the West*, the great significance of this common speech. The tongue, he says, which Bacon feared to use in his writings, lest they should remain for ever unknown to all but the inhabitants of a relatively unimportant insular kingdom, is now the speech of a new continent. The common law which Coke jealously upheld in the southern half of a single European island, is now the law of the land throughout the vast regions of America north of the Rio Grande. The names of the plays that Shakespeare wrote are household words in the mouths of a mighty nation, whose wide domains were to him more unreal than the realms of Prester John. Besides the common language, and all that a common language means, the colonies had in common, if not to the same extent, some form of local self-government. Each colony, that is to say, had in differing degree the right to make its own laws. One other fact was in the end common to all the colonies: they all in the end came under the sway of England, those colonies which had not originally been settled by Englishmen no less than those which owed their existence to English arms and English enterprise.

CHAPTER IV

THE INDIAN WARS

A NEW common factor came into the colonial problem. The dominion of Great Britain was found to be more or less galling by each and every colony. English rule was not always, nor indeed often, of a kind calculated to knit her colonies to her in a league of passionate adoration. But during the greater part of the eighteenth century, during the years in which the latent disaffection of the colonies was almost unconsciously growing into an active force, a semblance and more than a semblance of allegiance was kept up in the face of a danger that was at the same time imperial and colonial. Putting aside the brief Dutch dominion of half a century, three European powers had dreamed of supremacy on the continent of America—Spain, France, and England. In the eighteenth century, the really important claimants were reduced to two—France and England. Spain might be troublesome over some boundary question, might fight spasmodically with some colony that was neighbour to her possessions, but she was not to be considered as a serious rival for the rule of the New World. France was just such a serious rival. The colonial history of the last decade of the seventeenth century and more than the first half of the eighteenth century, is the history of what were called

THE INDIAN WARS 69

the Indian wars. These were really a series of French wars waged against England under cover of a line of painted savages. It must be admitted that, on the whole, the French managed the Indians better than the English did, treated them with more kindness, used them more gently, and were in consequence more successful in winning their alliance if not their allegiance. There were Indians shrewd enough to see that, French or English, the White Men were much the same, and that the Red Man would have to go to the wall for the one as well as the other. But for the most part the Indians were easily to be influenced by the French against the English, and the French did so influence them from 1689 to 1763. Colonial history between those two dates is practically the history of one long war, fought against Englishmen by savages armed and inspired by Frenchmen, to decide the great question whether America was to be under the sway of French or English. This long Indian war, or long succession of interrupted but continuous Indian wars, renewed the endless fears and ceaseless horrors of King Philip's days. Man, woman, or child, no one slept sound or slept safe in a small village or a lonely farmhouse during all that bloodstained three-quarters of a century. As often as not these savage raids were commanded by some French officer who cared little what happened to the victims of his savage allies, so long as one more village of the English-speaking race went blazing up to the midnight sky. The attack on Deerfield village, in the February of 1704, was made by a mixed force of French and Indians, led by a Frenchman, Hertel de Rouville, whose name was a terror to the colonists. The story of this foray has been brought of late very vividly before the eyes of all lovers of romance by Miss Wilkins's beautiful story, *Silence*. To read its early pages is to live in imagination through one night of all the many hundred nights when sounds like the laughter of fiends scared villagers from their sleep, and when men, women, and children huddled together in some house well built to stand a siege. The women loaded as fast as the men fired, using the spent bullets of the Indians to return against them. When lead gave out they melted precious pewter and precious silver to make yet more precious missiles. Long years of stealthy, murderous warfare, of ruined villages, of white captives tortured or sold into slavery, of Indian wigwams heavy with the scalplocks of slaughtered settlers, drove the colonists into a desperate hatred of the Indian as keen as that which burns to-day amongst the frontiersmen of the far west. That the only good Indian is a dead Indian, is the maxim of a soldier of to-day, but it expresses the general thought of those who offered a money reward for every Indian killed, and gladly paid it in the thought that the world was quit of one more painted devil.

The most serious episode in this episodical war came in 1753, when France and England faced each other on the banks of the Ohio. A map of North America for this period, painted in three colours to represent the claims of the three countries competing for the continent, will show that a narrow crimson strip running a thousand miles along the Atlantic coast represents the English colonies. A large crimson patch to the North denotes the territory of the Hudson Bay Company, founded in 1670. A vast green space covering Canada and all the interior region from the St. Lawrence to the mouth of the Mississippi represents the claims of France. Below this, tinted yellow, lie the great territories of New Spain. A governor of New York wrote back pathetically to his king that if the French were to be permitted to hold all the country over which the French claimed command, the King of England would not have a hundred miles from the sea anywhere. The French supported their claim strenuously. When the Ohio Company attempted to make a settlement in the valley of the Ohio, the settlers were driven out by French soldiers. The governor of Virginia resolved to send a special envoy to the French officer commanding on the Ohio to remonstrate with him. He chose for this duty a young gentleman of Virginia, who was quite unknown except to his intimate friends, but who was destined to become the most famous man in the history of America, and one of the most famous men in the history of the world. Young Mr. George Washington was a major in the Virginia militia. He was only twenty-three years of age, but he had done enough and more than enough in his three-and-twenty years to justify Governor Dinwhiddie's choice of an ambassador on a dangerous as well as a delicate embassy. Washington was left fatherless when he was eleven years of age. He owed his early education and his moral training to the care of his mother, Mary Washington. The son loved the mother as the mother loved the son. He had had some schooling, which came to an end when he was sixteen, and left him with enough of the essential knowledge, some geometry, and a considerable skill in surveying, an athletic body, and great mastery in horsemanship. This equipment for the world's adventure came near to being lessened when he was fourteen by the chance of his entering as a midshipman in the naval service of England. The opposition of his mother saved the boy for greater things. He left school to become a surveyor of lands, and worked hard and well at his business, as he worked hard and well at every business life offered him. At nineteen he received his command in the Virginia militia, and at twenty-three Governor Dinwhiddie, confident in his ability and his courage, chose him as the man to carry the message from England in Virginia to France on the Ohio, asking what France meant to do.

Young Mr. George Washington carried out his mission at the daily risk of his life. The vast and desolate region that lay between him and his goal was called the Wilderness, and through the Wilderness for more than five hundred miles Washington made his way in hourly jeopardy from hostile savages, from murderous guides, from the wild forces of nature. The expedition, says Irving, was 'the foundation of his fortunes. From that moment he was the rising hope of Virginia.' When Washington got to the French commander, and put his query, the answer was simple and straightforward enough. The French commander said that his immediate purpose in life was to hold the Ohio Valley, and to drive the English out of it. Washington had travelled his five hundred miles of ceaseless peril to learn so much. He turned on his heel, and traversed the five hundred miles again through the same ceaseless perils to tell Governor Dinwhiddie what the French commander had said. After that, Governor Dinwhiddie, as the

THE INDIAN WARS 73

representative of the offended majesty of England, knew that the one essential thing was to give the French a beating. This did not prove easy to do. In the year that followed Washington's mission, a small force was sent against the French under the command of Washington himself. The envoy of peace was now the herald of war. He had his little battle with the French at the Great Meadows, carried himself with valour and honour in the face of greatly superior numbers, made an honourable capitulation and returned with credit, if not with glory, to his own country.

A very harsh action by the English authorities at this time has been excused, if not justified, as a necessary military measure. Early in the war the British had conquered Nova Scotia, or Acadia as it was usually called, from the French. The inhabitants, simple Breton peasants, disliked the British rule; and now, at a time when it seemed likely that the French might endeavour to recover the place, they refused to take the oath of allegiance to the British government. The British government settled the question by a wholesale expulsion of the Acadians from their homes. More than six thousand were removed by force by British soldiers and dispersed among the English colonies. The act was carried out with so much needless cruelty and carelessness, that families were separated, and for long afterwards the colonial newspapers contained advertisements for the missing members of sorrowing families. The sad story of the Acadians was the inspiration of Longfellow's *Evangeline*.

A proposed reorganisation of the Virginia militia led Washington to resign his command; but when

General Braddock came over from England with two regiments of regular troops for the chastisement of the French, Washington gladly accepted an appointment as aide-de-camp on his staff. General Braddock, who had crossed the Atlantic to chastise the French, was a jovial man of the world from London, who loved wine and woman and song, but it may be especially wine, with all a soldier's cheerfulness, and who was prepared to meet and beat his enemy with all a soldier's bravery. But something more than bravery was wanted for the kind of war that Braddock was called upon to wage. He had to fight not merely the French, but the French allies. He had to contend with the Red Men, who knew every stone and tree that afforded shelter, who could hide in their hundreds and seem invisible, until the moment came for them to cry their cry, and hurl themselves upon the helpless enemy. Braddock marched gallantly to meet his enemy in proper military order, 'as if in St. James's Park,' with his bands playing, and his flags flying. Washington represented to him in vain the unwisdom of his action. Braddock was bull-headed and not to be advised. He had been warned before, and had disdained the warning. With the lightest heart he marched his men into an ambuscade where his whole force was at the mercy of the Red Man, and where the Red Man showed no mercy. It is one of the most tragic routs in history. Less than half of the British force escaped to tell of that fearful day. Washington was in all parts of that fatal fight; his clothes were torn with bullets; one chief afterwards related that he and his braves aimed at the young officer again and again: Washington seemed to bear a charmed life: he escaped without a wound. 'I have been protected beyond all human probability or expectation,' he wrote to his brother, 'for I had four bullets through my coat and two horses shot under me; yet I escaped unhurt, though death was levelling my companions on every side.' Death was indeed levelling his companions. Of the twelve hundred men who marched so blithely with all the gaudy circumstance of war against Fort Duquesne less than five hundred escaped to spread the tale of England's defeat through the English colonies. For three hours the unequal fight lasted. The Virginia riflemen with their native knowledge of woodcraft, and their experience of warfare in the wilderness, fought from behind trees as their opponents did. But the British troops, in their regular formation, fighting according to the regular rules of war as if against a regular foe under regular conditions, were steadily shot down by the Indians, to whom they offered a too easy target. At last they broke and fled in helpless panic, in hopeless rout. Braddock himself behaved very valiantly; if his bravery could have atoned for his blunder, the day would have been a British victory. He was carried off the field mortally wounded. Nothing in his life became him like the leaving it. The jovial general, who was so popular in London clubs, and at London dinner-tables, died like a gentleman and a soldier, with some splendid words upon his lips. 'I must do better another time.' The words showed that there were the makings of a hero in the rash, intemperate soldier. As the chaplain of the forces was wounded in that fight, it fell to George Washington to read the funeral service over his dead body. The curious might find an allegory in this picture of the pale, handsome young Virginian gentleman reading St. Paul's words of hope and comfort in the Resurrection and the Life over the dead Englishman.

The news of Braddock's defeat spread dismay throughout the colonies and roused fury in England. The colonists' first duty was defence; England's first desire was revenge. The colonists were in some alarm for their negro slaves, who believed that the victorious French would give them their liberty. The French encouraged the Indians in their furtive war against the colonists; and the Indians, convinced of the invincibility of the French and the weakness of the English, were unflagging in their attacks. Perhaps the most disastrous result for England of Braddock's defeat was not the triumph it afforded the French, the hopes it gave the slaves, and the ferocity with which it inspired the Red Man, but the knowledge now plainly presented to colonial minds that the soldiers of King George were not all-conquering, but might be defeated and put to flight like other men, if the odds or opportunity were against them. The knowledge counted for much in the years to come. In the meantime the colonists had their hands full. Washington, in command of the Virginia forces, toiled ceaselessly to defend the frontier from the Indian raiders, who were ever ready to swoop unexpectedly upon defenceless places, and leave behind them their record of blood and fire.

Gradually the wheel of fortune turned; gradually the French began to lose ground. Washington marched once more against Fort Duquesne, and on the 25th of November 1758 he took it, and was able to plant the British flag on the yet smoking ruins of the stronghold that was thenceforward to be called Fort Pitt, in honour of England's minister. The capture by the English of forts Niagara, Ticonderoga, and Crown Point were blows to France. The heaviest blow was now to be delivered. The hour had come and the man. A great expedition was planned in England against Quebec. The command fell to General Wolfe, a young soldier of thirty-three, who had served with great distinction in Germany in the Seven Years' War. In command of some eight thousand men, Wolfe encamped on the island of St. Orleans in the St. Lawrence River, eight miles below Quebec.

Wolfe attacked Quebec and was repulsed; the place seemed impregnable. But there was a soldier in Wolfe's army, a Lieutenant M'Culloch, who had been a prisoner in Quebec three years earlier. He thought there was a spot on the south side where the steep hills of the Heights of Abraham might be scaled with success. Wolfe resolved to make the attempt. He sent Captain Cook, afterwards a famous traveller, to divert attention by a feigned attack elsewhere, while he and his party were rowed along the St. Lawrence to the narrow path that might lead to victory. All the world knows the story of that night on that river, of the young, ambitious soldier repeating in a low voice Gray's 'Elegy' to the officers in his boat, and assuring them that he would rather have written that poem than take Quebec. It was a fine saying; it need not be taken too seriously as the expression of Wolfe's very soul. At least he did take Quebec. He and his party climbed unopposed the narrow path, and when the day dawned, Montcalm, the French commander, found an army ranged against him on the heights of Abraham. Montcalm marched out against the English with an army twice as large, and was hopelessly defeated in less than a quarter of an hour. Both generals were killed. When Montcalm was told that he was mortally wounded he said, 'So much the better; I shall not live to see the surrender of Quebec.' Wolfe lying dying on the battlefield heard the cry, 'They run.' It roused his sinking senses, and he asked, 'Who run?' He was told it was the French. 'God be praised!' he said, 'I die in peace.' He had done his great task. Quebec surrendered five days later. The surrender of Quebec meant the end of the supremacy of France in Canada. Four years later France had yielded to England every foot of her territory in the New World, except a few fishing-stations near Newfoundland.

One immediate result of the overthrow of the French was a great Indian conspiracy against the colonists, as deeply laid, and as deadly as that which led to King Philip's war. With the withdrawal of the French troops, the Algonquin Indians found themselves abandoned by the allies, whom they had thought irresistible, and left to face their English and their Indian enemies. There was an Ottawa chief, named Pontiac, who had helped to defeat Braddock's army, and who dreamed, as Philip had dreamed, that a union of the Indian tribes might yet drive the English back into the sea. He sent his envoys throughout the country; he persuaded the majority of the tribes to join his league; he even prevailed upon the Senecas of the Six Nations to enter the alliance. He made an attempt to secure the fort of Detroit by treachery. The attempt failed.

THE INDIAN WARS

Then Pontiac began his war in earnest. It lasted for nearly two years, during which, one after another, nearly all the forts held by the English in the region of the Great Lakes were taken by the Indians. Detroit held out successfully after sustaining a siege of five months, the longest siege ever made by Indians. The war was a succession of massacres, a record of hideous butchery, and yet more hideous cruelty. In the end, however, after the fiercest fight ever fought between the White Men and the Red, the Indians were defeated. Pontiac was compelled to sue for peace, and soon after he was murdered by another Indian. The conspiracy of Pontiac closed the long and cruel series of French and Indian wars. There was to be peace now on the American continent for a season. It was not destined to be a very long peace. It proved to be, as it were, a breathing space in which the colonists, resting from the struggles with the Frenchman and the Red Man, might have leisure to reflect upon their own place in the world, upon their relationship to the mother-country, and upon the direction in which they would wish their future career to go. These were problems that asserted themselves, problems that had to be solved.

CHAPTER V

HOW NOT TO GOVERN

THE American colonies never seemed more closely knitted to England than at the moment when the triumph of British arms wrested Canada from the French and set the colonists free from their most dangerous enemy. Kinship of race, joint pride in success, the common advantage of union, all seemed to point to an enduring bond between the colonies and the mother-country. That the bond did not endure was entirely the fault of the mother-country. The relationship of the colonies to England was, and had long been, strained. The descendants of the early settlers were jealous of their political liberty, were keenly watchful of the authority which England claimed to have over them. The English theory roughly was, that the English Parliament ultimately possessed absolute authority over the American colonies. That theory the American colonists strenuously denied. With the accession of George the Third the theory was to be maintained more pertinaciously and resisted more stubbornly than ever. From the very first, George was determined to play a prominent part in the political life of the country he governed. Thus a king's party and a people's party came into existence in England as a king's party and a people's party came into existence in the American colonies.

It might go hard even with an imaginative politician to devise a more unfortunate system of colonial administration than that which England chose to impose upon her children across the Atlantic. We know now, though the world does not always act upon the knowledge, that the only way to keep colonies loyal and contented, is to leave in colonial hands the management of colonial affairs. That unfortunately was not then nor for long later England's way. She chose to regard bodies of proud-spirited and high-tempered men as voiceless and spiritless dependents on whom she was at liberty to practise any perversion of justice that the home government was pleased to regard as an administrative system. The administrative system was farcical in its simplicity and inadequacy. At its head was a body in England, a standing committee of the Privy Council, known at length as 'The Lords of the Committee of Trade and Plantations,' and known familiarly as 'The Lords of Trade.' This body had been in existence since the year 1675. To this board in England the English governors of the American colonies addressed, on the one hand, full reports of all the legislative, financial, agricultural, and commercial conditions of the colonies they swayed; and, on the other hand, voluminous and querulous private letters relating the difficulties they had to encounter and the hardships they had to endure in maintaining the authority and dignity of the mother-country over stiff-necked and semi-mutinous subjects. It is hard, in an age when news travels with the swiftness of the wind, to realise the

F

immense and disastrous influence which such communications could have and did have upon a home government. Nowadays the internal affairs of England's most distant dependencies may be known in a few hours to an Englishman with the ability to read a newspaper and the intelligence to consider and to discuss its contents. Two hundred years ago, one hundred and fifty years ago, one hundred years ago, news could only travel with the speed of the sail and the speed of the horse. In the last third of the eighteenth century there were few people in London, and fewer still in the provinces, who knew much, or who cared much, for the condition of the American colonies. The public at large, when it thought of them at all, thought of them merely as so many commercial advantages to England. The minority who were really interested, really willing to be informed, were generally men in public life whose information was for the most part based upon such reports and letters as were submitted to the Lords of Trade by the colonial governors. As the colonial governors were always at odds with their governments, they sent home the most unflattering pictures of the colonists, whom they represented as whimsical malcontents, whose one desire was to cut themselves adrift from England. Though these fantastic representations could not influence the opinions of the few who really understood the position of affairs in America, they generally had a great effect upon the Lords of Trade. The Lords of Trade sympathised profoundly with the protesting governors, and showed their sympathy by encouraging them in the most foolish and ill-judged acts of interference with popular rights. Naturally, the

HOW NOT TO GOVERN

governors had a good deal of power in their hands, chiefly in the way of appointment: they had such influence as a mimic court can give. But their power was always checked by the fact that they were dependent upon their assemblies for their salaries. The Lords of Trade resented the strength of the Assemblies as much as the governors could do. They were always dreaming of some scheme for bringing the colonies under one head or viceroy, in a way that would minimise the legislative freedom while it increased the military force of the colonies. There were wise men in America who had dreamed of a union of the different colonies, but not such a union as would have pleased the Lords of Trade, who went on their blundering way, doing everything that lay in their power, and a great deal lay in their power, to foment the difference between the assemblies and the governors, and to provoke difference between the colonies and the mother-country.

With George Grenville's accession to power as head of the English Cabinet in 1763 began the presentation of the new colonial policy which was destined to develop so remarkably. The new policy was a combination of three intentions on the part of the home government: the intention to enforce very rigidly the Acts of Trade, the intention to establish permanently British garrisons in America, and the intention to impose taxation upon the colonies for the partial support of these British garrisons. Such a policy was exceedingly easy to propose at Westminster. It was exceedingly difficult to carry into effect in New England. As regards the first portion of the policy, that which aimed at enforcing obedience to the navigation laws, English statesmen believed, and few American statesmen would have denied, that England was legally in the right. After the weary business of the Seven Years' War, with its battle-grounds in Europe and its battle-grounds in America, England, drained by the struggle, and at her wits'-end for money to fight abroad and to feed at home, suddenly discovered that a species of smuggling was being carried on with a lively boldness in her American dependencies. Elaborate Acts of Trade, passed for the protection of British interests, were ignored. They were suffered to fall into disuse through the indifference or the defiance of those to whom they were addressed. They became a dead letter through the audacity of the colonists and the venality of the officials whose duty it was to enforce them. Angry imperialism strove to assert its authority by means of general search-warrants, or Writs of Assistance as they have come to be called. Probably no one now denies the legality, as the law then stood, of these Writs of Assistance. Under the law and the constitution by which the English colonies were then administered, these increased powers for the detection of uncustomed merchandise were, if not justified, at least authoritative and defendable. But to be within the letter of the law is seldom the justification for acts which can only mean a surrender to tyranny or a resort to revolution. The colonists were not yet ripe for revolution, but they were not raw enough for patient submission to tyranny. Public feeling raged against the Writs of Assistance. A government official, James Otis, the king's advocate, resigned his office formally to be free to protest against their issue. Otis was technically in the wrong: Otis was ethically in the right.

HOW NOT TO GOVERN

A rising young lawyer, John Adams, destined to undreamed-of fame, declared that American independence was born when 'Mr. Otis's oration against Writs of Assistance breathed into this nation the breath of life.'

The proposal to establish a permanent garrison of about ten thousand men in America was very distasteful to the colonists. More English soldiers might have been of much help in the French and Indian wars. But now France was out of the field; the Pontiac conspiracy was like to be the last united stand of the Red Man against the White. The colonists were content with their own militia, and they entertained some fear that the presence of a British garrison might be used by a British ministry to minimise their liberty. As they neither asked for nor wished for soldiers, they resented having soldiers imposed upon them. It is not probable that their resentment would have gone as far as actual resistance in any form to the proposed garrison, if it had not been for the conditions that accompanied the proposition. It would cost about three hundred thousand pounds to keep up a permanent garrison. Of this it was proposed that one hundred thousand pounds should be raised from the colonies by taxation. The question of taxation was the question that caused most difference of opinion, and aroused most irritation. England, harassed by her recent war, was driven to increase her taxation in order to replenish her exhausted exchequer. In an evil hour for themselves the ministry resolved to avoid unpopularity at home by courting it abroad. In order not to offend the English people by a too grave increase of taxation, they decided to offend the

American colonies by putting in force the often-dreamed-of scheme of applying taxation to them. It must always be remembered, however, that it was never proposed to tax America for the support of the English government. When Grenville brought forward his famous resolution, declaring that it was fit to impose certain stamp duties upon the North American colonies, he did so for the purpose of meeting portion of the expense entailed by the proposed American garrison. The resolution was passed without much difficulty, and the actual date of imposition of the duties was fixed for the following year. This taxation, exasperating in itself, was not the only interference with the colonies. Other resolutions, as lightly passed, imposed new duties on the colonial trade of a kind peculiarly aggravating to the colonists.

In itself the Stamp Act was not a flagrantly objectionable measure. It provided that all deeds and receipts and other legal documents of any kind should be written or printed on stamped paper. This stamped paper was to be sold by the government tax-collectors, and the money paid for it was to go to the government. Stamps were to be placed on printed books, on newspapers, and on playing cards. The advantages of the tax, from the point of view of those concerned for the revenue, was that for the most part it might be said to collect itself. As it did not include receipts for money paid and papers of exchange, it was not a specially onerous form of taxation, less onerous, indeed, than the law now is in England. It was not so much the measure itself, however, as the principle involved that aroused colonial opposition.

HOW NOT TO GOVERN 87

The colonists were not prepared to suffer in silence. New England and New York had long led the van of protest against the right of taxation of the home government. Seventy years earlier, the general court of Massachusetts by enactment denied the right of any other legislature to tax the colony. A little later the Assembly of New York did even more when it denied the right of any other legislature to exercise any legislative authority over the colony. Colonies that had asserted themselves so stoutly against possible aggression were not likely to remain passive when aggression had become not merely probable but actual. Boston led the van of protest. Samuel Adams, a cousin of John Adams, drew up the first resolutions denying the right of Parliament to tax the colonies against their will. The provincial Assemblies rained petitions upon the king, showered memorials upon Parliament. King and Parliament showed themselves equally indifferent to the prayers and to the dangers that lay behind the disregarded prayers. There were, however, individual members of Parliament who were not indifferent, and one of these was Colonel Barré. Charles Townshend asked why the Americans, 'children planted by our care, nourished by our indulgence, till they are grown up to strength and opulence, and protected by our arms,' should grudge to contribute their mite to relieve the English government from the weight of its heavy burden. Barré promptly replied by a series of scornful denials of all Townshend's statements. 'They planted by your care? No, they were planted by your oppression. They nourished by your indulgence? They grew up by your neglect. They protected by your arms? They have nobly taken up arms in your defence.' Barré went on to describe the colonists as a people jealous of their liberties and who will vindicate them if ever they should be violated. This daring speech made a sensation in England, but a much greater sensation in America. Its eloquent words were soon in every man's mouth, and it did much to encourage the colonists in their action against the measure.

No time was lost by the American colonies in combining against the execution of the law. The colony of Virginia was prominent in its conduct. Among the citizens of Virginia was a young gentleman of nine-and-twenty, who, in spite of his youth, had tried many things and failed in most of them. If life could have been successfully based on a taste for and skill in dancing and hunting, fishing and riding, young Mr. Patrick Henry of Studley, in Hanover County, Virginia, would have been a happy man. As he had little taste for book-learning, he tried commerce, and failed in that. Then he tried farming, and failed in that. Then he tried trade again, and failed again, and finally, at the ripe age of four-and-twenty, he devoted himself to the bar, and at the bar at last he attained success. He first steps into history as the opponent of the Stamp Act in the Virginia House of Burgesses in 1765. Every one is familiar with the famous speech in which he declared that, 'Cæsar had his Brutus, Charles the First his Cromwell, and George the Third——' Here he was interrupted by cries of 'treason.' As soon as the clamour had died away, Patrick Henry calmly concluded, 'And George the Third may profit by their example. If this be treason, make the most of it.' Undoubtedly to Patrick

HOW NOT TO GOVERN

Henry belongs the credit of being one of the earliest and one of the most advanced of the leaders in that movement which ended in the American Revolution.

The Virginia Assembly, inspired by Patrick Henry, passed resolutions, declaring that it and it alone had the right to lay taxes and impositions upon the inhabitants of the colonies. Other colonial assemblies followed the example of Virginia. Massachusetts, on the advice of James Otis, went a step further, and advocated the calling of a congress of all deputies from the colonial assemblies to consult upon the common danger. This congress was called and met in New York on the first Monday in the November of 1765. Massachusetts, South Carolina, Pennsylvania, Rhode Island, Connecticut, Delaware, Maryland, New Jersey, and New York were represented. The congress drew up a series of resolutions setting forth the rights and grievances of the colonists. In the meanwhile, public agitation against the Stamp Act increased. Wild riots broke out in Boston. The mob made an effigy of Andrew Oliver, the newly appointed collector of the stamp taxes, hung it on a tree, then cut it down, carried it through the streets to Oliver's house, and burnt it at his door. It then attacked and destroyed his house. It ravaged the house of Chief Justice Hutchinson, and flung his possessions into the street. The manuscript of his *History of Massachusetts* is still preserved, its pages stained with the Boston mud in which it lay that day. There were other riots in other colonies. Most of the stamp officers were forced to resign, and the colonists, to avoid using stamps, abandoned for the time all law proceedings and took to arbitration instead. By this time the English ministry had changed. The Rockingham administration was in power. Pitt denounced the Stamp Act. 'I rejoice,' he said, 'that America has resisted.' The act was repealed, to the joy of the friends of colonial liberty and the despair of the followers of the late ministry, though the colonists were offended, and the king's men comforted, by the passing of another act, asserting that Parliament had full power to make laws 'to bind the colonists and people of America subjects to the Crown of Great Britain in all cases whatsoever.' The news of the repeal of the Stamp Act was received with the wildest joy in Boston. Bells were rung, flags flown, prisoners for debt were set at liberty to share the common satisfaction. The colonists had reason to be hilarious. They had learnt the initial lesson of the good effects of union.

The repeal of the Stamp Act did not, as it was hoped that it would do, herald an era of happier relations between England and her American colonies. The resolution affirming the right to tax the colonies was not allowed to remain a dead letter. The Rockingham ministry had crumbled away and Pitt was Prime Minister in name but not in fact, when a second and yet more fatal, yet more foolish attempt was made to force obnoxious taxation upon the American colonies. Pitt was away in the country, prostrate, well-nigh insane with one of his terrible attacks of gout in the head, wholly irresponsible for his own actions, wholly incapable of guiding the course of the administration. His Chancellor of the Exchequer was Charles Townshend, and to Charles Townshend is due such a kind of fame as the fool earned who fired the Temple of Ephesus. Charles Townshend had a passion for popularity, and many qualities which deserved popularity. It is impossible even now to read without emotion the eloquent tribute of Burke to his memory, the tribute of Burke who, while he detested the measure, finely appreciated the temper of the man. He called Townshend the delight and ornament of the House of Commons, the charm of every private society which he honoured with his presence. According to his eloquent judge, there never arose in this country or in any country a man of more pointed and finished wit, and, where his passions were not concerned, of a more refined, exquisite, and penetrating judgment. But his great failing was his immoderate passion for fame—a passion, says Burke, with stately generosity, which is the instinct of all great souls. 'He worshipped that Goddess wheresoever she appeared, but he paid his particular devotions to her in her favourite habitation, in her chosen temple, the House of Commons.' It is the peculiar irony of fate that this passion for fame should have been gratified, and yet gratified in such a way as would have broken Townshend's heart if he could have foreseen the result. He has earned his fame as the supporter of a weak and evil measure, as the cause of a fatal quarrel and a fratricidal war, as the man who inflicted upon England the greatest loss her dignity and her fortunes ever received. The repeal of the Stamp Act had become as unpopular in Parliament as the Act itself had been a little earlier. To dissipate that unpopularity, Charles Townshend declared that revenue must be had out of America, and proceeded to undo all the good effects of the repeal of the Stamp Act by imposing a tax upon glass, paper, and tea. To please universally was the object of Townshend's life, but as Burke says, to tax and to please, no more than to love and to be wise, is not given to men. Townshend attempted this impossible feat. He was truly, to use again the words of Burke, the child of the House of Commons. He never thought, did, or said anything but with a view to it and to its judgment, and he adapted himself daily to its disposition, and adjusted himself before it as at a looking-glass. He accepted the passing temper of the House of Commons as an infallible guide towards the course prescribed by statesmanship, and in doing so he ruined his own reputation, and very nearly succeeded in ruining his country. Not often has it been given to any statesman to make so colossal a blunder as the blunder which is associated eternally with the name of Charles Townshend.

Though the repeal of the Stamp Act had brought about a measure of tranquillity in the colonies, a fire still smouldered. The colonial authorities had irritated the colonists by their attitude towards the offenders in the late riots against the Stamp Act. Governor Bernard of Massachusetts, a hot-headed, rash man who lives for us in Hawthorne's portraiture, offended the provincial legislature by his domineering conduct. The fact that his action was supported by Lord Hillsborough, then Secretary of State, kept distrust and disaffection alive. The legislatures of New York and of Massachusetts refused to execute the Mutiny Act, a measure quartering the king's troops upon them, on the ground that it involved the principle of taxation. Parliament immediately passed an Act restraining the New York legislature from passing any law whatever until it had complied with the principles of the Mutiny Act. New York did comply. Massachusetts, more sternly resolute, refused. It issued a circular to the other colonies, urging them to co-operate in taking measures to obtain redress for the recent Acts of Parliament. The home authorities were greatly alarmed at this second instance of combination amongst the colonies, against the parental authority of Parliament. Lord Hillsborough immediately called upon the blundering, bellicose Governor Bernard to have the circular rescinded. Governor Bernard was willing enough to obey, but he could not compel the indignant legislature to obey him. James Otis declared that the Massachusetts legislature would not yield, and that the British Parliament must give way. Let Britain rescind their measures, or they are lost for ever. Governor Bernard answered his bold language by dissolving the legislature. But the example set by Massachusetts was followed by other colonies. Maryland, Delaware, Virginia, Georgia, New York, spoke boldly out against Lord Hillsborough's action. The English Parliament owned its appreciation of the gravity of the situation by making a new office, that of Secretary of State for the Colonies, and by appointing the obnoxious Minister, Lord Hillsborough, to fill the post. Even if he had not already made himself unpopular with the colonies, he was one of the last men for such a duty. Though we may assume, in spite of the bitter saying of Horace Walpole, that he was something more than a pompous composition of ignorance and want of judgment, he certainly had neither the temper to appreciate, nor the tact to deal with, such a movement as was taking place across the Atlantic.

Lord Hillsborough imagined that a little of what he thought to be firmness would soon settle the American difficulty. But the abiding firmness was on the other side. The colonists, finding that their prayers were unavailing, combined once more in the determination not to import British goods. Boston once more took the lead in the new crusade. At a great meeting held in Faneuil Hall, one of those meetings which gave Faneuil Hall its well-deserved name of 'Cradle of Liberty,' the citizens resolved to encourage domestic manufactures, and to eat nothing, drink nothing, and wear nothing imported from Great Britain until the duties should be taken off. The principle spread among the States. Everywhere men and women banded themselves together, as Sons of Liberty and Daughters of Liberty, into associations pledged to the principles of Faneuil Hall. Even tea, so dear to the women of the last century, they consented to forego in their determination to resist the illegal encroachments of Great Britain.

CHAPTER VI

THE BOSTON TEA-PARTY

IN such a condition of public feeling, some trifling act may serve to set great forces going. The trifling impetus was afforded by the officers of the Board of Commissioners of Customs appointed under the new law. The sloop *Liberty*, belonging to a then little-known citizen of Boston, Mr. John Hancock, was seized by them for a violation of the revenue laws. As the customs officers fancied that the sloop would not be safe at the wharf, they cut her loose and towed her under the guns of a British man-of-war, the *Romney*, which happened to be lying in the harbour. The people of Boston immediately rose in insurrection. The houses of the commissioners were attacked, the custom house officers were beaten, the commissioners had to fly for safety on board the *Romney*, and afterwards to take shelter in Castle William, a fortress on an island in the mouth of the harbour. Bernard seized the excuse afforded by the *Liberty* riot to call for military aid, and Hillsborough answered the demand by pouring in troops from Halifax. Boston was quick with excitement, indignation, and anger. Faneuil Hall rang with the protests of Adams, and the exhortations to arms of Otis. As Bernard stubbornly refused to convene the Assembly, the Boston leaders called upon all the

towns of Massachusetts to send representatives to a
general convention. Only one of the towns invited
declined the summons. The representatives of all
the other towns and districts met in Faneuil Hall on
the 22nd September 1768, drew up a temperate and
respectful petition to the king, and passed a resolution
asserting their desire to preserve peace and order.

On the very day when the convention rose from
its task, eight British ships-of-war sailed into Boston
Harbour. On the first of October, two regiments of
British troops, with a portion of a third regiment and
a train of artillery, entered Boston with bayonets
fixed, drums beating and colours flying, and marched
to the Common. The Select-men of Boston absolutely refused to quarter the two regiments in the
town. One regiment had to find shelter in Faneuil
Hall. The next morning the State House was
opened for the soldiers by the governor's command, and two field-pieces placed in front of it. The
indignation of the people of Boston grew keener every
hour. The presence of the military in Faneuil Hall,
the encampment on the Common, the drumming and
fifing on the Sabbath, the marching and countermarching, the challenging of citizens, were so many
wounds to their pride and disturbances to their peace.
There was worse to come. Yet more troops were
poured into Boston, converting its quiet into all the
seeming of a garrison town.

At first the feeling between the citizens and the
soldiers was friendly, but this friendliness did not last
long. The Bostonians did not conceal their indignation at the presence of the military, who in their turn
began to treat the townspeople with contumely. The
very children took part in the quarrel. The soldiers

destroyed the snow-slides they had made for their sleds. A deputation of boys waited upon the British general to complain of this conduct. The general asked them if their fathers had sent them to display their rebellious spirit. The boys' leader answered that no one had sent them, that they had come of their own accord, as they would no longer bear the obstruction of their pastime. The general gave orders that the damage should be made good, declaring that it was impossible to beat the idea of liberty out of a people who had it so firmly rooted in them in childhood.

In England the feeling against the men of Massachusetts grew very bitter. Wild schemes were suggested for bringing the colonists to their knees. 'We can grant nothing to the Americans,' Hillsborough declared, in a moment of more than usual folly even for him, 'except what they may ask with a halter round their necks.' In order to place this halter round their necks it was proposed to revive an old law of Henry VIII., by which Boston citizens could be brought over seas and tried in England. Against the madness of the administration the voice of Burke, the voice of Barré, were raised in generous and eloquent protests. The protests had some effect. It was proposed to repeal, not indeed all, but at least some of the obnoxious taxes. To Lord North is due the discredit of deciding that the tax on tea should be retained. The good intentions of the government, limited as they were, were conveyed to the colonies in a peculiarly ungracious letter from Lord Hillsborough. It is not surprising that they had but little effect upon the colonists. Men who protested against the principle of taxation and the presence of masses of soldiers meant to overawe them, were not likely to be placated by some few poor concessions unwillingly made and uncivilly communicated. Even the recall of Governor Bernard was not now enough, though Boston went wild with joy on the day of his departure. Once again flags waved, bonfires blazed, bells rang, and cannon boomed to celebrate a brief felicity.

On the 5th of March 1770, the very day when Lord North was moving in Parliament for a repeal upon all the duties, with the single exception of tea, a conflict broke out between the citizens of Boston and the British troops. It is impossible now to know exactly what happened. Provocation was given and taken on both sides. An officer, Colonel Preston, interfered without success. Some of the soldiers fired. Several of the townspeople were killed and more wounded. Immediately the alarm spread through the city. Drums beat to arms, and thousands of the citizens assembled to join in a general attack upon the military. The lieutenant-governor succeeded, however, in calming the people. Colonel Preston and the soldiers under his command were committed to prison, and duly and fairly tried. Captain Preston and six of his men were acquitted, and only two soldiers were convicted of manslaughter. The fairness of the trial reflected the highest credit upon the Boston jury, and upon John Adams, who defended the arraigned soldiers. The people of Boston gave a public funeral to the victims of the Boston massacre, as it was called, and for long years after the commemoration of the martyred citizens was kept up with all honourable pomp and tragic circumstance. The first struggle of the Revolution had taken place.

Massachusetts was not the only disturbed colony. There was a rising in North Carolina in 1771, a rising that was bloodily suppressed by the governor and the loyal militia. But it was on the New England States that the eyes of politicians at home were fixed. It was the affairs of New England that were discussed. New England was the centre of the agitation. It was in New England that an event occurred, now only second in importance to the Boston massacre, the episode of the *Gaspee*. The *Gaspee* was an English ship-of-war of eight guns, whose commander, Lieutenant Duddington, had shown himself especially active in the enforcement of the Revenue Acts along the Rhode Island coast. His fiery zeal had brought him more than once into conflict with the state authorities, but his action had been supported by his admiral, and Duddington went his way zealously, defying and deriding the civil authorities.

'The civil authorities, or at least the citizens whom they represented, resolved to strike a strong blow in defence of their rights. An opportunity was soon afforded them. On the 9th June the *Providence* packet was entering Newport Harbour, when Lieutenant Duddington, full of his pride of office, called upon her to lower her colours in salutation as she passed. The American captain refused. The *Gaspee* fired at her to bring her to. The American captain ran his course, keeping in shallow water, and the *Gaspee*, hotly pursuing, ran aground. The tide was ebbing; the *Gaspee* was fast ashore for the night, the packet went its way triumphantly, and brought the news of what had happened to Providence town. Soon a drum began to beat through the Providence streets, summoning all willing persons to meet at the house of a well-known citizen. At ten o'clock, eight boats, manned by well-armed Rhode Island fishermen, and prominent citizens of Providence, put out from the town, and, rowing with muffled oars, reached the *Gaspee* where she stuck stranded. She was immediately boarded. Her crew, taken by surprise, could make little or no resistance. In such scuffle as there was, Lieutenant Duddington was badly wounded. Duddington's wounds were dressed carefully. He and his crew, with all their personal property, were conveyed on shore. Then the *Gaspee* was set on fire and left to burn to the water's edge, its flames blazing up into the bright dawn of the June morning.

This daring enterprise galled the government to the quick. But the government sought in vain any satisfaction for the affront. Though a reward of five hundred pounds was offered for the apprehension of the offenders, and though, as a matter of fact, the names of those who had planned and executed the enterprise were familiar to many, no evidence could be obtained against them. The *Gaspee* burned unavenged. The men of Providence, true to one another, and to their common cause, held their heads high, and boasted that the antique virtues were not confined to Boston.

Events like these quite unhinged the reason of the more hot-headed politicians at home. Their actions and utterances fanned a flame of fury against the colonies in England. The hostility of England towards her turbulent colonies served the purpose of one man more than all others. That man was the king. Ever since he came to the throne, his one dream was to restore, as far as might be possible, compatible with the conditions under which he held

THE BOSTON TEA-PARTY

the sceptre, absolute power to the monarch. In North, and in North's ministry, he found creatures excellently suited to be the tools of his intent. North's weak nature easily moulded itself in obedience to the bull-dog stubbornness of the king's temper, and what North did, his followers did.

In point of fact, while North was minister in name, the king was minister in deed. The administration of the country lay in the hollow of his hand. North and his weak or supple followers were but puppets that gyrated as the king pulled their strings. The familiar phrase of the power behind the throne had no meaning at this epoch in English history. The power was on the throne, and on the throne alone. The king guided all home and foreign policy, directed the course of debate in Parliament, handled his majority in the House of Commons and in the House of Lords as a skilful chess-player handles his men and his pieces. In an age when patronage was one of the principal factors in the administration of the state, the king reserved to himself the full use of this formidable weapon. The members of a ministry were nominated by the king. The English and Scotch judges were nominated by the king. They owed their promotion to the king. The preferments of the Church came from the king. Promotion in the army came from the king. The titles and the pensions dear to the adventurous placeman and prize-hunter were to be had only from the king. It was from the king and from the king alone that all these blessings flowed which ambitious or esurient spirits could sigh for, and which in the last century had so enormous an influence in shaping the course of politics. 'It was all for our rightful king,' sighs the gallant soldier of the Jacobite ballad. 'It is all from our rightful king,' might have been the burden of the placemen in the high noon of George's reign. Seldom had a constitutional monarch more power in his hands. Never did a constitutional monarch use that power so badly.

If the agitation in America served George's purpose in some degree by stimulating England in favour of the ministry that was his mask, it irritated him by the way in which it called into question his dreamed-of supremacy. What were the colonists that they should dare to disagree with measures passed by the king's ministers? He had been furious at what he called the 'fatal compliance of 1766,' and he thought that the time had come for undoing that compliance, and even more for avenging it.

The imbecile policy of Lord Hillsborough was the imbecile policy of the king. Lord Hillsborough dreamed his dream of dictating terms to the colonists when the colonists came, suppliant, like the burgesses of Calais, with halters around their necks. The king was convinced that if only England were resolute, the colonists would be found to be very meek. In George's view, the burgesses of Boston and Providence were only lions when the English were lambs. The king was hot to play the lion in his turn, and he set about his leonine game in earnest. If North had any vague dreams of conciliation, the king would not listen to them. America was to be sharply dealt with, swiftly brought to her knees. George was convinced that he was the very man to do it. A couple of remarkable events gave the king his opportunity.

Massachusetts, Virginia, and other colonies established certain committees. They were to make

THE BOSTON TEA-PARTY 103

colonial grievances public. They were to keep the provinces in touch with each other, and with the world outside. They were to obtain accurate information of all that happened in England which concerned the welfare of the colonies. To carry out this latter portion of their scheme they sent various agents to England. One of these agents was a famous man.

In the second half of the eighteenth century there was no more conspicuous man among the American colonists than Benjamin Franklin. He was born in obscurity when the century was six years old. He had worked his way from poverty to high state office and ample means. The printer's apprentice of the first quarter of the century was in its third quarter a recognised author, a respected statesman, a renowned man of science, a remarkable journalist. In the dawn of journalism in America, Franklin was one of the first to recognise the value of the new force and to lend all the weight of his shrewd intelligence and straightforward style to make the power of the press a living power in the land. As a student of science, it had been Franklin's rare privilege to make one of the greatest discoveries of all time, the discovery of the identity of lightning with the electric fluid. As the author of *Poor Richard's Almanac*, he did more than any other man to spread knowledge and a love of knowledge throughout the length and breadth of the colonies. As a statesman, he had attained the high office of Deputy Postmaster-General for the Colonies. His son was the last royal governor of New Jersey.

In choosing Benjamin Franklin for one of their agents in England, the discontented colonies could hardly have pitched upon a man better able to serve them, and at the same time to prove the entire loyalty of the colonies to the Crown. Franklin was himself, if not exactly a Tory, very much what in later times would be called a Conservative. He had not in the early days of his agency in England any other idea than that of preserving the union between the Crown and the colonies. Indeed, he seems to have believed that any severance of the union could only be disastrous to the colonies. But his affection for the English authority was never greater than his affection for the welfare of his own country. He proved his affection under conditions which brought down obloquy upon him, and which helped to precipitate the final struggle.

Somehow, probably no one ever will know how, several very important state papers came into Franklin's hands. These were certain letters of Hutchinson, a governor-general of Massachusetts, and of Oliver, the lieutenant-governor, written to Whately, who had been private secretary to George Grenville, and who had died in the June of 1772. In these letters, Hutchinson and Oliver expressed themselves very freely concerning the condition of America, and both declared themselves in favour of limiting the liberties and privileges of the colonies. These letters were absolutely confidential. Neither Hutchinson nor Oliver ever imagined that they would be made public. But after Whately's death they were stolen by some one unknown, and brought to Franklin. Franklin asked and obtained permission to send them to Massachusetts. He only obtained the permission on the strict condition that the letters should be neither copied nor printed, that they should only be made known to a few of the leaders of colonial opinion, that they should be returned, and that the source from which they came should be maintained in profound secrecy.

Franklin agreed to all these conditions, but it was perhaps impossible to expect that he could enforce them upon men three thousand miles away into whose possession such important political papers had fallen. Indeed, Franklin does not appear to have been over-anxious that the conditions should be observed. He pointed out that the restraint upon copying the letters did not prohibit talking of them. They were talked of by the leaders of colonial agitation. They were brought to the knowledge of the Massachusetts Assembly. The Assembly immediately petitioned Parliament to remove Hutchinson and Oliver from their posts. Hutchinson, soon made aware of the circulation of his letters, gave a sort of permission to make them generally known. At least he used words which were seized upon by his opponents as signifying permission. Thousands of copies of the letters were printed and sent all over the colonies.

In England the news of the promulgation of the letters aroused the keenest excitement. William Whately, brother of Hutchinson's correspondent, fearing popular suspicion might turn upon him, accused a Mr. Temple, to whom on a certain occasion access to his brother's papers had been granted, of stealing the letters. Temple challenged Whately, a duel was fought, and Whately was wounded. Then Franklin came forward, declaring that he was the means of making the letters known in America, and completely exonerating both Whately and Temple from any share in the business. Franklin immediately became the object of the bitterest public indignation. When the colonial petition, praying for the removal of Hutchinson and Oliver came before the Committee of the Privy Council, Wedderburn, the Solicitor-General, who opposed the petition, made a malignant and most telling attack upon Franklin. He branded him as a thief, almost as a murderer. He gibbeted him as a foul example of a man lost to all honour, lost to all decency. Franklin, who stood at the bar of the House, listened with unalterable composure to the terrible indictment, while all the Privy Councillors, with the exception of the Prime Minister, laughed at every stroke, and applauded every stab of Wedderburn's envenomed speech.

The event was memorable. The Committee, flushed with delight at Wedderburn's invective, declared that the colonial petition was false, groundless, and scandalous, and only made for the seditious purpose of keeping up a spirit of discontent in the province. The king confirmed the action of the committee, and completed it by dismissing Franklin from his office of Postmaster-General. Thus the Province of Massachusetts was doubly affronted in the contemptuous rejection of its prayer, and in the successive insults offered to its representative and most illustrious citizen. Franklin himself, though he bore with a stoical composure the taunts of Wedderburn, was converted from a sympathiser with, into an opponent of the English government. The English government did not think it mattered. They had yet to learn that in deriding Massachusetts and dismissing Franklin they had helped to divide their empire.

THE BOSTON TEA-PARTY 107

It is not too easy to pass an impartial judgment upon Franklin's behaviour in this business. Franklin himself always strenuously defended his conduct, and declared that he was bound to act as he did act, as a loyal and dutiful citizen and colonist. The letters were brought to him. They revealed a grave danger imminently menacing the liberties and the privileges of his fatherland. They were given to him under certain restrictions which, as far as in him lay, he observed. He had never made any secret of being the means by which they were conveyed to America. They were private letters, it is true, but the privacy of letters was not in the eighteenth century regarded with any peculiar sanctity by the government. Wedderburn himself, in all the fine frenzy of his denunciation, must have been well aware that his masters habitually did what Franklin had not done, and themselves intercepted and opened private letters; nay, more, that Franklin's own letters had been tampered with.

It does not of course follow that because a government did an unworthy act, therefore Franklin was justified in acting unworthily. But if certain private letters had been brought to Franklin's notice in which his own life was threatened, it would be strange indeed to blame him had he taken steps to protect himself against the machinations of his enemies. How much more was he then bound to save his country from the treachery that was being employed against her? The defenders of Franklin argue that the letters of Hutchinson, the letters of Oliver, were private and confidential only for the person to whom they were addressed. If by chance or folly they passed out of the possession of that person, it would be but pedantry to insist that those against whom their intentions were levelled should refuse to profit by the discovery because treason chose to inscribe its treachery as private and confidential.

While the public feeling on both sides of the Atlantic was thus inflamed by Wedderburn's speech and the affronts to Franklin, another event occurred which served to intensify the passions of both parties. The government, goaded by the king, was brisk in its determination to noose the colonists in Hillsborough's halter. The tax on tea existed. It should be sternly enforced. Boston was still resolute in its refusal to purchase imported tea. That resolution it was proposed ingeniously to undermine. There was a vast quantity of tea lying unsold in the warehouses of the East India Company. The company obtained from the government the privilege of exporting that tea direct to America instead of having to sell it in England to merchants who exported it to America themselves. Tea thus directly sent and relieved from export duty could be sold very cheaply indeed in the colonies. It was hoped that this cheapness would break down the resolution of the colonists, and cause the tea to be bought readily in Boston.

The hope on which the government built was a serious fear to the patriot party in Boston, who knew how hard it would be for men to resist temptation for the sake of a political principle. The patriot party accordingly took prompt measures to meet the emergency. Just as the principal citizens of Providence had banded together to burn the *Gaspee*, so the principal citizens of Boston banded together to resist the imported tea. Three ships laden with tea sailed into Boston Harbour in the December of 1773. In the dusk of the evening of the 16th, the crews and captain of these ships were suddenly surprised by the attack of what seemed to be a party of Mohawk Indians, painted, feathered, and frightful. These were no Indians, but reputable Boston citizens directly inspired and guided by John Hancock, Samuel Adams, and other patriot leaders. The accoutrements of the red men were merely assumed to render identification difficult, if not impossible. The supposititious Mohawks held the ships at their mercy. Sentinels were carefully posted on shore to keep all agents of authority at a distance. In some two hours' time the entire cargo of tea, amounting in all to three hundred and forty-two chests, was flung into the sea. Having done their work, the mysterious Mohawks retired not merely unattacked but absolutely uninterfered with and unopposed. No more emphatic protest could well have been made against the action of the English government.

John Andrews of Boston was busy in those days writing letters to a relative describing the events of that busy hour. He heard and saw much of the Boston tea-party. ' They say the actors were *Indians* from *Narragansett.* Whether they were or not, to a transient observer they appear'd as *such*, being cloath'd in Blankets with the heads muffled and copper-color'd countenances, being each arm'd with a hatchet or axe and pair pistols, nor was their *dialect* different from what I conceive these geniusses to *speak*, as their jargon was unintelligible to all but themselves.' Andrews goes on to say that not the least insult was offered to any person, save to one man ' who had ript up the lining of his coat and waistcoat under the arms, and, watching his opportunity, had nearly fill'd 'em with tea, but being detected, was handled pretty roughly. They not only stripp'd him of his cloaths but gave him a coat of mud, with a severe bruising into the bargain; and nothing but their utter aversion to make *any* disturbance prevented his being tar'd and feather'd.' Some of the tea, however, was unwittingly carried away by some of the actors in the comedy, for we are told elsewhere that next morning the shoes of at least one eminent citizen of Boston were found to contain tea leaves which had lodged there during those vivid hours in which the sober father of a family renewed his youth and masqueraded in the trappings of a Mohawk Indian.

CHAPTER VII

THE EMBATTLED FARMER

THE example set by Boston was swiftly followed by other colonial towns. Charleston allowed a cargo of tea to be landed only to insist upon its being immediately stored up in damp cellars, where it rotted unsought for and unbought. New York and Philadelphia compelled the masters of their tea-ships to put to sea again and carry their cargoes back to the Thames. The news of the Mohawk raid stirred a whirlwind of fury in England. Even men who had advocated the claims of the colonies were, or professed to be, shocked at the daring deed of the men of Boston. Former friends declared that mutinous colonies were no gain to England, and had better be allowed to depart. Even to Chatham the action of the Boston people seemed criminal, prompted by passions and wild pretences. While he strenuously denied England's right to tax America, he insisted that he would be the first to support the authority of the mother-country against separation. In America it is remarkable to find that George Washington condemned the exploit. On the other hand, in the record made on the authority of Burke, the *Annual Register*, there is no condemnation of the action of the Boston citizens.

The East India Company, whose finances were in

a desperate condition, clamoured for redress. The king was resolved upon revenge. Under his instigation Lord North, in the beginning of 1774, introduced the famous measure for closing the Port of Boston against all commerce.

This was not all, this was not enough. The mutinous spirit of Boston was to be chastened by comprehensive alteration of the laws of the province. The rights it had enjoyed since its existence began were removed. Its charter was changed. The council for the province which had hitherto been chosen by the people was now to be chosen by the Crown, 'agreeable to the practice now used in respect to the appointment of counsellors in such of his Majesty's other colonies in America, the government whereof are appointed by commission under the great seal of Great Britain.' The bill transferred the nomination of the judges of the province to the Crown. Another act allowed the governor to send loyalists implicated in the disturbances to England for trial. To support these intolerable measures, troops were poured into the country, and General Gage, the commander-in-chief in America, was made governor of Massachusetts. The king had indeed asserted himself. It now only remained for Massachusetts to play the lamb's part set out for it, to be meek and wear the Hillsborough halter. Unfortunately for the plan, Massachusetts did not meet these infringements of her liberties in any meek or lamblike spirit. Nor did she find herself standing alone in her resolute attitude of resistance. If England could thus in three successive coercion acts cripple the commerce, change the charter, and jeopardise the free trial of one province, she could do so for another. Colonial jealousies gave way before the common danger.

General Gage did not find his office as governor of the province of Massachusetts an agreeable one. Although he was personally not disliked, although he was closely linked with colonial society by his marriage with an American woman, he came to his high office as the representative of an unjust tyranny and a peculiarly odious aggression, and his popularity suffered accordingly. He was burnt in effigy by the people of Boston on his accession to the post of governor. Such welcome as he received came solely from the official classes, who would have welcomed anybody coming with the authority of the home government. His position was a most unhappy one. Coming in on the heels, as it were, of three coercion acts, he was regarded as in some degree their representative, and as such he was hated.

The hostility of the people of Boston to the new measures did not limit itself to passive dislike of the new governor. It took more active form. The colonists were angered by the rashness of England, but they were not alarmed, and they certainly were not cowed. The hated Acts of Parliament were, we are told, 'printed on paper bordered with black, hawked about the streets as a barbarous, bloody, cruel, and inhuman murder, and in some places burned with great solemnity.' The people of Boston were determined, however, to do more than to burn bits of paper 'with great solemnity.' They were resolved to resist to the utmost of their power the encroachments of the English ministry. At pitch of noon, on the first of June 1774, the Port of Boston was formally closed, and its commerce devoted to destruction. The ceremony aroused the liveliest feelings in the sister colonies. In Virginia, George Washington joined with his fellow-citizens in prayer for the avoidance of civil war, and George Mason bade his family go about in mourning. In Philadelphia the inhabitants closed their houses, knelled their church-bells as if for the dead, and hoisted their flags half-mast high. From all the provinces came words of sympathy with and deeds of friendship for Massachusetts. The Southern provinces poured in offerings of corn and rice for the benefit of the poor who were thrown out of employment by the closing of the port. Salem and Marblehead, rival ports to Boston, immediately offered her townspeople the use of their wharfs and harbours. Money came from all quarters, and what was better than money, the resolutions of colony after colony, passed at meeting after meeting, calling upon the people of Boston to resist the new tyranny. Boston was not slow to answer to the appeal. When Gage summoned the Assembly of Massachusetts, it immediately proceeded to denounce the British government. It declared its intention of resisting to the last, and of abandoning all intercourse with England until the injuries of the colonies were redressed. Gage promptly dissolved the Assembly, but he was powerless to check the expression of popular feeling or the growth of popular sympathy.

The colonies were not content with mere expressions of sympathy. They were determined upon more overt acts of protest against the encroachments of Great Britain. A Continental Congress of deputies from each of the provinces was proposed, approved of, and energetically carried out, in spite

THE EMBATTLED FARMER 115

of all the efforts of the colonial governors to prevent the various Assemblies from nominating delegates. Every province, with the exception of Georgia, sent its delegate to the Congress, which assembled in Philadelphia, on the 4th September 1774. Peyton Randolph of Virginia was its President, Charles Thompson its Secretary. Its meeting in the Carpenters' Hall was one of the turning points in the story of the struggle. The fifty-five delegates who represented the twelve colonies that had agreed to join the Continental Congress were composed of men of almost every variety of creed, of race, and of character. To the Congress came native-born Americans, men speaking only the English speech, men who had always regarded themselves as Englishmen, or at least as loyal subjects of the English Crown. With them were Dutch settlers, German settlers, French settlers, Scandinavian settlers, and this strange blend of races meant a no less strange blend of creeds from Calvinists to Quakers.

Almost all the ablest men in colonial political life came to the Congress. Washington came from Virginia with Patrick Henry, Richard Henry Lee, and Peyton Randolph. Samuel and John Adams came from Massachusetts, John Jay from New York, Stephen Hopkins from Rhode Island, John Dickinson from Pennsylvania, Roger Sherman from Connecticut, and John Rutledge from South Carolina. Some eminent names, indeed, were absent from the list of delegates. Franklin was away in England. Jefferson had not been chosen by the Virginia convention as a delegate. James Otis, the eloquent, the patriotic, could not come. He had been brutally attacked in 1769 by a Commissioner of Customs named Robinson, and a party of officers. He was cruelly beaten, and received a blow on the head from a sword in the struggle. Otis brought an action against his assailant Robinson, and recovered two thousand pounds, but refused to take the money when Robinson confessed himself in the wrong and begged Otis's pardon. Robinson's repentance came too late. The injury to Otis's head affected his reason. The fine intellect that had been devoted to freedom was overthrown.

The Congress began its business by declaring its absolute approval of the action of the people of Boston in resisting the coercive measures. It called upon them to continue that resistance to the last, and urged the other colonies to support them materially as well as mentally in that resistance. It next drew up what have been truly called a series of extremely able state papers, defining and defending the position of the colonies. Lord Chatham, when they came to his knowledge, compared them with the masterpieces of Greek and Roman statecraft, and gave the voices of Philadelphia the pre-eminence. It cannot be said that the Congress was aggressive towards the mother-country when it is remembered that in the famous Declaration of Rights which it drew up, these words are to be found. 'From the necessity of the case, and in regard to the mutual interests of both countries, we cheerfully consent to the operation of such Acts of the British Parliament as are *bonâ fide* restrained to the regulation of our external commerce for the purpose of securing the commercial advantages of the whole empire to the mother-country, and the commercial benefits of its respective members.' This act of concession indicated no subservient spirit. The

Congress was as firmly emphatic against Imperial taxation, against the quartering of troops, against the three recent coercion acts, as the most impassioned patriot of Faneuil Hall could wish. It protested uncompromisingly against the exercise of legislative authority in several of the colonies by a council appointed by pleasure of the Crown, against such a system of legislature in fact as had just been applied to Massachusetts. It voted addresses to the people of Great Britain, to the people of Canada, and to the American people. In each of these addresses it reasserted the wrongs of the Colonists and appealed for sympathy and for support in redressing them.

It is, and always must be, something to marvel at that the majority in the English government, that the majority of the English people, thought, as they undoubtedly did think, that the colonists could be easily beaten into obedience, could be ultimately compelled to accept the despotic dominion of the mother-country. That George could conceive the conquest of the American colonists to be not merely possible but feasible is not surprising. George was not an Englishman. He was only third in descent from the autocratic Elector of Hanover, who wore unwillingly the English crown. All his racial interests, all his hereditary disposition, led him to believe that obedience to a royal will was part of the eternal principles of earth and heaven. The English people, the leaders of the English people, ought to have known better, ought to have estimated more accurately the forces with which they were now going to contend. These stubborn colonists were largely men of the same blood, the same race, the same creed and speech as themselves. They were near kinsfolk, children of the same ancestor. The war that was about to be fought would be a fratricidal war. If victory was one of the traditions of English arms, those arms were now to be employed against men who boasted of the same tradition. It was to be Englishmen against Englishmen in the shock of civil strife.

There were, it is true, men in England of finer temper, men who better understood the nature of the struggle that was about to begin, men who saw with clearer eyes the inevitable end. Many of the advocates for reconciliation between the colonists and England were advocates because of the injury which the certain struggle and the possible severance must inflict upon British commerce. But the greatest champions of conciliation based their prayers and their pleadings upon the principles of justice, of international rights, of imperial policy, of religion, as well as of statecraft. Chatham's great voice was raised again in favour of peace, in favour of proper concessions to the American people. He made no half-hearted proposals of compromise, of peddling, insufficient concession. He knew, and said, that the mere cancelling of the late obnoxious laws would not be enough to pacify the colonists. Their fears had been awakened, their resentment aroused. It was necessary in order to allay these fears, and to placate that resentment, to approach the subject in a wide and generous spirit. Chatham did as a wise man should do when he consulted with the man who was best able to set forth the claims of the colonists, Benjamin Franklin. The great English statesman and the great American statesman drew up a bill which, if it had been accepted, might have averted for long enough the separation between England and America.

The joint measure drawn up by Chatham and by Franklin provided for the repeal of the late Acts. It abandoned the taxation claim as a matter of course. That was the least any measure of the kind could do. It ordered the recall of the troops, and promised security to the existing colonial charters. But it did more than this. It empowered a Colonial Assembly to meet and to arrange some means by which the American colonies should contribute towards the payment of the public debt. What Chatham was preparing to do in the House of Lords, a greater than Chatham was preparing to do in the House of Commons. Burke drew up a measure that was very similar to the measure devised by Chatham and Franklin, a measure leaving it to the General Assemblies of the colonies to grant supplies and aids, instead of giving and granting supplies in Parliament, to be raised and paid in the colonies. It has been justly asserted that Burke's speech on Conciliation with America forms, with the earlier speech on American Taxation and the later Letter to the Sheriffs of Bristol, the most perfect manual for any one who approaches the study of public affairs, whether for knowledge or for practice. But though Burke spoke with the tongue of angels, he could not prevail. If Burke had been wisely listened to, if Chatham had been wisely listened to, if even the voices of the great merchants of London and of Bristol had been listened to, things would have gone very differently. But they were not listened to. The House of Lords rejected the measure of Chatham and of Franklin. The House of Commons rejected the measure of Edmund Burke. The king rejected the earnest petition of the City of London in favour of the colonial claims. Nothing was listened to by the administration or by the king, save proposals for the prompt, stern, uncompromising punishment of the men who dared to resist taxation and to resent coercion.

Under these conditions, it was pretty plain that little was left but war. If the king and the ministry, strengthened by the strong majority gained in the recent General Election, were stubborn in repression, the colonists were no whit less steadfast in their resolve to resist oppression. The Massachusetts Committee of Public Safety proceeded to organise resistance, to enrol militiamen, to collect arms. Gage, who had been fortifying Boston, provoked the first collision. The Massachusetts Committee sat at Concord, the beautiful little New England village which was destined in later days to be a kind of Tusculum for American philosophy. Gage resolved to make a raid upon the stores of arms collected there and to disperse the growing body of militiamen. Franklin had said that at any moment a casual squabble between a drunken porter and a hot-headed soldier might kindle the flames of civil war all over the country. It was the action of a hot-headed soldier which did kindle the flames of civil war. Gage's attack upon Concord was the beginning of the end.

The expedition to Concord was to be a secret expedition. Eight hundred men under the command of Lieutenant-Colonel Smith were carried in boats across the Charles River to East Cambridge on their way to Concord, on the night of the 18th of April.

To preserve the secrecy of the expedition, Gage had given orders that no American was to be permitted to leave Boston, but the order had been given too late. Gage had counted without Paul Revere. Paul Revere was an able engraver who had lived forty years of uneventful life to taste at last the joys of eventful living and gain an honourable immortality. He was a warm patriot. He expected, as many another did, that sooner or later an attempt would be made upon Concord. A hint had come of the threatened attack. A friend in Boston was pledged to put a lantern in the belfry of the North Church tower if the British did set forth. On the opposite shore, Paul Revere waited, booted and spurred and ready to mount. The signal was given. Paul Revere saw it, mounted, and rode as for his life through the quiet night, making it unquiet with his cries as he roused the sleeping villages of Middlesex with the warning to be up and to arm, for the enemy was upon them.

Everywhere on Paul Revere's track came the ringing of bells and the clatter of arms as the sleepers awakened sprang from their beds, caught up their weapons, and swelled the alarm that was stirring the whole countryside. The English soldiers marching along heard the sounds and shouts ahead of them, and knew that those whom they were sent to surprise were forewarned and forearmed. Colonel Smith went on steadily to his fate, and the fate of English dominion in America. In the grey morning an advanced body of the English troops under the command of Major Pitcairn of the Royal Marines marched into Lexington. There they found some seventy militiamen, duly armed, drawn up under

Major Parker on the village green. Parker told his men not to fire unless they were fired on, 'but if they want a war,' he said, 'let it begin here.' Here it did begin. Major Pitcairn immediately rode up to them, addressing them as rebels and calling upon them to throw down their arms and disperse. As they did not obey, he fired his pistol at them, ordered his men to fire. The soldiers fired. Seven of the militia were killed and nine wounded. The rest, firing at random and doing almost no damage to the British, fled in confusion. After a while they rallied, followed the British, and captured some stragglers, the first prisoners of the war.

Two hours after leaving Lexington, the British troops marched into Concord. Some two hundred militiamen were posted upon an adjacent hill, but on seeing the superiority of the British force, they withdrew to some distance. Colonel Smith, paying no heed to them, proceeded to search the town for artillery and military stores. He found little either of the one or of the other, for the Americans had concealed or carried off almost all their arms and ammunition. He found and set fire to some gun-carriages. He cut down the Liberty pole. This was all the spoil of the Concord raid. By this time the militia on the hill had been stiffly reinforced by large bodies of armed men that came from all directions aroused by the general alarm. They stood on the hill watching the movements of the soldiers in the town and the rising flames. Anxiously the leaders consulted together. Would it be anything less than madness for these countrymen, unsifted in such perilous enterprise, to attack the disciplined, experienced royal troops? The fate of the American continent hung upon the decision of that instant, upon the action of that hour. The colonists decided to attack. One gallant spirit, Captain Isaac Davis of Acton, said, 'I hav'nt a man that is afraid to go.' He and his party led the advance upon the bridge. As soon as the colonists came 'pretty near,' to use the words of Colonel Smith, the troops opened fire. Isaac Davis was killed by the first discharge. There was just a moment when it seemed as if the colonists would fall back. Then the militia major, John Buttrick of Concord, shouted out to his fellow-soldiers, calling upon them in the name of God to fire. In the name of God he called, and in the name of God they obeyed. They followed up a fierce volley by a fierce charge. The soldiers retreated into the town to join the main body, leaving the bridge in the possession of the Americans. The battle of Concord was fought and won. Bancroft with pardonable pride calls it more eventful than Agincourt or Blenheim. The 'Embattled Farmer' had won the first toss in the great conflict.

The old bridge has vanished long since, but the people of Concord delight to take the traveller from afar to the spot where it crossed the sweet river that 'slumbers between broad prairies, kissing the long meadow grass, and bathes the overhanging boughs of elder-bushes and willows, or the roots of elms and ash-plants, trees, and clumps of maples.' A granite obelisk marks the spot where the fight was hottest. The grave is shown of two British soldiers who were slain in the skirmish, and have slept, says Hawthorne, ever since peacefully, where Zechariah Brown and Thomas Davis buried them. 'Soon was their warfare ended ; a weary night march from Boston, a rattling volley of musketry across the river, and then these many years of rest. In the long procession of slain invaders who passed into eternity from the battlefields of the Revolution, these two nameless soldiers led the way.'

Smith made no attempt to retrieve the defeat of the bridge. The country was thoroughly aroused. In answer to the firing and the ringing of bells, armed reinforcements were continually swelling the ranks of the militia and the farmers. The best, if not the only thing he could do, was to retreat as fast as he could to Boston. The retreat was no easy business. All the way from Concord to Lexington the country was alive with assailants. It seemed, said a British officer afterwards, as if men had dropped from the clouds. Behind every tree, and wall, and fence, and hedge, the Americans waged an Indian warfare. From every point of cover a merciless fusillade was kept up on the retreating British by almost unseen foes. Just before reaching Lexington the retreat had become well-nigh a panic-stricken flight. Luckily for the king's despairing troops, there was help for them at Lexington. News of the condition of the country had reached Gage at Boston, and Gage sent out reinforcements under Earl Percy, which arrived at Lexington just in time to save the hunted soldiers from destruction. 'Earl Percy sees me fall,' says the stout-heart in the brave border ballad. The Earl Percy of the Lexington relief might have seen many tall soldiers fall as they staggered into the hollow square which his detachment formed to shelter and defend the fugitives. We learn that the tongues of the flying men were hanging out of their mouths like those of dogs after a chase. Their ammunition was expended, their nerve was gone.

Even with the reinforcements, the British troops were still in a bad way. The English officers appear to have been very angry because their antagonists did not come into the open and face them in a pitched battle. But the opportunity and the strength of these skilled marksmen lay in thicket fighting, and they kept up the sharp-shooting all along the line of retreat, until the fugitives were in sight of Charleston Harbour and under the protection of the guns of some British men-of-war. They got to shelter just in time. A body of the Essex Militia, seven hundred strong, were on their way to intercept the fugitives. Had the Essex men come between the flying soldiers and their goal, the British would probably have been compelled to surrender. They had suffered disaster enough. Nearly three hundred men were killed or wounded on the English side during the dismal day. The colonial loss was only ninety-three.

It would be hard to say whether loyalists or patriots were the more astounded by this victory of raw militiamen and simple farmers over regular troops. It had been the complacent English conviction that the American farmers would prove much too cowardly to face the military, yet here were the military put to flight by these very cowards. It was not to be believed, only it had happened. In America the great day was recognised as the beginning of the revolution. 'Oh! what a glorious morning is this,' said Samuel Adams when he heard the sound of the guns at Lexington. The colonists hastened to follow up their victory. From all parts of the country armed men made their way towards Boston. From every part of New England militiamen, farmers, and volunteers hurried towards the capital. An extemporised army of sixteen thousand men was preparing to beleaguer Gage in Boston.

From that moment it was obvious that the arbitrament of arms could alone decide the quarrel. While Gage and his soldiers were penned in at Boston, while the colonists were assembling in their armed thousands, tidings of the disastrous day of Concord and Lexington were carried to England as swiftly as winds and waters would allow. The news was received with fury by the royal party; with grave regret by the men who, with Burke and Chatham, sympathised with the efforts of the colonists; and with cynicism by such witty onlookers at the game of life as Horace Walpole. While the followers of Lord North were shrieking for vengeance upon the rebels, while Burke was courageously expressing his opinions, Horace Walpole contented himself with quoting, not unhappily, from *Chevy Chase*. 'The child as yet unborn shall rue the hunting of that day,' he wrote. Fribble though he was, professed wit and affected man of the world, he saw that the issues were grave, and that the result would scarcely fail to be injurious to England.

The day of Lexington served to teach the statesmen at home that the theories of Lord Sandwich as to the cowardice of the colonists were not theories that it was reliable to build upon. When Chatham's proposals of reconciliation were being discussed in the House of Lords, Lord Sandwich added a darker stain to the infamy of his name by his attack upon the Americans. He laughed contemptuously at the numbers of the colonists, called them 'raw, undisciplined, and cowardly,' and expressed a wish that 'instead of forty or fifty thousand of these brave fellows they would produce at least two hundred thousand. The more the better. The easier would be the conquest.' Probably Burke had these words in his mind when he wrote in his account of the event at Lexington that it 'sufficiently showed how ill-informed these were who had so often asserted at home, that a regiment could force their way through any part of America, and that the very sight of a grenadier's cap would be sufficient to put an American army to flight.' It is, indeed, little less than a delight to read the impartiality and justice with which Burke was able to record, or cause to be recorded, the events of that memorable war, with an impartiality and a justice that most other men would have found it hard indeed to preserve in that heated atmosphere.

CHAPTER VIII

BUNKER HILL

THREE weeks after the battle of Lexington, the second Continental Congress met in Philadelphia. It was a curious body with ill-defined functions, with ill-defined powers. Indeed, in the strict sense, it had no powers at all. It was not a legislative assembly. It was a mere meeting of delegates summoned to consult together and to report back to the colonists that they represented. The Congress was only entitled to advise, it was not entitled to direct, the colonies. From the first, however, it assumed a certain measure of authority by passing resolutions which were to take immediate effect without the formal ratification of the different legislatures. It was of course essential that, in the bustle and confusion of the hour, some body should exist, enabled to take prompt action for the common good. The Congress was uncompromising in its patriotism, in its stand against oppression. Nevertheless, it still recognised the authority of the British Crown, for its earliest acts included the framing and sending of petitions and addresses to the king, as well as to the people of Great Britain. It began foreign relations by establishing a 'Committee of Correspondence with our friends abroad.' It gradually took over to itself those matters of administration which had been in the hands of the home government. It established a large paper currency. It resolved that an American continental army should be raised. In fact, it acted as a sovereign power, though no sovereignty had been given to it. Its first acts of sovereignty were to do the very deeds which the colonists were fighting England for doing. It enforced regulations on trade. It maintained troops without the consent of the colonies. It raised money by national authority. The difference of course was, that the acts of the Congress were done for the people by the people themselves, through their representatives, and were not the arbitrary enforcements of a foreign power. The Congress was the makeshift for a non-existing government. It had much to do, and it did much, and, on the whole, well. The most important act of the Congress was their choice of a leader for their newly formed army. George Washington of Virginia was unanimously chosen commander-in-chief of the continental forces.

During the years that had passed since he had avenged the destruction of Braddock's army by the capture of Fort Duquesne, Washington's life had been for the most part relatively uneventful, and positively happy. Washington's heart had always been lightly inflammable. Passion followed passion in the picture-gallery of his loves. Many of these early affections are the puzzle of the persevering, who yearn to know who the 'Lowland Beauty' was, and who 'Young M. A. his W.,' to whom Washington offered adoration in verse, and who was Frances Alexander, and who the mysterious 'Mrs. Neil.' We know that he was very anxious to marry Mary Philipse, a New York beauty, who declined him and married Roger Morris. It has been said, but we need not believe it in the absence of any proof, that he was in love with Sally Fairfax, the wife of his friend, George William Fairfax. In 1758 he met the woman who was to be his wife. He had gone to Williamsburgh to consult doctors, believing himself to be in very bad health. 'My constitution is much impaired,' he wrote, 'and nothing can retrieve it but the greatest care and the most circumspect course of life.' At Williamsburgh he met Mrs. Martha Custis, a young widow of six-and-twenty with two children. He fell desperately in love with her, succeeded in winning her affections, and was married to her on the 6th of January 1759. A great deal has been said in praise, and not a little in dispraise, of Martha Washington. It is enough for us to believe that she made George Washington happy. It would seem to have been his ideal to live a quiet country life with his wife and her two children, at his home, Mount Vernon. It probably never occurred to him that he might have again to carry arms. But, though he had retired from military service, his life was not permitted to be entirely that of an easy-going country gentleman, content with his farming, his hunting, his fishing, his rural pleasures, and his rural friends. He was elected a delegate to the Virginia House of Burgesses, and he remained a member during the fifteen years between 1759 and 1774. When he first entered the Assembly, the speaker presented the thanks of the House to him for his distinguished military services. Washington, much embarrassed, did not know which way to look or what to say, whereupon the speaker said to him courteously and graciously, 'Sit down, Mr. Washington, your modesty equals your valour, and that surpasses the power of any language I possess.' In spite of the fact that Washington never took any prominent part in the debate in the House of Burgesses, his fellow-citizens appreciated his worth well enough to choose him as one of their delegates to the Congress. Patrick Henry said of him enthusiastically, that for solid information and sound judgment, Washington was unquestionably the greatest man in the Continental Congress.

During the agitations that immediately preceded the affray at Concord, Washington, like the other patriotic leaders, had ardently espoused the colonial cause, but like the other patriotic leaders, with no thought or purpose of separation from England. Now, however, he was prepared with the others to resist British domination to the bitter end, and his appointment as commander-in-chief gave to one of the greatest men in all history his greatest opportunity. There is no nobler, no sweeter figure in the chronicle of any country. With his unalterable calmness, his grave dignity, his antique courtesy, his modesty, and his unselfishness, he had naturally earned the respect and the admiration of those who knew him or knew of him. But his countrymen could not know, and did not know, that he possessed those qualities of greatness for which later generations revere his memory. He had tasted more experience of war than his fellow-leaders of the patriotic party. He had great influence in a colony whose assistance was of infinite moment to the colonial cause. But it was impossible that even his closest friends, his warmest admirers—and he had many friends and many admirers—could guess at the absolute genius for generalship, the marvellous instinct both for soldiership and statesmanship which the sweetly austere Virginian gentleman was yet to display. It was not as yet that even his enemies were to recognise in him, the first, the last, the best, the Cincinnatus of the West.

Washington had not reviewed his army by the historic elm-tree on Cambridge common, when two remarkable events bore, the one success, the other defeat, to the colonial arms. After the affray at Lexington, the Congress had declared that as General Gage had utterly disqualified himself for serving the colony as a governor, no obedience whatever was due to him, and that he ought to be considered and guarded against as an unnatural and inveterate enemy to the country. Gage may be said to have retaliated in a proclamation in which he offered a pardon in the king's name to all who should at once lay down their arms and return from the field to their respective occupations and peaceful duties. From the proclamation's promise of pardon were, however, especially excepted Samuel Adams and John Hancock. Their offences were said to be of too flagitious a nature to admit of any other consideration than that of condign punishment. The most significant answer which the absurd proclamation received from the colonists was the appointment of the proscribed Hancock as the President of the Continental Congress. The proscription and the promotion alike must have been exquisitely pleasing to Hancock. The weakness of his loyal nature was an overweening vanity, easy to offend and impossible to flatter too highly. If Gage did little or nothing beyond the issuing of proclamations which were not worth the paper that they were printed on, the colonists were not so idle. They struck at once a gallant and successful stroke.

Among the many who had rallied to Boston after the battle of Lexington, was a young man named Benedict Arnold, who had managed to live a great deal of queer, and not altogether admirable, life in his five-and-thirty years. His youth was noted for its turbulence, its audacity, its more than common love of mischief. His early life reads like some Picaroon story from the pages of *Gil Blas* or *Lazarillo del Tormes*. He had been apprenticed to an apothecary. Finding this little to his taste, he ran away and enlisted as a soldier. This too soon wearied him, and he deserted. Then he became a merchant in New Haven, engaged in a large trade with the West Indies which ended in a bankruptcy that did not leave his reputation for honesty wholly unclouded. Such was the man who collected sixty volunteers from New Haven and marched at their head to Cambridge on the 20th of April 1775. He at once suggested that an expedition should be sent to seize upon the fortresses of Ticonderoga and Crown Point, which commanded, by their situation upon the great Lakes, the passes between the colonies and Canada. Arnold's proposal was accepted. He received a colonel's commission from the Massachusetts Congress. He raised a small force of four hundred men, and set out for Ticonderoga. But on his way he met with a rival adventurer, and a rival expedition. The idea of seizing upon Ticonderoga had not been confined to Benedict Arnold. There lived in Vermont a very able, very eccentric man from Connecticut, named Ethan Allen, two years Arnold's junior. He was the extremely popular leading spirit of an association known as the Green Mountain Boys, which had been formed to resist the jurisdiction of New York over the Vermont region. He had dreamed of capturing Ticonderoga. He raised an expedition for the purpose, and was on his way, when he ran counter to Arnold and his party. Arnold immediately claimed command of the expedition because of his Massachusetts commission. Neither Ethan Allen nor those who were with him were men readily disposed to yield to the authority of others. In the end, Arnold joined Allen's party as a volunteer. At daybreak on the morning of the 10th of May, Allen and Arnold, with eighty-three men, rowed across the lake and entered Ticonderoga. The little garrison, taken wholly by surprise, could not make, and did not attempt to make, any resistance. Ethan Allen with an alert eye to the dramatic effectiveness of the situation, called upon the sleep-ridden commandant to surrender ' In the name of the great Jehovah and the Continental Congress.' It has been asserted that Ethan Allen made no such heroic flourish, but it would be hard to disassociate the sonorous phrase from the taking of Ticonderoga. Crown Point surrendered to Seth Warner, another Green Mountain Boy. By these two captures the adventurers secured in the forts more than two hundred pieces of cannon and many valuable stores.

The next serious struggle was not a triumph for the continental arms. While the colonials maintained their siege of Boston, troops came pouring into the city from England under three generals—Howe, Clinton, and Burgoyne—and it was evident that a serious contest between the royal and the continental forces must soon take place. On the English side, victory was confidently anticipated. The affray at Lexington, the capture of Ticonderoga, and various small scuffles near Boston Bay, in which the colonists had had the best of it, had at least taught the royalists that their enemies were not wholly to be despised. But the British generals were convinced, from the number and quality of the troops now under their command in the beleaguered city, that the result of the quarrel could not long be doubtful.

It may have been an absorbing sense of this confidence which led Gage first into the grave error of not earlier attacking the continental forces, and, secondly, into omitting to fortify the suburb of Charlestown, which should as a strategic point have been of the utmost importance to Gage. The occupation of Charlestown was eagerly desired by the colonials, and they resolved to make a daring attempt to secure this advantage. A little before twelve on the night of the 16th of June, a body of some thousand men under William Prescott, a hero of the French war, was secretly dispatched to take possession of Bunker Hill, one of the heights at the back of the suburb. The expedition acted so quickly, that before the morning dawned it had a small but strong redoubt, some entrenchments and some breast-work completed on Breed's Hill, which was connected with Bunker Hill. So quietly was this important work carried on that, though the peninsula was surrounded by the British ships of war, no sound of the operations betrayed the toilers. Prescott himself more than once during the night walked down to the shore of the Charles River, and listened to the sound of the British sentries going their rounds and relieving guard.

When morning dawned, Gage discovered to his dismay what the colonists had done, and made immediate efforts to dislodge them. The guns of the *Lively*, man-of-war, and the battery from Copp's Hill opened fire upon the Americans, who, however, continued their toil, undismayed, cheered by the encouragement of Prescott, of Israel Putnam, and of Joseph Warren, the youthful president of the Massachusetts Congress. As the fire from the ship and from the battery failed to dislodge the colonists, Gage determined to try to storm the position. After three in the afternoon, Lord Howe's detachment of some two thousand men landed at Charlestown and ascended the hill. The colonists suffered them to advance to within a few yards of their entrenchments before Prescott gave the word to fire. Under the terrible volley the British troops paused, reeled, wavered, many even retreated. 'Are the Yankees cowards?' the defenders of the hill shouted as they saw the British falling back. Again and again the soldiers were rallied to the attack. Again and again they fell back dismayed before the murderous colonial fire. Again and again Howe, whose gallantry on this occasion was conspicuous, found himself almost alone on the field. At last he withdrew to rally his men for a fresh attack.

In the meantime, the British, under General Clinton, had set Charlestown on fire by red-hot shells, and soon the stately town was in a blaze. Then came the third assault. Howe's men, reinforced and lightened of their knapsacks, swept up the hill, and, in spite of the desperate opposition of the militiamen, carried the redoubt at the point of the bayonet. The Americans were forced to fly. The carnage in the redoubt was terrible. The battle of Bunker Hill ended as a British victory. It was a dearly bought victory. The British lost more than a thousand men; the Americans not quite half that number. But the Americans lost a valued leader in young Joseph Warren, so good and true a man, that the royalists are said to have looked upon his death as equivalent to a loss of five hundred men for the colonists. He was the intimate friend of Samuel Adams. He was the close ally of John Hancock. The peer of Adams, he was more than the peer of Hancock. His chivalry and his wisdom had raised him to a first rank among the revolutionary leaders, and his chivalry sacrificed the life that his wisdom might have preserved for his country. The most conspicuous officer who fell on the British side was Major Pitcairn, who had led the British advance at Lexington. The colonists lost five of their six pieces of artillery, and the strategic position which they had so daringly striven to secure was in the enemy's hands. It was not for long of much service to them. Washington now took command of the colonial forces. Gage was recalled to England. Howe remained in command at Boston, but he was compelled by the superior generalship of Washington to evacuate Boston in the early March of 1776. The royalists were allowed to retreat to their ships without hindrance, as it was feared that any attack would incite them to burn the town. The royalist fleet sailed away, and the American army under Washington marched for New York, whither Washington believed the British to have gone.

Washington no longer commanded a purely New England army. Virginia, Pennsylvania, and Maryland had helped to swell the muster. He was surrounded by a group of officers who were for the most part men of ability, of courage, and of honour. Nathaniel Greene was the ablest, Nathaniel Greene the scholar blacksmith, who foresaw the coming struggle and studied the art of war, that he might be ready to serve his country. His lofty spirit, his tender heart, his rare intelligence, rank him with the noblest soldiers of the world. David Morgan, the Virginian frontiersman, and John Stark of New Hampshire, were splendid specimens of rough-hewn heroism, men of the Viking mould, of the Spartan courage, men who in another hemisphere and an earlier age would have ridden with the lances of Hawkwood, or tramped with the Beggars of Brederode. Another son of New Hampshire was John Sullivan, lawyer by profession, student by inclination, soldier by patriotism. Israel Putnam of Salem had been saved from the Indian stake in the French wars to serve his country now with the same wild courage that killed the wolf at Pomfret. Henry Knox, the Boston bookseller, brought from his shelves and volumes a knowledge of artillery not to be over-valued. Others there were, but these were the best of the good. Worst of the bad were Benedict Arnold and Charles Lee. Bad enough, though not so bad as these, was Horatio Gates, the jealous intriguer, the unready, the unreliable, vain, foolish, and untrue. All these men rallied under the new American flag, which was composed of thirteen red and white stripes to represent the thirteen States, but which still carried in its top corner the British Union Jack. A year later, Congress banished the Union Jack and substituted the abiding blue square with the white stars, one for each State. It is told that the first Stars and Stripes ever hoisted after an American victory was hurriedly patched together from a white shirt, a blue jacket, and a red petticoat.

While New England was thus blazing with civil war, other parts of America begun to be stirred by the effects of the struggle. The Continental Congress had from the first directed its thoughts to Canada. It had made various attempts to secure the co-operation of the Canadians in resistance to England, or at least to command their neutrality. The efforts of the Congress were successful only in the second particular, and only partially. The Canadians were on the whole ready enough to be neutral. They were not willing to join in arms against the mother-country. The Congress conceived that the time was propitious for an attempt against the Crown in Canada. The successes at Crown Point and at Ticonderoga had cheered them. They knew that there were very few troops actually in Canada. These facts, and the assumed sympathy or neutrality of the Canadians themselves led the Congress to take decisive action. An expedition was sent into Canada under General Schuyler, with General Montgomery as his second in command. An unsuccessful attack was made upon Fort St. John on the River Sorel in the September of 1775. General Schuyler fell ill, and returned to Albany. Montgomery, a young and very able officer, was left in command. He renewed the attack with a reinforced army in November and captured Fort St. John after a vigorous resistance. He then marched on Montreal. Montreal had already been attacked by Ethan Allen, the hero of the capture of Ticonderoga, but the attack had failed, and Ethan Allen had been taken prisoner. Montgomery was more fortunate. Montreal was not in a position to resist the large force at his command, and he entered it without striking a blow. The British force capitulated, and the governor escaped with difficulty to Quebec.

Montgomery was an able man. He was also a very ambitious man. Though it was winter, though his force, never very large, was daily lessening as the terms of service expired, he resolved to make a bold stroke to secure Quebec. Already an American army, under the command of Benedict Arnold, had made its way through the wilderness, suffering the severest hardships. It had climbed the heights of Abraham by the very path Wolfe climbed, and it lay before Quebec, which it had in vain summoned to surrender. On the 1st of December Montgomery joined Arnold, full of courage, full of confidence. The united American force did not amount to more than nine hundred men, while the garrison of Quebec numbered some fifteen hundred. But in spite of this disproportion, Montgomery attempted to take the town by storm. Montgomery was shot dead in the first assault. Arnold, who accompanied him, was badly wounded. Many of the best American officers were killed, many prisoners were taken. The assailants had to fall back in despair. Reduced by death and capture to little more than four hundred effective men, they made Arnold their commander, and resolved to remain before Quebec in the hope of receiving reinforcements.

Some small reinforcements did arrive, and for a time Arnold kept the English closely cooped up within their walls, but many things were against the Americans. The Canadian inhabitants, upon whose sympathy and aid they had reckoned, had been alienated by the high-handed conduct of the American troops, and were becoming actively hostile to the invaders. A terrible attack of smallpox raged through the army. In a few months, out of a force of some two thousand men, but nine hundred were fit for service. Moreover, the frozen river was opening, and a British ship was able to force its way through the ice and land reinforcements of British troops. The Americans resolved to retreat. Before a threatened sortie they retreated precipitately. Reinforcements kept pouring in of English and German troops. Disaster after disaster fell upon the American troops in Canada. At last in June the final retreat was made, when Arnold withdrew from Montreal to Crown Point. Thus there was not an American soldier left in Canada. The great invasion that was to have done so much for the American cause had only resulted in catastrophe, in the death of some gallant and gifted soldiers whom a young cause could ill spare, and in the alienation of those upon whom the Continental Congress had counted so confidently for support. At least the Canadian expedition had served to show Benedict Arnold at his best. He was never to play so great a part again. It would have, been happier for Arnold if he had fallen as Montgomery fell, a brave soldier dying for his country. His memory would have been kept green by a grateful people, his name treasured by the republic he had helped to raise. There were many more years of life waiting for Benedict Arnold. Fate reserved for him no more years of honour.

Defeat in the North was compensated for six months later by success in the South. Charleston in South Carolina was supposed to be especially threatened by the English levies, and Charleston was promptly placed in a condition of defence by Colonel Moultrie. By the end of June, when the British armament had made its appearance off Charleston and prepared to attack, the insurgents were quite ready to receive them. The attack was made with great fury. It was desperately resisted. It ended in triumphant victory for the American forces. The British fleet, gravely crippled, withdrew to New York. This success brought many waverers into the ranks of the Congressionists. The numbers of what were called the loyalists were so much reduced as to make their position in the southern provinces one of complete insignificance. The successful resistance of Charleston preserved the southern colonies from war for some years to come.

By this time there was very little prospect of reconciliation between Great Britain and her revolted colonies. The petitions of Congress to the king were treated with contemptuous silence. Tidings came to the continental leaders of the most determined preparations by the English to crush the rebellion out. Legions of German mercenaries were being bought, regiments of English soldiers were being raised for the final discomfiture of the Congress and its supporters in arms.

It should never be forgotten, though it would sometimes seem to be forgotten, that the revolt of the American colonies was not regarded with indignation by the whole of the people of England. If the Tory party, if the men who rallied around Lord North's ministry, were bent on war and eager for revenge, the Whig party, and all the men who lent a splendour to the Whig party, were as ardent in their advocacy of the rights of the American colonists as if they had themselves been born on the farther side of the Atlantic. An English duke, the Duke of Richmond, hoped that the Americans might succeed, because the Americans were in the right. The greatest of the orators of the age, the greatest statesman, perhaps the greatest man then living—Edmund Burke—declared that he would rather lie in prison than enjoy freedom in company with the men who were seeking to enslave America. The eloquence of Charles James Fox asserted itself in sympathy with the revolutionary cause. There were men among the admirers of Burke and the adorers of Fox who were in the habit of alluding to the army commanded by General Washington as 'our army.' It would be unfair to attribute this championship to the readiness of one political party in opposition to use any weapon against its opponents in office. Men like Burke, men like Fox, lesser men like the Duke of Richmond, and the followers of Burke and Fox, were inspired with an honest devotion to principles of liberty, which they believed to be most shamefully assailed by the policy pursued by King George towards the American colonies. This very attitude on the part of the Whigs made them the less able to render much service to the cause they applauded and the principles they upheld. They had against them the great mass who earnestly believed, if they did not openly profess, that the interest of England should have precedence over the demands of justice, and who did not, and perhaps could not, appreciate that the interests of any nation are best served by her steadfast adherence to justice.

CHAPTER IX

INDEPENDENCE

IN 1776 the colonies took the most momentous step in their career. The obstinacy of the king, the folly of his advisers, and the ferocity with which the war had been prosecuted, had already convinced the Continental leaders that their struggle must end in absolute liberty or absolute defeat. Their convictions were prompted and strengthened by the extraordinary success of a pamphlet which made its appearance in the January of 1776 in Philadelphia. The pamphlet was called *Common Sense*. It was published anonymously, but there were plenty of people who knew that the author was an Englishman named Thomas Paine, who had arrived in America not many months earlier. Paine had the spirit of a revolutionist, and many of the qualities which make a successful revolutionist. He was a grateful recipient of all the new vague ideas that were in the air about the Rights of Man, ideas which had been fostered by the genius of Rousseau and the genius of the Encyclopædists. He regarded revolution against constituted authority as in itself a virtue. His heart went out to revolutionary America, as it was some years later to go out to revolutionary France. He crossed the Atlantic to lay his ready wit, his rough-and-ready reasoning, and his powerful prose, at the service of the rebellious colonies. The value of his service it would be difficult to overestimate. *Common Sense* was one of the most potent factors in the events that led to the Declaration of Independence.

Common Sense is not a masterpiece of political reasoning, but it served the purpose for which it was intended better than if it had been argued with the logic of Burke. Its theories, as ancient as they were vague, of ideal democracy; its denunciations, as vehement as they were comprehensive, of kings in general and of the English king in particular, were well calculated to appeal to the passions, the hopes and the fears of men who found themselves involved in a doubtful and dangerous struggle. Paine scoffed at any sentimental associations with the mother-country. He argued—and the arguments were more influential than the scoffs—that the very moment had arrived when the colonies, if they wished to be released from the authority over-seas, had the best opportunity of setting themselves free.

The pamphlet had an enormous sale. It went into every part of the colonies, and wherever it went, it set men longing for independence and planning its attainment. Washington himself has testified to its great influence. It only put into a more definite form ideas that had long been fermenting in the minds of many of the leaders and many of the followers, in the struggle against Great Britain. An alliance with France had for some time attracted the congressionalists, but an alliance with France was only possible if the colonists declared themselves free from their allegiance to France's traditional enemy. Still, there were many opponents of any scheme of separation, and it was in the end the arbitrary and unreasonable action of England which forced the hands of the Americans, which strengthened the hands of the revolutionists, and enabled the extreme leaders to carry out their purposes.

When the Continental Congress was called together, the name of Thomas Jefferson was not included among the delegates from Virginia. Jefferson was at that time one of the most important public men in Virginia. He was very soon destined to be one of the most important public men among the English-speaking race. He was thirty-two years of age. He had been for eight years one of the most distinguished lawyers at the Virginia Bar. He had been for six years a member of the Virginia House of Burgesses. He was a man of great physical health and strength, a skilful horseman and zealous hunter, an earnest and practical farmer. He had received a sound, and for its time, a wide education, within the walls of William and Mary. He loved learning as he loved the law, and he was an excellent performer on the violin. In 1772 he had married a beautiful, childless and wealthy widow, Mrs. Martha Skelton. The union of his and her fortune made Jefferson a wealthy man.

His life was as happy as it promised to be tranquil. Like Washington at Mount Vernon, Jefferson at Monticello found perfect content in his peaceful life, planning gardens, looking after his farms, turning his little portion of primæval forest into a park, and domesticating many kinds of trees and shrubs. This bucolic existence was not to be long-lived. In 1774 he prepared the Draught of Instructions for Virginia's delegation to the Continental Congress. The Draught was an extremely able and extremely radical expression of the rights and liberties of American citizens. The Draught was not accepted by the convention. It was published as a pamphlet, and republished in England by Edmund Burke. It earned for its writer 'the honour of having his name inserted in a long list of proscriptions enrolled in a bill of attainder.' After this his life moved rapidly. There came a vacancy in the delegation of Virginia to Congress. Jefferson was naturally chosen to fill the place. On the very day when Washington received his commission as commander-in-chief of the Continental army, Jefferson reached Philadelphia. The next day he took his seat in the Congress, where he proved a most active and useful member.

By this time the growing desire for independence began to take a practical shape. One by one the more eager of the colonies had declared themselves in favour of asserting their freedom. One by one the colonies that were either actively or sluggishly opposed to the idea of independence were brought over to agreement with it. On 1st June a committee of five was appointed to draw up a Declaration of Independence. The five men were Jefferson, Franklin, Adams, Sherman, and Livingstone. Jefferson, as the chairman of the committee, was privileged to write the paper. His draught was written in his lodgings on a little writing-desk of his own invention, which still exists. When the draught was submitted to Congress it was much altered, and generally for the better. Its author, stoically silent under sharp, even carping, criticism, was soothed by Benjamin Franklin with diverting anecdotes. It was discussed through the 2nd, 3rd, and 4th of July. Jefferson in later days delighted to tell how the final vote upon the Declaration was hastened by the extreme warmth of the weather and by the presence of swarms of flies that came from a neighbouring stable, and added much to the discomfort of members already exhausted by debate and heat. Lawyer John Adams was the most eloquent advocate for Independence; Lawyer John Dickinson was the most stubborn, the most serious of its opponents. He thought it premature, and said so stoutly, and lost his popularity, to win it back again by fighting as a private soldier against the English. The arguments in favour of Independence finally triumphed. Twelve of the colonies agreed to act unanimously. New York, unhappily, persisted in abstaining and had no share in the great action. On the second of July the Congress had declared that the United Colonies were, and ought to be by right, free and independent States, that they were absolved from all political allegiance to the British Crown, and that all political connection between them and the State of Great Britain was and ought to be totally dissolved. On the fourth of July Jefferson's Declaration was, after some slight changes, adopted and duly signed by the members of the Congress. It was publicly proclaimed to the people from the steps of the State House in Philadelphia, and was received by the populace with the enthusiasm of joy-bells and salvoes of artillery. John Adams predicted rightly that those demonstrations of joy would be repeated year by year by the people of a free country.

The hall in which the Congress had assembled was christened Independence Hall. The square in which the Declaration was read aloud was called

Independence Square. The chief charm of the Declaration of Independence to the men of a later world lies in its noble beginning and its no less noble end. The faults and the follies of King George have faded into the past. They have no direct bearing upon the lives men live to-day. The great assertions of great truths with which the Declaration begins appeal as warmly to the mind to-day as they did when they were first written, and will appeal as warmly to generations yet to be. 'We hold these truths to be self-evident—that all men are created equal; that they are endowed by their Creator with certain unalienable rights; that among these are life, liberty, and the pursuit of happiness; that to secure these rights, governments are instituted among men, deriving their just powers from the consent of the governed; that whenever any form of government becomes destructive of these ends it is the right of the people to alter or to abolish it, and to institute a new government, laying its foundation on such principles and organising its powers in such form as to them shall seem most likely to effect their safety and happiness.' The sonorous words ring with a free music. There is an antique dignity and gravity in the conclusion of the Declaration, where 'the Representatives of the United States of America' declare the Colonies to be free and independent States with 'full power to levy war, conclude peace, contract alliances, establish commerce, and to to do all other acts and things which Independent States may of right do. And for the support of this Declaration, with a firm reliance on the protection of Divine Providence, we mutually pledge to each other our lives, our fortunes, and our sacred honour.'

For good or evil now the great step was taken. The free American States had no choice left them but to win by the sword the rights they had so proudly asserted or to be blotted out by their enemy.

The difficulties of the Continental government were now only beginning. Washington was at New York, which had become the centre of revolutionary activity. In August Howe prepared to attack New York at the head of a large army of nearly thirty thousand men. Washington's position in New York was very difficult. Disaffection to his cause was all around him, for New York was largely loyalist. Even amongst those who were supposed to be devoted to the Continental cause discontent was rife. Washington's army, numerically much smaller than Howe's, was torn by faction, weakened by sickness, enervated by the news of the Canadian disasters, imperfectly armed, badly trained, lacking in discipline. Almost all were depressed; many were despairing. To these raw, disheartened forces General Howe opposed well-equipped, practised English troops, and a large number of the recently raised German mercenaries. On the 23rd August he occupied Long Island. On the 27th the Americans, who were defending the entrenchments, were totally defeated, and the entire force only escaped capture through the skill of Washington under cover of a heavy fog. It was clear that New York could not be held much longer. Washington had momentary thoughts of destroying the city rather than allow it to fall into the enemy's hands, but the suggestion was rejected by Congress. Washington retired to New Jersey, and New York was captured by Howe on the 15th of September.

It is not surprising if Washington felt profoundly

discouraged. His soldiers had made themselves extremely unpopular by their severity to the loyalists and their disorderly behaviour. The inhabitants of Long Island and of New York City had hailed the arrival of Howe as the arrival of a liberator and a friend. Washington began to fear with justice that the English would soon be able to recruit as fast as the Americans. At this period of the struggle there seems to have been but little patriotic feeling animating a large part of the American army. Again and again, as soon as their terms of enlistment expired, whole regiments disbanded and returned to their homes. It seemed at one moment as if the struggle would come to an end because of the total disappearance in this way of the Continental army. The term of enlistment for the bulk of the army was but one year, and it looked very probable that the end of the year would find Washington without a man at his back. He appealed in vain for aid to Gates at Ticonderoga, to Lee on the east side of the Hudson River. Gates could do nothing. Lee would do nothing. Lee was a man of a wild courage, of a wild genius. He had fought in many lands and under many flags. He was remarkable for his quarrelsome nature. He was remarkable for his mental accomplishments. These have earned for him the honour of being included in the varied company of persons to whom the authorship of the *Letters of Junius* was attributed. It was his misfortune to misunderstand the character of Washington, and not merely to misunderstand, but to regard it with a jealous contempt. This queer mixture of the man of letters and of the soldier of fortune appears to have seriously believed that Washington was a well-nigh incapable man, under whose authority disaster must inevitably fall upon the American cause.

At first Lee treated the summons of Washington with a dogged disobedience. At last he yielded to the imperative orders of his chief, and entered into Jersey only to fall into the hands of the British. Like many other adventurers of his class, he seems to have lost heart and head when the turn of the luck seemed to be against him. No baser spirit than Lee's degraded either army. While in captivity, and shaken with fears for his life, the captive condottiere declared to his captors his conviction that the game of American insurrection had nearly come to an end. He came to an agreement with his captors to play the traitor to his cause. When he was set free, through the firmness of Washington in demanding his release, he did his best to bring about a defeat of the Continental army at the battle of Monmouth. He not merely refused to obey Washington's orders, but he gave false orders as from Washington to others. Washington placed him under arrest; he was tried by court-martial, his treachery was not as patent as his incapacity, he was given the benefit of the doubt and suspended from the army for a year. From this point his insane hatred of Washington grew more rancorous. He wrote foolish scurrilous letters to the newspapers. One of these led to a duel in which he was wounded. He died in 1782, in a tavern in Philadelphia. His last wish was not to be buried in consecrated ground. He had kept too much bad company in his life, he said, to desire more of it after life. His last wish was not gratified. He was buried in the cemetery of Christ Church. Many decent people attended his funeral, who would scarcely have done so if they had known how absolute a traitor the man was. His treason was only made plain seventy-five years later. Then a full plan in his handwriting for destroying the Continental cause was discovered among the Strachey archives in Somerset, where it had no doubt been placed by Sir Henry Strachey, who was private secretary to Lord Howe in 1775. Lee's treason was worthy of the man. It was fortunately as unsuccessful as his own career.

The American cause would soon have come to an end if all its leaders had been as hot-headed and as hysterical as Lee, as imbecile and deceitful as Gates. Fortunately in Washington a great cause had found a great leader. Driven back by the British troops from one New Jersey town to another, until at last he was forced to cross the Delaware river to Pennsylvania, Washington never lost heart. He complained bitterly indeed to Congress of the passive as well as the active treachery of the militia and the people to the national cause. But he was not the man to give up a great struggle in despair because every New Jersey farmer was not a hero and every raw militiaman not a patriot. When the stars in their courses seemed to fight against him, he remained, like Sisera, undismayed. Things looked to be at their worst for the American insurgents, at their best for the English. On all sides the fainthearted were making piteous appeals for peace. The demoralisation was general and terrible. Washington still remained firm, and his courage inspired courage. The Congress retreated to Baltimore, investing Washington for six months with what have been truly termed dictatorial powers for the raising of troops and the provisioning of his forces. His hands thus strengthened, Washington resolved to make a bold stroke. General Howe, serenely confident of victory, issued a proclamation offering pardon to all who would desert the American cause. Many eagerly seized at the offer, including, unhappily, two members of the Congress, Allen and Galloway. Suddenly Howe's confidence and the confidence of the renegades was shaken. A series of attacks by Washington ended, after some changes of fortune, in clearing the Jerseys and forcing Howe to fall back upon New York. Thus the year ended more hopefully for the American cause.

CHAPTER X

SARATOGA AND YORKTOWN

NEITHER difficulty nor defeat weakened the spirit of the American Congress. It bore its many disasters with the same composure with which it welcomed its few successes. It seemed as if consciousness of the justice of its cause not merely upheld it in adversity, but inspired it with a conviction of ultimate success. It did wise things. It did courageous things. It placed great, almost unlimited powers in the hands of General Washington. It gave the country a new sense of national existence by the proud decision that the United Colonies should henceforward be called the United States. It resolved on appeal to France. In the straits to which the country was driven, the Congress felt bound to seek for aid wherever aid could be honourably found. If France would consent to recognise the independence of the United States, then the United States would accept the money and the arms of France to be employed against the old enemy of France. To this point had the English government of her American Colonies come, that men of the English race and of the English tongue turned for aid and comfort to the country that had been England's enemy for centuries. If anything could have impressed the king and the king's ministers with the earnestness of the struggle in which they had engaged with such light hearts, that fact might have done so.

Benjamin Franklin, Arthur Lee, and Silas Deane were the colonial Commissioners appointed to plead the colonial cause at the court of the French king. Franklin, still smarting under the sense of the insult that had been put upon him by the English government, may well have been gratified by the enthusiasm with which he was received in Paris. Philosophers and statesmen, soldiers and courtiers, beautiful court ladies and princes of the blood-royal greeted the American emissary with a warmth which was not all insincere. If court and courtiers could have guessed at the results which were in no small degree to come from Franklin's visit to Paris, the welcome would have been very different. But Rousseau and the philosophers had made the desire for liberty, in other countries, fashionable in the places of the great, and Franklin appeared to be the incarnation of the phrases and theories of the hour.

Franklin's popularity, however, did not so far serve him as to enable him to get all or even much that he wished to get. He wanted public recognition of the United States, he wanted open and liberal support, and he could get neither. Underhand assistance, covert support, large words for small deeds, these were readily forthcoming. Arms might be secretly bestowed; American privateers might be permitted to sell their prizes in French ports, while French authority closed its eyes. But this was all, or well-nigh all. France was not going to recognise, as yet, the American rebels—was not going, as yet, to appear as their ally in arms.

It was at this moment that the action of a young

French nobleman had a grave effect, not merely upon the fortunes of the American cause, but upon the destinies of his own country. The Marquis de la Fayette had fed his mind largely upon the new doctrines. He felt himself prompted by the inner voice to put his sword and his fortunes at the service of the struggling American colonies. It matters very little whether in doing this he was spurred solely by a passion for freedom, as his admirers maintain, or by the restless ache of personal ambition and the desire to figure largely on the world's stage. Whatever the spur may have been—and there was so much that was generous in La Fayette's nature that we may wisely assume the nobler purpose to have dominated—the result, as far as its effect upon the history of two countries was concerned, was the same.

La Fayette offered himself to the Commissioners as a volunteer. The Commissioners told him frankly that they were too poor even to provide him with a vessel to take him to the States. La Fayette was not to be refused. Out of his own fortune he carried himself across the Atlantic, offered his sword to Washington, and received from the Congress the rank of Major-General in the Continental army.

His example was largely followed. It was followed by Thaddeus Kosciusko, the young Polish gentleman fresh from his military studies at Versailles. It was followed by other high-spirited youths, men of position, men of wealth, who thought that their swords were rusting ingloriously while the American cause was to be fought for. They crossed the Atlantic on La Fayette's traces, and found, as he had found, warm welcome and swift employment on active service. One of the almost inevitable results of this new crusade was the French alliance of February 1778, and the recognition by France of the United States. But there were deeper results yet, when those chivalrous French officers, who had crossed the seas to fight for an idea, came back again to their own country with the wider thoughts of freedom and democracy which were to have their issue in the summoning of the States-General.

If France, in the person of La Fayette, gave to Washington a devoted comrade and a brave ally, she was no less generous in giving to the Continental cause the services of Baron von Steuben. Baron von Steuben was one of the ablest and the best trained soldiers in Germany. He had distinguished himself during the Seven Years' War. He had served on the staff of Frederick the Great. He had left the army, and he happened to be in Paris when Franklin was enlisting the sympathies of the French court. The French minister Vergennes thought that an experienced soldier like Steuben would be the very man to lick the raw American levies into shape. Steuben was persuaded to enter the American army, and his future career proved the wisdom of Vergennes' advice. Steuben saw that the ragged regiments before him contained the material from which to build a magnificent army. He at once devoted his great energy, and his even greater scientific knowledge, to convert an untrained and undisciplined into a trained and disciplined force. With a musket in his hand and fierce foreign oaths bubbling on his lips he set to work, and worked so hard and so well that he altered the whole military condition of the army he was remoulding. He practically taught the American soldiers the value of the bayonet, and the American leaders the value of a good staff. It would be hard to overrate the services of Steuben to the American cause.

Another foreigner rendered priceless service to America in another way of war. This was Paul Jones, the Scotch sailor. He had been a Virginia trader; he had lived in Virginia; he loved Virginia, and his heart went with Virginia's cause. He was an experienced, fearless mariner. He was given a captainship in such poor navy as the Continental cause could muster. He soon made his name a terror to the enemy. He ranged the British coasts in his ship, the *Bonhomme Richard*, carrying the colonial war into the ports and havens of Great Britain. He destroyed British vessels in the Humber. He entered the Firth of Forth and made to capture Leith, but was swept away by an unconquerable west wind. He was consoled for this disappointment by his famous fight off Flamborough Head with the British warship *Serapis*, while his consort the *Pallas* engaged the *Countess of Scarborough*. Both the English ships surrendered to the American vessels after one of the most desperate and bloody battles recorded in the story of the sea. This was Paul Jones's greatest battle. It made him famous all over the world; it has given him lasting fame. He had thirteen years of life yet to live and many wild things to do in them, and many strange experiences to taste of the early years of the French Revolution. But he reached the high-top-gallant of his life in that wild long fight off Flamborough Head when the *Bonhomme Richard* and *Serapis* were lashed together, and the battle raged along the burning decks in the cloudy autumn night.

SARATOGA AND YORKTOWN

Before the French alliance was concluded defeat after defeat fell upon the Continental arms. Washington was defeated at the battle of Brandywine, where La Fayette fought his first fight on American soil and got his first wound. The Continental Congress had to fly from Philadelphia, which was occupied without opposition by General Howe. By the subsequent capture of Redbank the British opened the Delaware and secured a free passage for their fleet to Philadelphia. Washington retired to winter quarters in Valley Forge, where his heroism and the heroism of those that were with him gave to the great struggle its noblest glory.

The British successes in the middle states were accompanied by successes in the north. On the Canadian frontier General Burgoyne had massed a large army of more than seven thousand men, together with a great number of Canadians, and unhappily a great number of Red Indians, whom he should have been ashamed to use. It is true that Burgoyne professed to believe that his savage allies would obey the laws of war and attack only those who appeared in arms against them. As a matter of fact, the Indians fought after their own barbarous fashion, sparing neither women nor children. The atrocities that they committed only deepened the hate with which the English cause was regarded by the rebels.

At first Burgoyne had everything his own way. He and his savages captured Ticonderoga, one of the strongest positions held by the Colonists in the north. Its loss was one of the greatest blows their pride had suffered. But after this success Burgoyne's luck began to turn. He was defeated again and again, until defeat degenerated into disaster. Burgoyne was forced to retreat to Saratoga, where he was surrounded by the Americans under General Horatio Gates. No serious attempt was made to relieve him, and after some days of communication with Gates, he and his army were obliged to surrender. The terms were not dishonourable to the vanquished, while they were eminently serviceable to the victors. The British were to march out with the honours of war, give up their arms, and return to England on the express condition that they were not to serve again in North America during the progress of the struggle.

This was the first great triumph of the American arms, and it raised the hopes of the colonists as high as before they had been cast down. Men who hitherto had either held aloof from the cause of the Congress or had professed loyalist sentiments now began to rally to what they saw to be the winning side. If England had been blessed with a wise king, or if the king had been blessed with wise counsellors, the fall of Saratoga would have ended the conflict. But the king was not wise. His counsellors were not wise. They resolved to continue the war in the wild hope of even yet breaking the spirit of the rebels and punishing them for the humiliation of Saratoga.

The humiliation of Saratoga had an additional advantage for the Continental cause beyond the first advantage of an honourable victory. It settled the vacillating purposes of the French court. The French King formally recognised the independence of the United States, formally entered into a treaty of commerce and alliance with the United States. This was, of course, meant to be taken by the British

SARATOGA AND YORKTOWN 163

Government, and of course was taken by the British Government, as equivalent to an act of war. The new danger for a moment woke something like a sense of intelligence in the advisers of the king. Lord North proposed measures of conciliation which were ludicrously inadequate to the original demands of the colonists. They were promptly rejected by the Congress. He sent over a Commission, which tried alternately to bribe and to menace, and which failed ignominiously in both, and soon returned from the States in all the disgrace of ill-success. The war had still to go on.

But England as a whole was getting weary of the war. There was a daily increasing party in England which was compelled by its sense of justice to sympathise with the revolted colonies. That party of which Burke was the most illustrious member had shown its sympathy outside Parliament by its indignation at the cruelty with which the American prisoners had been treated and by the subscription that was raised to relieve their sufferings. In Parliament its sympathy was shown by a proposal to recognise the Independence of the United States, a proposal chiefly memorable as being the cause of the last speech ever made by Chatham. He was carried to the House to raise his protest against 'the dismemberment of this most ancient and most noble monarchy.' He was trying to explain the policy he recommended, a policy which would have been directed to the winning back of the States upon the most generous terms. The policy was never to be formulated. The great statesman fell fainting in his place. He was carried out of the House and taken to his country seat in Kent to die.

The saddest pages in the story of the war which had still to go on are those which tell the tale of the treason of Benedict Arnold. Few of the Continental soldiers had done so much, still fewer had done more for the cause of American Independence. Handsome, brave, rarely gifted, honoured with the attached friendship of George Washington, happy in the companionship of a young, beautiful and devoted wife, Arnold might well seem a man specially aided by Providence to pursue the path of duty and integrity. Unhappily his mind was ill-balanced. His passions overcrowed his judgment. He got into a quarrel with Congress. He believed himself to have been wronged. It must be admitted that he was not altogether well-treated. But he brooded over his injuries till the thought of them warped in his mind every noble instinct and extinguished every sentiment of honour. His distorted brain conceived the horrible idea of avenging himself upon Congress by betraying his country to the enemy. He persuaded Washington, who loved and trusted him, to give him command of West Point. He entered into a treasonable correspondence with the English commander Clinton, in which he proposed to betray West Point to the British. Arnold's insane ambition was here prompting him as well as his sense of wrong. He thought that this deed coming on the heels of so many American disasters would completely ruin the Continental hopes, would overthrow the hated Congress, and would hand the colonies back to their old allegiance. The glory and the triumph of all this would be due to him. The magnitude of the success would compensate for the magnitude of the crime.

The particulars of the treason were planned between Arnold and Major-General John André of the English army. The scheme for the surrender of West Point was deeply laid, and only a chance prevented it from being carried out. André visited Arnold within the American lines to settle all the plans. He left Arnold to rejoin the English, carrying with him papers in Arnold's handwriting concerning the plot. On his way back André fell into American hands and was made prisoner. The officer in whose charge he was placed, not understanding what the papers were, at once sent word to Arnold of the capture of a spy with compromising documents in his possession. Arnold fled to the shelter of a British ship and escaped. André was tried by court-martial as a spy, sentenced to death and hanged. A great deal of pity has been expressed, and very naturally expressed, for André's fate. He was young, he was brave, he was gifted. It was indeed a tragedy that he should have perished so miserably through association with so base a traitor. But he undoubtedly was playing the part of a spy, and he undoubtedly deserved his punishment by all the laws of war. It has been said that Washington might have saved him, that Washington ought to have saved him. Washington's duty clearly was to accept the finding of the court-martial, whatever his inclination may have been. Lord Mahon has impugned the authority of the court-martial itself on quite unjust ground. He assumed that the American generals 'had probably never so much as heard the names of Vattel or of Puffendorf,' and could therefore 'be no fit judges on any nice or doubtful point' of military law. As a matter of fact, Nathaniel Greene knew his Vattel very well, and Vattel was much read by the American leaders of the time. Most of the members of the court-martial were well-educated men. Four had taken University degrees. La Fayette was a member of the court-martial, and so was Steuben, who had been a staff officer of Frederick the Great. It is to be regretted that André's request to be shot instead of hanged could not be granted, but the court probably remembered the case of Nathan Hale, the young soldier-graduate of Yale, whom Howe had captured and hanged as a spy four years earlier.

Many years later André's remains were removed to England and placed in Westminster Abbey. The renegade and traitor, Arnold, fought under the English flag for a time and dragged on a dishonoured life for many years in England till his death in 1801. His wife remained loyal to him in his exile and his shame. The last act of his ruined life was to dress himself in the old American uniform that he had always preserved and had never worn since the day when he drew a traitor's sword against his comrades and his countrymen. He wished to die, he said, in the old uniform in which he had fought his battles, and he asked God to forgive him for ever putting on another.

The war went on with varying fortunes for two years more—two years which served only to add to the lustre of Washington's genius and to emphasise the folly of the British ministry. It is not necessary to follow in detail all the changes of fortune or to note every battle that took place during these memorable years. With Spain against her, with France against her, England still fought desperately for her supremacy in America. The war had chiefly

SARATOGA AND YORKTOWN 167

drifted into the southern states, where one or two conspicuous victories won by Lord Cornwallis revived the hopes of the ministry, and depressed the spirits of the colonists, who found the aid of France of less value than they had expected. But the whole condition of things was changed by a crowning disaster to the English arms.

Cornwallis, baffled in an attempt upon North Carolina, had shut himself up within the lines of Yorktown in Virginia. Washington by a forced march came in front of him at a time when the sea was held by the French fleet. Washington on one side, the French fleet on the other, and famine within his lines, forced Cornwallis to submit. He negotiated for a surrender, by the final terms of which he had to give up his troops as prisoners of war to Congress, and his naval force to the French fleet. On the 19th he marched out with folded colours, and formally surrendered to General Lincoln.

This practically ended the war. Though Lord North still blustered, and still urged the king to bluster in vague terms which talked of the continuance of the struggle, the minister knew in his heart that all was over. The House of Commons was against him, the country was against him. The Commons sent up an address to the King pleading for peace. As the royal answer was thought to be equivocal, the Commons passed a resolution that any person advising the king to persevere in the war against America should be considered as a public enemy. This hint was strong enough even for Lord North, even for the king. Lord North resigned, and Lord Rockingham took office for the express purpose of bringing about a peace. Lord Rockingham died soon after taking office, and was succeeded by Lord Shelburne. Shelburne was no less an advocate of peace, and negotiations were opened to that intent in Paris. Franklin, Jay, Adams, and Laurens represented America at the Court of France. At first they acted with the co-operation of Vergennes, the French minister, but becoming suspicious of his good faith, unreasonably as it would now appear, they turned away from him and conducted their negotiations directly with the English envoys. The treaty naturally was concluded on conditions agreeable to the new country. By its provisions the United States extended from the Atlantic coast to the Mississippi River. Florida, which included parts of what are now Alabama and Mississippi, was restored to Spain, which retained her hold upon Louisiana. The nine years' struggle had beggared England of her best colonies, and had converted those colonies into a new English-speaking nation.

CHAPTER XI

THE CRITICAL PERIOD

THE six years from 1783 to 1789 have been happily called the critical period of American history. Gargantua had been born, but Gargantua had yet to live, and there were moments in his fierce infancy when it seemed as if he must perish prematurely.

The States of America were free. The States of America had asserted and attained their independence. The States of America were avowedly united. But for a time the Union seemed to be little more than nominal, and for a time the independence appeared to be little more than the privilege to perish in isolation. The new country had no government. It had no army. It had no political or social organisation. It was weltering in a financial waste, almost without credit, almost on the edge of national bankruptcy. Its commerce was so limited as to be practically crippled. It was torn by terrible internal dissensions. State quarrelled with State over questions of territory. It alienated foreign sympathy by the general treatment of the loyalists who were still left in the country. This treatment was very often unjust to a party that had stood by the opinions that had been everybody's opinions twenty years earlier. The treatment was sometimes absolutely cruel. If it were true, as anti-colonial historians assert on doubtful evidence, that loyal women were stripped naked, tarred and feathered, and so exhibited through the streets of Boston, then Boston contained citizens who would have made agreeable companions for Carrier of the Loire and Jourdan of the Rhone. Most cities did, most cities do contain such citizens, eager to take their base advantage of a time of tumult. If men were hanged by the victors only because they had been loyal to King George, they suffered martyrdom as much as the victims of the Boston massacre. Reprisals are seemingly the unhappy, inevitable incidents of revolutions. A great cause and a glorious victory cannot be degraded by the excesses of a few camp-followers. But if the victory had been glorious, the great cause was still in peril. The country seemed leaderless. Congress seemed leaderless. Congress seemed helpless for good. Long years later, Gouverneur Morris and Jay were talking over the events of the years in which they had helped to make history. 'Jay,' said Morris, 'what a set of damned scoundrels we had in that second Congress.' 'Yes,' answered Jay, 'we had.' The story is dear to the anti-colonial writers, who love to swell their indictment of the Continental cause by cataloguing every folly and every offence that can, rightly or wrongly, on good evidence or on bad evidence, be laid at its door. The real significance of the story is the reverse of what such writers find in it. It is possible that there were scoundrels in the Continental Congress. It shares that misfortune with most large assemblages of men. But it did a great work, and on the whole it did that great work well. Its honour in accomplishing the task is only the greater in proportion to the difficulties it had to encounter, within and without its ranks.

The worse the condition of the country appeared to be in the six years that followed the war, the more remarkable was the way in which it rescued itself from the Slough of Despond in which it was floundering. Threatened with financial ruin, with faction, with anarchy, the new country made an effort even greater than its effort for independence. It shook itself free from the dangers that were closing about it and choking out its life. It showed itself worthy of the independence it had won. When an armed mob of mutineers clamouring for arrears of pay practically drove the Congress out of Philadelphia, when State after State threatened secession from the Union, when a former captain of the Continental army, Daniel Shays, headed an armed rebellion against the State government of Massachusetts, when the currency of the country was scarcely worth the paper it was printed on, America had indeed come to the moment when the choice lay between death and life. A little longer in that Valley of the Shadow, and the new country must have ceased to be. But the new country had too much vitality to fall ignobly under its burdens. It chose to live and not die. It braced itself to make its freedom real. It called order out of chaos, it welded a meaningless and unstable league of jarring and factious states into the greatest republic that the world has yet seen.

'We are one nation to-day,' said Washington, 'and thirteen to-morrow: who will treat with us on those terms?' The attempt was now made in 1787 to make the thirteen nations one nation, with whom all the world would be glad to treat. A great convention was held in the Philadelphia State House, to which all the States, except New Hampshire and Rhode Island, sent delegates. Most of America's leading public men were sent to the convention, Washington of course, and Franklin, and James Madison, whose gifts and learning have earned him comparison with the younger Pitt, and Elbridge Gerry and Francis Dana, and perhaps the noblest American after Washington, Alexander Hamilton.

Alexander Hamilton is in many regards the most personally attractive figure among the heroes of American Independence. His physical charm, the vivacity of his genius, which asserted itself when he was still a boy, and which persisted through his life, his courage, conspicuous in an age and fellowship of brave men, his tender humanity, his devotion to his own exalted standard of right and duty, compel the attention and command the regard of the men of to-day as they did those of his contemporaries. No one would dream for a moment of asserting that he was Washington's equal as a soldier, as a statesman, or as a great man. But he was endowed with qualities that were wanting, or were less marked, in Washington. Washington in history as in life seems to stand further apart from his fellows, to breathe a rarer, if not a colder atmosphere. If Washington is the father of his country, Hamilton is the brother of his countrymen. Hamilton was born in 1757 in Nevis of the West Indies, the child of a Scottish father, of the ancient house of Hamilton, and of a French Huguenot mother. A paper descriptive of a hurricane, which the boy wrote when he was fifteen, saved him from a counting-house in Santa Cruz and

THE CRITICAL PERIOD 173

sent him over-seas to pursue his studies in New York. He worked hard at King's College, which George the Second had founded. He took a living interest in the political events that were gradually thickening around him. When war appeared probable, he set to train himself seriously for a soldier, and when war came it found Hamilton ready to take up arms. His military career was remarkable. Men called him 'the little lion.' As Washington's secretary he served Washington and the cause well. His devotion to Washington was neither blind nor unquestioning. He was strongly opposed to the form of André's execution. 'The refusing him the privilege of choosing the manner of his death will be branded with too much obstinacy,' Hamilton wrote. Shortly after his happy marriage in 1780 to the daughter of General Schuyler, some disagreement with Washington, not precisely understood, caused him to surrender his office as secretary, and no inducement could induce him to resume it, in spite even of a personal appeal from Washington himself. When the war was over, Hamilton devoted himself to, and distinguished himself at, the New York bar; and when the time came for calling the American nation into existence out of a chaotic confederacy, Hamilton played the most conspicuous part in winning order from disorder and turning darkness into light.

After incessant debate, much wrangling and many compromises, the Convention of 1787 succeeded in shaping the Constitution under which, with some modifications, America still lives. All legislative powers are vested in a Congress consisting of a Senate and a House of Representatives. The House of Representatives is composed of members chosen every second year by the electors of each State having the qualifications requisite for electors of the most numerous branch of the State legislature. A representative has to be over twenty-five years of age, a citizen of the United States for seven years, and an inhabitant of the State in which he was chosen. The number of representatives must not exceed one for each thirty thousand inhabitants. The House of Representatives choose their own Speaker and other officers, and have the sole power of impeachment. The Senate is composed of two senators from each State, chosen by the State Legislature for six years. A senator must be thirty years of age, nine years a citizen, and not an inhabitant of the State for which he is chosen. The Vice-President of the United States is by virtue of his office President of the Senate. The Senate chooses its other officers, and has the sole power to try all impeachments. Members of both Houses are paid for their services. They can hold no public civil office while they are members of Congress. All revenue bills originate in the House of Representatives, but the Senate is free to propose amendments. The President has a power of veto on any bill. If, however, it is still approved by a vote of two-thirds of both Houses, it becomes law. Congress has powers of taxation, borrowing money, regulation of commerce, naturalisation, coinage, declaration of war, providing for army, navy, and militia, and discharging all the usual duties of a government. The different States are left free to manage their local government in their own way, but they are bound by the Federal law in all matters relating to war and peace, military matters, tariff, treaty, and finance. The President and Vice-President must be natural born citizens of the United States. They are elected for four years by electors of each State, equal to the whole number of senators and representatives to which the State is entitled in Congress. No senator or representative or person holding any office of trust or profit under the United States may be an elector. The electors vote by ballot for a President, and by a separate ballot for a Vice-President. One of the two officers must not be an inhabitant of the State. Whoever obtains a majority of the whole number of electors appointed by all the States is chosen as President, and the same rule governs the choice of Vice-President. The judicial power is invested in a great tribunal called the Supreme Court, and in inferior courts. Members of the Supreme Court hold their office 'during good behaviour.' Their places are filled by the President, with the consent of the Senate. The Supreme Court is perhaps the most independent body in the world. It has no initiative, but with it rests the final decision as to the interpretation of the Constitution. Congress is enabled, on the wish of a majority of two-thirds in both Houses, to propose amendments to the Constitution, which become law if ratified by a majority of three-fourths of the several States.

Undoubtedly the unanimous consent of all the States was legally essential to the creation of this constitution, and undoubtedly the constitution was created by only eleven States, as Rhode Island and North Carolina refused to ratify, and kept out of the Union for some time. In point of fact the eleven ratifying States seceded from the existing Confederation and made a new government. They made it very well, and it has endured with occasional emendations, and proved itself adapted to very different conditions of social and political existence from those it was framed to rule. Both by his voice and by his pen Hamilton laboured splendidly in the creation of the Constitution. When it was created he laboured splendidly in its service through several years of public office.

The new constitution came into force in 1789, and the same year witnessed the beginning of the destruction of the old monarchical system of Europe. George Washington was elected as the first President of the United States, and he took the oath in the old Federal Hall in New York City on the 30th of April. Two months and a half later, over in Paris, the Bastille was taken. Its great key was sent across the Atlantic as a present to the President of the American Republic. The American Revolution had ended. The French Revolution had begun. The American Republic did not start under conditions of what are called republican simplicity. Washington's own personal tastes were not exactly simple, and were not altogether democratic. He had indeed disdained the idea of being made a king, but he liked a show of dignity and display in his high office. He had a weakness for sonorous, even pompous address, and had strongly desired that the official designation of his office should be 'His High Mightiness'—a form of ceremonial salutation which happily was not adopted. It was the close of a formal and elegantly dressed age, and Washington loved formality and elegance in dress. At his levees his own attire was punctiliously rich and stately. He expected those who attended what might almost be called his court to attire themselves with a fastidious regard for the dignity and decorum of the occasion. There were many, of course, who resented the show and splendour of Washington's administration. They sniffed at the coaches and four. They resented the scarlet and white liveries. They thought Mrs. Washington dressed far too gorgeously. They dimly discerned a danger to the commonwealth in the pearl-coloured waistcoats of the President, and the President's powdered hair. But the last century still lived; and Washington was very much the child of his century, with its belief in deportment and the mode and the grand manner, and the aptness of splendour to splendid occasions and splendid individuals.

Washington was President for two terms of four years each, which were sufficiently eventful for the young Republic. In the very beginning of Washington's presidency, the young Republic lost one of the most famous of her founders. Benjamin Franklin died on the 17th of April 1790, mourned by the whole civilised world. Eli Whitney's invention of the cotton-gin revolutionised the trade of the South, and played its unconscious part in a quarrel that came near to destroy the Union. In the meantime the Union grew. Rhode Island and North Carolina came in. The 'Old Thirteen' were increased by the addition of three new States. Ethan Allen, Seth Warner, and the Green Mountain boys carried their point at last. Their independence of New York or New Hampshire was recognised. Vermont entered the Union as a separate state. Kentucky, famous for furious Indian fights and for the adventures of Daniel Boone, the hunter and trapper, joined the Union in 1792. Tennessee was added in 1796.

The Union was thriving, but its hours were not all propitious. Washington had many difficulties to deal with. There were financial difficulties, difficulties with the National debt, which Alexander Hamilton dexterously disposed of or minimised. There were difficulties with hostile Indians, causing defeat and slaughter of many hundreds of United States troops before the red men were defeated by General Wayne. There were difficulties with insurgents in Pennsylvania, who proposed to resist by force of arms the imposition of a tax on distilling whisky, and who were only reduced to submission by force of arms. There were difficulties over a treaty which John Jay made with England as Washington's envoy, and which many Americans thought conceded too much to Great Britain. Over all these difficulties the people who disliked Washington and the people who distrusted Washington made a great ado. They reviled him as bitterly as if he had been a traitor like Arnold or a traitor like Lee.

Perhaps the greatest difficulty Washington had to deal with was the difficulty of keeping the country neutral when revolutionary France declared war upon England. Washington's firmness saved the United States from involving themselves in a foreign war. An absurd French envoy named Genet came over to the States, and acted for a season as if America were not merely an ally but a subject of France. He fitted out privateers against England in American harbours, and when Washington remonstrated with him, he assailed Washington with abuse almost as bitter as that with which some of Washington's own countrymen loaded their President. Washington called upon the French government to recall Genet, and Genet was recalled. But he had fallen in love with a beautiful New York girl, and she had fallen in love with him. They married, and he settled down in New York and became a quiet member of society, and there was an end to his vapourings.

The cares of office were wearing Washington out, and the attacks of lesser men, and the failure of so many of his fellow-citizens to understand his motives or to appreciate his integrity. When his second term of office expired he was not to be persuaded to accept a third term, though many tried hard to persuade him. He was wise to refuse. The acceptance of a third term might have set a dangerous precedent. He was wise to refuse for his own sake. He was growing old. He was growing deaf. He wanted rest. He retired to Mount Vernon to end his days. He issued a farewell address to his fellow-citizens which remains one of the monuments of American wisdom, American statesmanship, and American eloquence. Washington retired amidst the regrets of the nation and the insults of a base, foolish or misguided minority. Washington knew two years of peace at Mount Vernon, and in the last year of the century he died.

It is hard to attempt an appreciation of Washington without drifting towards the danger of hyperbole. The man was so great and so unselfish, so successful and so modest, so illustrious and so simple, that he seems to stand alone in the possession of qualities that are seldom united. There have been greater soldiers, greater statesmen, greater rulers. Few men have united so many of the essentials of greatness in so admirable and so honourable a personality. Cæsar and Napoleon were greater captains. Burke was a greater statesman. Alfred was perhaps a greater ruler. It was given to Washington to be a great soldier, a great statesman, a great ruler, and as well one of the most pure-spirited, high-minded, honourable and lovable of beings, a true man and a true gentleman. 'First in peace, first in war, and first in the hearts of his countrymen.' The beautiful words were his greatest tribute while he lived. They serve for his fittest requiem.

There are those who in their desire to lessen all greatness delight to think that the man was not faultless. These would have us believe, what we need not believe, that he was unfaithful to his wife. These harp on his undemocratic richness of dress and his habit at his receptions of holding his hands behind his back to save him from shaking hands with his visitors. They are at pains to remind us that the hero wore false teeth. This is but labour lost. Washington remains the hero in spite of his false teeth, in spite of the pearl-coloured waistcoat and the powdered hair, in spite of his hauteur of state. Cromwell's wart, or Luxembourg's hump, or the satyr face of Socrates, the scar of Danton and the squint of Wilkes and the baldness of Cæsar—these are the patent blemishes that bind the great man to the little man and make them kin. In the genius there is no kinship, and it is the genius we remember when we honour the illustrious name.

CHAPTER XII

THE SUCCESSORS OF WASHINGTON

THE new president, John Adams, the portly gentleman with the twinkling eye, who looked like the typical John Bull, carried on that tradition of the eighteenth century which the first president so eminently embodied. His life was almost co-equal with the reigns of George the Second, George the Third, and George the Fourth. He had been a subject of the first monarch. He had rebelled against the second. In the reign of the third he was an old man who had been for years the free subject of a free republic. It was inevitable that his view of life, political and social, should be the view of the century to which the larger part of his life belonged. He was like Washington, a man with a respect for established forms, a respect for formalities, a regard for those external decorums and suavities which adorned the urbanity of the waning century.

In his day of administration, and after it, men and women still wore the habit and the manners of a modish age. Gentlemen still wore knee-breeches, leaving, like their fellows in France, the long trouser to the sans-culotte. They still made a brave show, on occasion, in periwigs and cocked hats and scarlet cloaks. The gentlewomen still rouged, and piled their powdered hair in a high mountain over the

forehead. People who wished to be thought
fashionable modelled their lives upon those of the
English gentry, drank tea and talked scandal, danced
old dances at Assemblies and Routs, gambled
gallantly at the card-tables, carrying themselves
quite joyously and frivolously, like the shepherd-
boy in Arcadia who piped as if he would never
grow old. They seemed to have little idea that
the world was changing all around them. They
regarded social distinctions with as grave a punctili-
ousness as if there had never been a Declaration of
Independence, and as if a French Revolution counted
for nothing in the experience of mankind. At
Harvard College, for instance, and at Yale College,
students were arranged in the catalogue, not by
order of alphabet, but according to the supposed
social position of their parents, so far as that could
be ascertained by minute scrupulous inquiry of the
college authorities. Scholarship could not raise the
low-born student from his place, and when he passed
upon the college stair his superior in birth, he was
obliged, by custom, to yield to him the balustrade.

The influence of the old world was still potent.
In many ways, the new republic resembled the
old monarchy in the days when John Adams was
president. John Adams had certainly deserved well
of the new Republic. The free-thinking graduate of
Harvard, the successful New England lawyer had
felt the spirit of patriotism quicken within him as
he listened to the glowing words of James Otis
against Writs of Assistance. From that moment
Adams was prepared to devote his gifts and his
life to his country. His defence of Captain Preston
and the other soldiers implicated in the Boston

massacre, proved his moral courage and firm impartiality. He played a prominent part in the first and second congresses. In his dealings with the French he showed himself to be an admirable diplomatist. He carried himself with discretion and tact when he acted as the first minister of the new Republic to England. He was an eloquent and logical thinker, speaker, and writer. It was not given to any one to have a vaster idea of John Adams' merits than John Adams himself. He was always chagrined to find that the country at large rated Washington so much higher than himself. It did not seem to him in accordance with the fitness of things that John Adams should only be poor Vice-President, while Washington sat in the President's seat, and came near to being addressed as his 'High Mightiness.'

Adams's view of his office was like that of Washington, the view of an eighteenth century statesman; a view that was aristocratic rather than democratic. He believed in a governing class whose place was at the head of affairs. Like Hamilton, he had a decided distrust of the masses. He was supposed to have a distinct affection for an etiquette, display, and ceremonial, that seemed in the eyes of the austere more suited to a regal court than to a presidential parlour. The extreme republicans believed that he loved these things too well, that his soul yearned for titles. There was an absurd story told against him. According to this story he harboured fantastic designs of marrying his daughter to a son of the British king. The English prince was to be proclaimed King of the United States. The legend went that Adams was only turned from his design by Washington himself, who paid him three visits, dressed the first time in white, the second time in black, and the third time in full uniform, with drawn sword, before he could dissuade him.

There were already two parties in the State. Human beings must needs divide themselves always into two parties, the party that wants to go on, and the party that wants to stay where it is. Adams was the leader of the party that wanted to stay where it was. He, and those who thought with him, regarded the Constitution with the applauding eye of Voltaire's Pangloss. It was the best possible Constitution in the best possible of worlds. There were, however, a great number of persons who declined to treat the Constitution as if it were a sacred covenant. They thought something very much better might have been done, and that they were the people to do it. Those who adored the Constitution called themselves, or came to be called, Federalists. Those who did not adore the Constitution called themselves, or came to be called, Republicans, a term which was afterwards changed to that of Democrat.

If Hamilton and Adams were in a sense rivals for the leadership of the Federalists, Thomas Jefferson was the unquestioned leader of the Republicans. The writer of the Declaration of Independence had an affection for the French Revolutionists who had taken that document for their charter and had done so many strange things in its name. He could regard the September massacres, not with sombre acquiescence like Danton, but with a cynical composure. He would have been at home at a meeting of the Jacobin Club. He would have enjoyed a quiet evening with Robespierre in the bosom of the Duplay

THE SUCCESSORS OF WASHINGTON 185

family. He had much in common with the philosophers who prepared the way for the Revolution. His literary tastes and his love for science would have made him an appropriate companion for Diderot, d'Alembert and Helvétius. His unquestioning faith in the democracy would have endeared him to Rousseau and to St. Just. As he adored France, so he hated England. The Federalists were all the other way. They were anti-Gallicans from their dislike of the extremes to which the French Revolution had gone. They were supposed to have a decided leaning towards England and towards the English method of government. They nick-named their antagonists disdainfully sans-culottes, and their antagonists retorted by deriding them as monocrats. Both parties resembled all other political parties since the dawn of time in being very keen, very hot, very deeply convinced that they were wholly in the right and their opponents absolutely in the wrong. The zest and heat of both parties prompted them to express their opinions of each other in speech and in print with an asperity, even with an acrimony, that added at least an excitement to public life. Of the two parties the Republicans were the most powerful in journalistic attack.

Adams had a bustling, stormy presidency. He had almost as much to contend against in the obvious distrust and veiled antagonism of Hamilton as in the opposition of Thomas Jefferson and the leaders of the Republican party. He made himself exceedingly unpopular by calling into existence two laws known as the Alien and Sedition Acts. The public press was very outspoken, very bitter in its attacks upon Adams and the Federalist party. Many of the journalists were English; many were French. The Federalists, excited and fearful, thought it necessary, for the salvation of the State and for their own preservation, to pass one law by which aliens could be removed from the country at the discretion of the President, and another by which the freedom of the press was threatened. The measures were extremely foolish. They failed to effect their purpose, as they were bound to fail in a free country. They gravely injured the party that had called them into being.

The one success of Adam's administration was the attitude maintained by the United States to France. The Directory was exceedingly hostile to America on account of the treaty which Jay had concluded with England in the previous administration. Diplomatic relations between the two countries had practically ceased to exist. Adams sent over three envoys in the hope of establishing a better feeling. An amazing attempt, presumably inspired by Talleyrand, was made to extort from these envoys fifty thousand pounds for the benefit of the Directory. The famous response, 'Millions for defence, not a cent. for tribute,' became the war-cry of the Federalists. The nefarious attempt was exposed by the publication of despatches in which the would-be extorters appear concealed under the letters X. Y. Z. America promptly prepared for war. It was a naval war, and it lasted some little while, and there were several sea-fights, and on the whole America had the best of it. When Napoleon overthrew the French Directory he made peace with America. So ended the first war waged by the new Republic.

Adams was not re-elected when his term of office expired in 1801. The country chose Thomas Jefferson for President, and a political colleague of his, Aaron Burr—who very much wanted to be President—for Vice-President. Adams was bitterly disappointed at his defeat, and he showed his disappointment in a way quite unworthy of him and of his honourable career. Instead of waiting, as Washington had done, to grace with his presence the inauguration of his successor, he hurried away to hide his mortification in his own home. He was always vain, and he knew it, but in this instance his wounded vanity quite overcame his better judgment and his sense of public decorum. He lived for a quarter of a century more in quiet literary seclusion; lived to see his son President of the United States; lived to die on the fiftieth anniversary of the Declaration of Independence and in the ninety-first year of his age.

With Jefferson a very different order of things came into being. He seemed as if he wished to take advantage of the dawn of the new century to inaugurate a new era for the Republic. The show, the pomp, the formality that had been so dear to the Federalists disappeared like the delusion of a dream. There were no more coaches and six, no more gorgeousness of presidential attire, no more splendidly-attired officials and splendidly-attended levees. Jefferson was twice elected to the presidency, and his eight years of office are memorable years. They chronicled the purchase of Louisiana from Napoleon, who had taken it from Spain. They recorded a law forbidding the importation of slaves from any foreign country into the United States after 1807. They witnessed a series of struggles with the Barbary pirates which added to the growing fame of the little American navy. They admired the launching of

Robert Fulton's steamboat on the Hudson. They welcomed the admission of Ohio into the Union as the seventeenth State. There had long been a difficulty about the Ohio valley. People argued as to whether it belonged to the individual States who claimed it, or to the United States as a whole. In the end the greater part of it was made over to the government and was known for a long time as the North-West Settlement. It was slowly settled. It was organised at last into a State, and as a State it kept the name of its fair river.

The dramatic interest of the Jeffersonian epoch belongs not to the President, but to the Vice-President; not to Jefferson, but to Aaron Burr. Few figures more sinister, more malign, than Aaron Burr trouble the page of history. Few men, having great gifts, ever misused those gifts to baser purposes. A corroding desire for personal success at any price seems from his very youth to have eaten away whatever there may have been of good, of honourable, of noble in Aaron Burr's nature. He had been Hamilton's rival in early days at the New York Bar. He had served, like Hamilton, in the ranks of the Continental army. When the Constitution was created he found himself in public life incessantly opposed to Hamilton. Hamilton seems to have in the end inspired him with a hatred so intense that nothing would satisfy him but an attempt upon Hamilton's life. In 1804 he failed to obtain the appointment of Governor of New York State. He attributed his failure to the action of Hamilton. He proceeded to force a quarrel upon Hamilton on the strength of the publicity given in a newspaper to some alleged severe comments made by Hamilton upon Burr's character. Burr demanded that Hamilton should either deny having ever animadverted upon his character or should meet him in mortal combat. Hamilton could not and would not deny that he had often in private expressed his opinion of Burr's conduct. Burr insisted upon a duel. The manners of the time made it hard almost to impossibility for any one to refuse such a challenge, just as it would still be hard almost to impossibility for a Frenchman of to-day to refuse such a challenge. The duel was fought on the 11th of July at Weehawken on the Hudson. Hamilton was mortally wounded, and died thirty hours later. The whole nation mourned for him with public show of sorrow. A coroner's jury returned a verdict of murder against Burr, and Burr had to fly for his life.

In killing Hamilton, Burr had killed his own career. Public life seemed closed to him. He made one wild despairing, almost insane attempt to gratify his lust for success. He schemed a scheme for invading the vast regions to the west of the Mississippi. He seems to have cherished some crazy idea of building up a new empire out of Mexico and Texas and making himself its emperor. He was arrested. He was tried for treason. Whatever his plot had been, the secret was closely kept; nothing definite could be proved against him and he was set free. But his ambitious dreams were ended; his ambitious hopes were dulled. He drifted hither and thither over Europe, a mean, dishonourable, unlovely figure. He was treated as a French spy in England; he was treated as an English spy in France. He was often in great straits for want of money. It is told of him, that once in his wanderings he came to Paris and

requested an audience of Talleyrand. Talleyrand
made answer that 'The Minister for Foreign Affairs
will be happy to see the late Vice-President of the
United States; but M. Talleyrand thinks it due to
Colonel Burr to state that he always has the minia-
ture of General Hamilton hanging over his mantel-
piece.' The tale may very well be true. Talleyrand
once said to George Ticknor of Boston, that 'he had
known nearly all the marked men of his time, but
had never known one on the whole equal to Hamilton.'
Burr made his way back to the United States at last,
and was suffered to live unmolested in obscurity in
New York. For all but a quarter of a century he
dragged on his degraded life, poor, lonely and dis-
eased. He died at last a paralysed pauper who had
once come near to be the President of the American Republic, who had once dreamed of being the
head of a new Mexican empire. History scarcely
holds record of a more overweening ambition more
ruthlessly foiled.

There is little doubt that Jefferson could have been
elected President for a third term if he had wished.
But like Washington he saw the unwisdom of establishing so dangerous a precedent, and in 1809 he was
followed by another Republican Democrat, James
Madison of Virginia. Madison had not begun as a
Democrat. He was one of the writers of the famous
series of papers known as 'The Federalist.' In his
elegant Augustan style he had advocated the doctrines dear to Hamilton and to Jay. But he had
been 'overlooked,' in the Shakespearean sense of the
word, by the attraction of Jefferson and had passed
from the camp of the Federalists into the camp of
the Republican Democrats.

THE SUCCESSORS OF WASHINGTON

Madison was now fifty-eight years old. He was probably the most learned living American in history and constitutional law. He was an enthusiastic champion of religious liberty and the freedom of conscience. He played a leading part in causing the convention to assemble which created the Constitution of the United States. He played a leading part in the work of the convention. The great event of his administration was a foreign war. Once again America and England were opposed in arms, and once again success was waiting for America.

CHAPTER XIII

WAR WITH ENGLAND NUMBER TWO

THE war of 1812 is not a war that can be looked back to with satisfaction by either of the belligerents. Neither side can be said to have entered on it from the highest motives. Neither side can be said to have come out of it with the highest glory. Undoubtedly America had much to complain of, not only from England, but from France. Napoleon's decrees were as inimical to American interests as the English claim of the right of search. If Napoleon had succeeded in his dream of conquering Europe, if the medal which his vanity caused to be struck, celebrating the conquest of England, had commemorated a fact and not a figment, there need be little doubt that the emperor would have turned his mind and his armies against the detested republic over-seas. America had a kindly feeling for France in spite of its offences against her commerce. For England she had only a dislike that often deepened into a stronger emotion. This was not surprising. France had helped the States to obtain the liberties which England had denied them, and of which, as many believed, England would deprive them if she could.

There was a party in America exercising a powerful dominion in political life which was hot for war with England. The chief leader, the chief orator of this party, was a young Virginian gentleman named Henry Clay. Clay had settled in Kentucky; he had earned name and fame and fortune at the bar. He had advocated the partial abolition of negro slavery. He had served his country in the Senate and in the House of Representatives, and had been speaker of the Lower House. In 1812 he was thirty-five years old and the principal inspiration of the political party known as the Warhawks. Clay turned his eyes towards Canada, and saw her in imagination added to the territories of the Union. He turned his eyes towards England and saw her clinched in a desperate struggle with Napoleon. Clay's actions and Clay's eloquence in stimulating the war feeling in America would have been unjustifiable if they had been prompted merely by schemes of territorial aggrandisement or the settlement of an old grudge. But the conduct of England offered America every inducement to go to war. The conduct of England was such as to compel any self-respecting State possessed of a dollar and a rifle to go to war. Even the eloquence of Clay would not have conjured a war party into existence and kept it alive with his breath, if nothing had been done by England to make war seem justifiable. The conduct of England had made war inevitable.

The doctrine maintained by England with regard to the rights of belligerents and neutrals was absolutely opposed to that held by the United States. England, roughly speaking, claimed the right at all times to stop American ships and search them for English seamen. Undoubtedly there were many English seamen serving under the American flag.

The reason for such service was easy to find. Englishmen took service under the Stars and Stripes to escape the brutal injustice of the press-gang, to escape from the evils which unhappily stained the English naval system. Between a tyranny at home and freedom abroad it is scarcely surprising that the oppressed seaman chose liberty at the cost of a change of country. This change of country was one of the most important factors in the quarrel between America and England. The right to extend its citizenship to foreigners was portion and parcel of the constitutional system of the United States. Any man of any nationality who chose to come to America, to fulfil certain conditions, to live a certain specified time on American soil, could take out naturalisation papers and could become in the eyes of the American law as much a citizen of the United States as if he had been born of American parents within the borders of the Republic. There was one difference, and only one, between him and the native-born American of native stock; the naturalised citizen could never become President of the United States.

England maintained that a British subject was always a British subject, and could not escape from his allegiance by going through any ceremony with any other State. England acted persistently in accordance with her theory. She stopped and searched American ships. Her naval officers acted according to their own judgment in deciding whether seamen were deserting English subjects or no. Many men who were unquestionably American were forcibly carried off under the pretence of being recognised as English fugitives. In 1812 thousands of native-born Americans were serving against their will in the battle-ships of England. American seamen had so served on board the *Victory* with Nelson, had even, it is said, acted as bargemen to the great admiral. There were, of course, some English seamen in the American navy; but the difference, the vital difference was this, that English seamen fled to the Stars and Stripes of their own free will, while American sailors were compelled to serve the Union Jack against their will, by the unjust application of an exceedingly unjust principle, the principle of the right of search. The right of search was simply the application of the press-gang to the high seas instead of to the streets of English seaport towns.

There was a commercial question involved in the dispute as well as a question of international law. England and France were each anxious to prevent the other from carrying on trade with the United States. Great Britain issued certain orders in council forbidding the United States to trade with France. America retaliated by passing an Embargo Act, which forbade any American vessel to leave port. This Act effectively prevented the United States from trading at all. The American merchants were by no means pleased at the interference with trade. They were not at all consoled by the appearance of President Madison, on his inauguration, dressed from head to foot in clothes of American manufacture, as a standing proof that the country could do without the products of foreign nations. The majority in the North, indeed, were so much against war, and acts that must or might lead to war, that there was a time when it seemed on the cards that the New England States might leave the Union.

The influence of Clay and his Warhawks carried the day. Diplomatic relations with England grew more and more strained. Mr. Erskine, the British Envoy at Washington, was very anxious to preserve peace. He made concessions which were disowned by the Home Government. Another envoy was sent in his stead, who pursued a very different, a very hostile line of policy, and had in his turn to be recalled. Manifestations of a desire for war increased daily in number and volume. In the southern States, men who were opposed to the war either kept their opinions prudently to themselves, or expressed them publicly at the risk of their lives. Editor Hanson of Baltimore was rash enough to oppose the war in his paper. A furious mob attacked his office. He and his friends, General Lee, the 'Light Horse Harry' of the Independence War, and General Lingan, another veteran of the war, defended the place for a time. At last the magistrates interfered, and lodged Hanson and his friends in prison for safety. The mob attacked the prison, broke into it, dragged out Hanson, Lee, and Lingan. Lingan, pleading hard, and pleading vainly for his life, was brutally killed. Lee was so injured that he never recovered.

America declared war on Great Britain in the June of 1812. There were many Americans who were willing, were even anxious, to declare war upon France as well. The young Republic was undoubtedly prepared to face tremendous odds. Even though England was busily engaged in her struggle with France, her unquestioned, her stupendous supremacy as a sea-power, made America's action in fighting for a principle the more daring. England had the greatest navy in the world, America one of the smallest. Against Great Britain's thousand sail, America could only oppose half a dozen frigates, and six or eight sloops and brigs. It was not surprising that Great Britain, in all the glory of her naval supremacy, should have regarded America as an insignificant quantity at sea. Hitherto the American seaman had only been tested in petty wars—in that quarrel with France which was barely a war, in those scuffles with the Moors of Tripoli which were scarcely to be called wars. Yet these same petty wars had raised the American marine to the highest standard of excellence. The United States Navy was only a few years old, but it had used those few years well and gallantly. The war of the Revolution was still in the minds of the elder seamen. Men still talked of Biddle and Barney, and of Paul Jones and the *Bonhomme Richard.* Younger men had learned their business in those sea-fights with France, in those scuffles with the Barbary pirates.

The American navy was especially fortunate in its men. The pressed British sailor went reluctantly to a kind of slavery. The American sailor served of his own free will as a free man. A son of the sea coast, he had learned the business of the sea from his boyhood. He was amphibious, one foot on sea and one on shore, equally at home in either element. He was only a trader or a whaler, but he was a trader and a whaler in days when all the world was at war, and when American merchant-vessels had to be ready to defend themselves from privateers and pirates. As the frontiersman, working his way in the illimitable regions of the West, learnt wariness and self-reliance and the art of war from the ever-present, ever-dangerous red man, so the American sailor learnt wariness and self-reliance and the art of war from those skimmers of the sea who carried the colours of France, or the flaunting flag of piracy. The American trader was as ready to fight for his own hand, and as skilled to do so, as any Viking who sailed with Erik or Leif. A free man, he had the virtues of free men. He was moral and religious in his rough way, blending often the daring of the buccaneer with the convictions of the covenanter. America could hardly have had a better seaman for her need.

It was this capability of the American seaman which made the war of 1812 as creditable to the United States at sea, as on the whole it was discreditable to her on land. On land, with one signal exception, the campaign was disastrous to the Americans. That conquest of Canada, of which Henry Clay had dreamed, was not to be realised. As if the odds against them were not sufficient, the United States Government had an Indian war upon their hands. An Indian prophet had arisen in the West, who strove to recall his people to the simple ways from which they had been perverted by the white man and the white man's fire-water. This prophet had a brother named Tecumseh, a bitter enemy of the American people. When the war of 1812 began, Tecumseh and his followers joined themselves to the British, and proved very formidable allies. To employ savages now as soldiers by either party to a war between civilised nations would be held an outrage on humanity. But the Red Man had been used as an ally in the War of Independence. He had been used as an ally in the earlier wars between the British and the French. To employ him once again did not seem so monstrous then as it would seem now. The war in the North-West was, for the most part, a war of Americans against Indians, as the Indians always formed more than half the British forces. The sea war was rich with successes for America. Those Americans who had disdained or distrusted their navy, who had wished their ships never to sail, and had believed that if they did sail they would never return, now heard of American victory after American victory. Success at sea was needed to console for disaster on land. The land war was a series of petty skirmishes as bloody as they were trivial, and, for the most part, the land war gave success to England. An old and feeble American general, General Hull, followed a futile invasion of Canada by an ignominious retreat to Detroit, where he surrendered his army to the English. Another American force surrendered at the River Raisin only to be massacred by the Indians who were with the English. The English general, General Proctor, who permitted, or who at least could not prevent this horror, was afterwards defeated by Harrison at the River Thames in a fierce battle, in which the Kentucky mounted riflemen behaved very gallantly, and in which Tecumseh was killed. Whatever other result the war of 1812 had, it ended the last chance of resistance for the red man to the advance of the pioneers of the new race. With Tecumseh, the power of the red man to act as a barrier against the westward course of empire was broken for ever.

The war came to an end with an English victory, and an English defeat. The victory was infinitely more disgraceful than the defeat. In the August of 1814, a British force was landed by Admiral Cockburn in Maryland, and marched on Washington. There was no effective resistance offered. The British troops entered Washington. To his lasting shame and the shame of General Ross, who acted with him, Cockburn ordered the public buildings to be set on fire. The President's house, the Capitol, the Arsenal, the offices of the State Departments, with a number of private houses and newspaper offices were given to the flames. Public libraries and public archives perished. It is enough to mention such a deed to brand it with infamy. Pakenham's defeat at New Orleans was glorious in comparison with such a shameful triumph. Andrew Jackson was shut up in New Orleans. In the January of 1815, General Sir Edward Pakenham resolved to take New Orleans by assault, and to drive Jackson out. The odds were all on Pakenham's side. He had nearly ten thousand men. Jackson had little more than half that number. Pakenham was superior to Jackson in artillery. But Jackson was the better soldier, and the English were hopelessly defeated, losing a quarter of their number in killed and wounded, General Pakenham being among the killed. A treaty of peace had actually been signed at Ghent when this battle took place, the last battle of the war. By the terms of the treaty things appeared to be left pretty much as they were before the war began. But as a matter of fact, no further attempt was made to impose the principle of the right of search upon American vessels.

CHAPTER XIV

FROM PRESIDENT TO PRESIDENT

IN one sense the history of America in the first half of the nineteenth century is identical with the history of civilised Europe. The amazing series of applications of the resources of science to the improvement of existence which distinguish the nineteenth century from all its predecessors found the new world as unprepared as the old and left both equally grateful. The steamship and the railway train, the electric telegram, gas, labour-saving machines, even the domestic match, all these gifts of science served to transform a world that had remained unchanged in such particulars for centuries. Up to this time men travelled on land as fast as a horse could carry or horses could draw them: on sea men were carried by sails at the favour of the wind. Young America was no better off and no worse off than ancient Rome. Washington travelled from Mount Vernon to New York as Cæsar travelled from Naples to Rome, under the same conditions and with the same possibilities of speed. The growing century changed the whole conditions of the world. Men were no longer dependent on lamp or candle for illumination, no longer had to struggle with a tinder-box to procure themselves fire and light. Men were able to journey across vast distances with an undreamed-of swiftness. The boon that the new discoveries conferred upon America was even greater than that bestowed upon Europe. If the discoveries which quickened communication had not been made the United States might have remained for generations, if not for centuries, a small civilised and civilising patch upon a corner of the surface of the North American continent. The power of steam on road and river and sea gave the little republic the strength to explore and settle and the right to hold and absorb the vast territories of the new world in a Union more stable and more splendid than the empire of Rome.

The history of that Union for many years was a history of territorial development, of increasing population, of commercial growth, of financial crises, the inevitable history of a new nation forming itself in an area which allowed it to assume gigantic proportions. It was a history of incessant struggles with the Indians, as the rough, rude, strenuous pioneers of progress, the advance-guard of civilisation, marched further and further into the regions where the Red Man strove to assert his last poor privileges of aboriginal sovereignty. It was a history of political battles waged by a people with a more than Athenian passion for politics. It was a history of the struggle of popular leaders to attain that power, almost supreme while it lasts, but which lasts so short a time, the power conferred by its constitution upon the President of the United States. For nearly half a century President succeeded President without adding to America's story one illustrious ruler—for even to Jackson the term illustrious cannot be applied —or inflicting upon it one dishonourable ruler.

During this long period American history was in a sense domestic, in a sense tranquil. It well-nigh included her in that order of country which is said to be happy in having no history, so far as history is assumed to be composed of stirring events that take the attention of the world by storm. The time ended in one of the greatest upheavals in history, and inscribed on the roll of America's presidents the most illustrious name since that of Washington.

James Monroe succeeded Madison at the end of the war with England. Monroe was an honest, earnest, able citizen, a plain, straightforward man, whose early passion for democracy had cooled to something closely akin, if not similar, to a kind of federalism. His long, if not always successful, experience of diplomacy abroad, in Paris and in London, had given him an intimate acquaintance with the men and the minds of the Eastern world. He had not to do what Talleyrand said that Hamilton did; he had not to 'divine Europe.' His name is given to the famous political doctrine which denies to Europe the right to establish influence upon the soil of America. In 1823 a certain number of European sovereigns banded themselves together in a league with the sounding name of the Holy Alliance. The object of the Holy Alliance was to oppose revolution and republicanism and to bolster up the autocratic monarchies of Europe with mutual aid. The Holy Alliance put the King of Spain back on his throne, and the King of Spain with the proverbial gratitude suggested that the Holy Alliance would be very kind to him and very consistent with its high mission if it helped him back to his authority in his American colonies.

When the United States bought Louisiana Spain had protested that the purchase did not include West Florida. The United States took possession of West Florida and was anxious to buy East Florida. Spain would neither sell East Florida nor resign her claim to West Florida. East Florida became a kind of Alsatia, a refuge for fugitives from and enemies to the United States, smugglers, Indians, adventurers of all kinds. Andrew Jackson made a raid into this nominally Spanish Alsatia in pursuit of a party of hostile Seminoles and punished the Spaniards who had supported and encouraged the Indians. After this Spain consented to cede her claim to Florida on certain conditions. She had, however, still a number of dependent colonies in Central and South America and Mexico, and these resenting the harshness, and taking advantage of the weakness of Spain, had rebelled and set up revolutionary governments. It was against these revolutionary governments that the King of Spain now wanted the Holy Alliance to act. This touched America nearly, for there was always the danger that American soil under the Spanish flag might easily get partitioned among other European powers who were stronger than Spain. It also touched England nearly in her commercial interest, for British merchants were doing a brisk trade with the colonies that had flung off their allegiance to Spain, and the British merchants were very far from willing to have these Spanish-American ports shut in their faces.

Canning was at this time the English minister for foreign affairs. He suggested to the American envoy that it would be a good thing if England and America were to combine to prevent any action of the Holy Alliance against the revolutionary Spanish States. America was already conscious of the danger of European encroachment on the American continent. Russia was in Alaska. Russia might dream of extending her influence beyond Alaska. Russia was the head and front of the Holy Alliance. Monroe was determined that the United States should deal with the problem alone. He declined Canning's suggestion, and in his message to Congress he showed what his Government's policy was. The policy asserted as a principle that the American continents, by the free and independent condition which they had assumed and which they maintained, were henceforth not to be considered as subjects for future colonisation by any European power. It declared that the United States could not view interference with the affairs of existing states in America by European power in any other light than as the manifestation of an unfriendly disposition toward the United States. This is the justly celebrated Monroe doctrine, which has been accepted as portion and parcel of the American principle ever since. The words were the words of John Quincy Adams; the policy itself was only an amplification of Washington's theory of neutrality; the immediate inspiration of that present action came from Canning. But Monroe accepted the responsibility for it, and it remains accordingly somewhat inconveniently associated with Monroe's name.

A whole army of new politicians had arisen, men of the post-revolutionary generation, men of the middle period in America's first century of political life. The names of Clay, of Webster, of Calhoun, of Adams, and Benton, and Randolph represent the most eminent incarnations of the various theories of political life, reason and principle. Henry Clay, to whom the war-party in America in 1812 owed its fierce impulse, was one of the greatest party leaders of an age that was rich in party leaders. His eloquence charmed its hearers with a spell for which it may be admitted that the modern reader seeks in vain. It is true that the modern reader seeks vainly for the spell that must have lain in Sheridan's Begum speech, if we believe, as we are obliged to believe, the unanimous testimony of Sheridan's splendid contemporaries. But Sheridan was at no pains to preserve his speech, of which but a paltry epitome remains to us, while Clay's speeches remain as open to study as the speeches of Daniel Webster. The speeches of Daniel Webster have and deserve a different fate. They are as attractive to read as they must have been attractive to hear. The magnificent voice, the magnificent mind were lodged in a magnificent body. Webster was more than common tall; his head was massive; his eyes were as dark and as luminous as night. This son of a New Hampshire farmer was the noble inheritor of the noble New England tradition. He was the first of the Federalists so long as the name of Federalist was worn by the new generation. He was the first of the Whigs when the name shifted to that venerable relic of English political phraseology. He was one of the greatest orators who had ever moved the American senate; he was also one of the greatest criminal lawyers that had ever adorned the American bar. If, like Shakespeare, he had little Latin and less Greek, his command of the English speech was that of a lover and a master. He had a royal presence and a royal carriage. Hallam said of him that he was 'worthy of Rome or Venice, rather than of our noisy and wrangling generation.' Carlyle said of him that 'As a logic-fencer, advocate, or parliamentary Hercules, one would incline to back him at first sight against all the extant world.' If he shared with his adored Addison that affection for wine which was the habit of his day, if he drifted into debt heedlessly, and could dismiss some urgent claim with a regal wave of the hand and a regal 'Let it be paid,' it must be remembered that his faults were in a measure the faults of genius, the faults of Mirabeau, the faults of Fox. Like Clay, Webster had a desire for the Presidency, and like Clay he was denied the gratification of his desire. Yet no one of his contemporaries could have been better fitted to hold that high office, or could have given greater lustre to it and to his country.

A man of a very different type was John Caldwell Calhoun of South Carolina. Calhoun was of Irish blood, but his nature had in it none of that bright ebullience which is so often the heritage of the Irishman in America. His view of life was austere even to gloom. On his grave, set face, shadowed by his shock of hair, and illuminated by his piercing eyes, sternness and sadness set their seal. He was a man of the highest public morality, according to his standard of public morality; he was entire of life and pure of offence, save in his fanatical devotion to the principle of negro slavery. In a sense this very devotion did its service to the world. It has truly been said of Calhoun that he failed in every object of his life except the one which was to force the slavery issue on the North. To force the slavery issue on the North was to hasten the inevitable end. Like Clay, like Webster, like indeed every prominent politician of the hour, and like many who were not prominent at all, Calhoun dreamed of the Presidency, but political quarrels and political intrigue denied him his desire.

Thomas Hart Benton was a politician of a rougher type than Clay, Webster, and Calhoun. He was a lawyer, but he was also a soldier. He came of a hot-tempered family whose hand was prompt with the pistol, as Jackson once learned to his cost when he raised his whip on Benton, and was wounded by Benton's brother. He was a man of wide political knowledge. He was a sturdy Democrat. His championship of a gold and silver currency won for him the nickname of Old Bullion.

By birth of North Carolina, and by adoption of Missouri, John Randolph of Roanoke in Virginia was another Democrat, of a lesser order of ability than Benton. He was of good family; he claimed descent from that Princess Pocahontas who married Rolfe, and who died in England long years earlier. He was rough in speech, rough in manner. He would swagger into the Senate in hunting-clothes, swinging his hunting-whip. His tongue was sharp, and his command of personal abuse hard to rival. He once grossly insulted Clay. The result was a duel, happily a bloodless duel. He was like an Ishmaelite, says a biographer, his hand against every man and every man's hand against him. He was a Democrat, but he was a Southerner before he was a Democrat, and he was a Virginian before he was a Southerner. 'When I speak of my country,' he said proudly, 'I mean the commonwealth of Virginia.'

There was a whole world of lesser politicians. These were the most conspicuous of that day and hour.

In the last year of Monroe's presidency, Lafayette visited the States. It was nearly half a century since the young Frenchman had offered his sword to the struggling colonists. Much had happened to the world in the long interval. The French Revolution had answered the challenge of Europe with the head of a king. Napoleon had come and gone like a dream. A son of the house of Capet sat again for his brief hour upon the throne of the Bourbons. Lafayette came from a changed Europe to a no less changed America. The thirteen colonies had grown into four-and-twenty States. The population had risen from three millions to nine and a half millions. The authority of the young Republic extended over a territory larger in area than that of most of the kingdoms of Europe put together. Lafayette would scarcely have dared to prophesy in the early days of Valley Forge that if Heaven gave success to the colonial arms it would accord the colonies such full measure of prosperity, such marvellous progress along the path of Empire. If the aged statesman could have been given but for one moment a glimpse into some Cagliostro's mirror, and shown what yet another half century should do for the commonwealth that he had helped to liberate, even with his knowledge of the marvel that had been wrought, he might well have refused to believe the vision.

Monroe's second term of office had been known as the Era of Good Feeling. Like other historical periods of peace, it was but the herald of an age of passionate strife. It was only natural that as the country grew in wealth and strength and territory, political feeling should grow keener and political parties more assertive. The early Revolutionary statesmen of the school of Washington scarcely realised the inevitableness of party in politics. Their ideal was the ideal of early Rome, where none were for a party, where all were for the State. The division into Federalists and Republicans which they regretted had persisted, as it was bound to persist, as it persists to this day under changed names and different conditions. New problems had arisen to deepen the depths of party difference, to widen the distance between party leaders. Financial and commercial questions were the great questions in dispute. Apart from the slavery question and all its consequences, the political history of the United States is largely a history of the struggle between those who advocate the policy of free trade and those who champion the policy of protection; between the advocates of one system of adjusting the financial machinery of the country and the advocates of another system. It is enough here to recognise these great divergencies of public opinion, divergencies as keen and as far from reconciliation or from compromise now as they were in the beginning.

Monroe was succeeded in the Presidency by John Quincy Adams, a son of Adams, the second President. He was followed in 1829 by Andrew Jackson, the hero of New Orleans, the 'Old Hickory' who was the adored idol of the American people. Jackson was the last of the American Presidents who had taken any personal share in the War of Independence. As the companions of Mahomet succeeded to the Caliphate one by one, till there was none left who had looked upon the face of the Prophet, so the comrades

FROM PRESIDENT TO PRESIDENT 211

of Washington sat in the Presidential seat till their number was exhausted. Jackson was an extremely earnest, honourable, upright man, who managed to do great harm to his country by introducing the principle of changing the officials of the civil service with the change of President. 'To the victor belong the spoils' was the phrase, not of Jackson indeed, but of one of Jackson's adherents, and it admirably represents the policy on which Jackson acted, and of which he set the example that was fatally and unfortunately followed by his successors.

Jackson's financial policy led to the great commercial crash in 1837, the first year of office of his successor, Martin Van Buren. The superabundance of paper money, the railroad craze, and the multiplicity of wild-cat banks led to disaster. Specie payment was suspended all over the country, and thousands of families were ruined. Van Buren did much to retrieve the financial position of the country by bringing about a separation of the government and banking. But Van Buren was not popular with the country. His opponents reproached him with aristocratic tastes, with using gold spoons, with possessing a silver tea-service. They ran against him and they carried against him for ninth President the General Harrison who had defeated Tecumseh's brother at Tippecanoe. Harrison died within a month of his inauguration and was succeeded according to the law by the Vice-President, John Tyler.

Tyler's term is remarkable for the settlement of a dispute with England which had been pending ever since the War of Independence, as to the boundary between Canada and the United States. The boundary was settled by a treaty negotiated by Daniel Webster and Lord Ashburton, from whom it is known as the Ashburton Treaty. It was during Tyler's administration that the attention of the world was directed to a new religious sect. Years earlier, a man named Joseph Smith had produced a singular book, which seemed to be a queer imitation of the Old Testament, and which claimed the authority of revelation. He called it the Book of Mormon, and he founded a sect of Mormons, one of whose doctrines was polygamy. These Mormons had made a settlement at Nauvoo in Illinois, and now in 1844 the people of Nauvoo attacked the Mormons, drove them out, and killed Smith. Smith was succeeded by Brigham Young, who led his people to Utah, to the Salt Lake Valley, where they founded Salt Lake City, and where they are to this day, though their territory has become a State of the Union and their practice of polygamy has been declared illegal by the law of the United States.

The name of James Knox Polk, the eleventh President, is associated with the satisfactory settlement of the dispute with England over the ownership of Oregon, and with the war against Mexico.

Polk was succeeded by General Zachary Taylor, a hero of the Mexican War. Taylor belonged to the Whig party. He was a successful soldier. He had no opportunity of showing what he might have been as an administrator, for he died in the second year of his Presidency, from an illness brought on by exposure to the sun during the heat of a public Fourth of July ceremony. His successor was the Vice-President, Millard Fillmore. Fillmore was a self-made man. Born in a log-cabin in the wilderness, brought up on a farm, educated on the Bible and a hymn book, apprenticed to a wool-carder, he won his way by his own efforts to the Buffalo bar, and from the bar to public life. During his Presidency the passing of a famous measure, the Fugitive Slave Law, gave a new interest to an old question, the question of negro slavery.

CHAPTER XV

NEGRO SLAVERY

THE history of America after the conclusion of the war with England is practically the history of one great question for nearly fifty years, the question of negro slavery. Negro slavery had been one of the difficulties in the way of the Convention that had called the Constitution into existence. It had been met at the time by a compromise, which staved off a definite settlement then, as compromises staved off a definite settlement again and again for the next couple of generations. The men of the Convention who were in theory opposed to negro slavery, with Washington at their head, thought that there could be little harm in any compromise which preserved peace and promoted union. They were convinced, and there seemed to be every ground for their conviction, that with the fulness of time the question of negro slavery would answer itself with the gradual disappearance of the negro slave.

In this way they were mistaken. The invention of the cotton-gin by Eli Whitney altered the whole conditions of the problem. Cotton became the staple produce of the Southern States. This notably increased the demand for slave labour and made the Southern States jealously suspicious of Northern designs against slavery. It also whetted the Southern

NEGRO SLAVERY 215

desire for increase of territory. Cotton is a plant that exhausts the soil it grows in, and that calls incessantly for new fields for its production. To provide these new fields the South was always eager to welcome the admission of new States into the Union, so long as they were States that could grow cotton, and so long as they were States that might have slaves. The men in the North, on the other hand, were opposed to slavery altogether, and were very unwilling to allow it to spread. An understanding, however, had grown up to the effect that a system of balance was to be respected in the unification of the States. There was to be a slave State for every non-slave State, so that neither party should have the advantage over the other.

Thus Indiana, which was a non-slavery State when it entered the Union in 1816, was balanced by the admission of Mississippi as a slave State in 1817. When Illinois entered as a non-slave State in 1818, it was balanced in its turn by the admission of Alabama as a slave State in 1819. In 1821 Maine came into the Union as a non-slave State, and to preserve the balance the Southern party called for the admission of Missouri in 1821 as a slave State. Over this, however, a fierce controversy rose. The Northern party were gradually growing more inimical to the spread of slavery in the Union. They were beginning to see with alarm that the old belief that slavery was a dwindling and would be soon a dying institution was baseless. Cotton, calling for ever more land and ever more labour, had defeated that dream. The North began to think that it was time to say that there should be no more slave States admitted into the Union. This raised a fierce protest from the South, which insisted upon preserving the tradition of the balance of State with State, and asserted vehemently the justice as well as the importance of slavery.

When the feud seemed at its hottest the ingenuity of Clay averted a quarrel by the arrangement which is known as the Missouri compromise. By this arrangement Missouri came in as a slave State, but it was agreed in Congress that slavery should be prohibited for ever to the north of the parallel of 36° 30′. South of this line any new States were to be left free to come in as slave States or not as they chose. The compromise only averted the inevitable reckoning. It procured a peace which was no peace, a sort of armistice which lasted for little more than twenty years, when the quarrel blazed up again with greater fury than before. Slavery was a national, not a domestic question; it might have been easier to settle it as a national question in 1820 than in 1860.

There is happily no need now for any one to be eloquent in protest against negro slavery, because there is no probability of any one being found eloquent in its favour. That question is settled for good and all as far as civilised humanity is concerned. It would be as reasonable to expect a man of intelligence publicly to applaud the political methods of the Old Man of the Mountains and his company of Assassins, as to expect from him any advocacy, any approval, any justification of negro slavery. There are certain phases of human existence which have to be blotted out of the world's story for good and all, at least so far as any particular æon of civilisation is concerned. Nobody

NEGRO SLAVERY

now is in favour, for instance, of taxation without representation, or of property qualifications for Parliament. In the same way nobody now is in favour of negro slavery. It is therefore hard to realise, but it has to be realised for the right understanding of the Civil War, that only a generation ago a great number of civilised men were in favour of negro slavery, and in favour of it in no vague, half-hearted, theoretical way, but with a passion which drove them to fight and to die rather than surrender it.

All the arguments by which the Southerners defended what they called euphemistically their 'peculiar institution' have long since been answered and dissipated. Those who turned to the Hebrew Bible and professed to find divine sanction there, forgot that a like divine sanction was sought and found in the same source by the New England Witch-hunters. On the same analogy they might have found a sanction for sacrificing animals to Jehovah in the cotton fields of Carolina, and for practising polygamy in the capital of Virginia. The more serious defence, that slavery was indispensable to the wealth and welfare of the South, to the growth of rice, of sugar, and above all of cotton, has long been abandoned. Universal economic opinion is now against this argument. It has been proved, as clearly as any problem of economics can be proved, that servile labour is in the end more costly and less efficient— looking at it merely from the material point of view— than free labour.

The attempt to associate the South with Athens, because both in the South and in Athens slavery existed, was as fallible as the rest. Modern civilisation owes almost everything to the Greeks, but not everything, and the fact that Cleon the poet from his sprinkled isles might thank Protus in his tyranny for a gift of slaves, was no authority for one Virginian gentleman to breed black children for the market as he might breed dogs or pheasants, or for another Virginian gentleman to entertain a servile seraglio. In fact there was and could be no serious defence of slavery. It was extremely bad for the South. It had naturally a debasing effect upon the moral character. Constant association with a race whose standard of morality was necessarily low had a contaminating influence upon the white youth. In some States of the South it was said that there was not a likely-looking girl who was not the concubine of a white man, nor an old plantation in which coloured grandchildren of the owner were not whipped in the field by his overseer. The constant sense of unquestioned ownership of human beings inevitably fostered cruelty. On coloured men, on coloured women, on coloured children the ceaseless scourge was plied.

Frederick Douglass said 'everybody in the South seemed to want the privilege of whipping somebody else.' Frederick Douglass was himself a Maryland slave, who had been taught to read by his Baltimore mistress until his master objected, on the ground that learning would spoil the best negro in the world by making him discontented. From that master's point of view the master was right. Learning did make Frederick Douglass discontented, and probably few men did more than Frederick Douglass to bring about the emancipation of his class. Being so far educated, when a book containing some of the speeches of Chatham, Sheridan and Fox came in his way, he was able to read those speeches, and to learn from them that if what they said about the rights of man were true, then he ought not to be a slave. Douglass managed to escape North and devoted himself to the abolition cause. He delivered lectures in the North and in England against slavery, which always had a great effect upon his hearers. 'He surpassed,' says Wentworth Higginson, 'in his perception of the finer felicities of the English language all other self-made men whom I have ever known.'

That degradation of one set of human beings by another, which brought with it the passion of lust and the passion of cruelty, brought with it also the passion of terror. Those black chattels had bodies that could writhe under the lash. They had hearts that could bleed when wife was parted from husband or children from parents on some public platform. They had hands too which might some day be lifted in revenge.

As in ancient Rome, the dread of a servile insurrection was always latent. As men and women lived in the early days on the Indian territories, so men and women lived in the civilisation of the South with the shadow of danger over them. Planters kept their weapons near their bed, ready for instant use. Mothers startled from their sleep by any sudden noise clasped their infants in their arms, roused to a sudden remembrance of the ever-present, ever-haunting fear of rebellious slaves. There had been one black rising, headed by a negro named Nat Turner, the terror and the horror of which lingered long in men's memories. What Nat Turner had done might be done again. What Nat Turner had tried to do another might more nearly succeed in doing.

Of course the history of slavery in the South was not all a history of luxury, of cruelty, and of fear. There were plantations where the slaves were very happy, where the whip was never lifted, where families were not separated by sale as callously as if they had been cattle, where the black man loved the white master with a dog-like devotion, and desired no release from a bondage which custom and kindness had made dear to him. But if this happy order of things, this constant service of the antique world, had been the rule, men would still have been bound to abolish slavery. If it had been the rule, the South could not have clung more closely to its peculiar institution. Perhaps it clung so closely partly from a spirit of opposition. The anti-slavery agitation had slowly been growing in strength for some years in the States to the North of Mason and Dixon's line. When Jackson was President a Quaker named Benjamin Lundy started a newspaper called *The Genius of Universal Emancipation.* Lundy advocated the gradual emancipation of the slaves. His views did not attract very much attention; the views of another apostle of the cause attracted a great deal of attention. William Lloyd Garrison, a young man who had been Lundy's assistant-editor, started in 1831 a weekly paper in Boston. *The Liberator* was the outspoken champion of the demand for the immediate emancipation of the negro slave. It roused the greatest enthusiasm among those whose ideas it represented in the North. It roused the fiercest wrath in the South. The State of Georgia offered five thousand dollars for Garrison's head.

Garrison's supporters grew in number with the growth of hostility to his teachings. His meetings were broken up in Boston. He was dragged through Boston streets with a rope round his body. He was rescued by the police with difficulty and placed in gaol for protection. His fellow-worker, the Rev. Elijah Lovejoy, was killed by a mob at Alton, Illinois. Garrison won great names to his side; prompted great voices to speak in his cause—the voice of Wendell Phillips, the voice of Theodore Parker. The genius of Emerson, the genius of Thoreau, the genius of Lowell, of Whittier, of Channing came to strengthen the cause and to win adherents. In the face of every danger, in defiance of every violence, the strength of the Abolitionists, as the anti-slavery party was called, grew and grew. As it grew, so hotter and hotter became the indignation in the South.

States are like human beings, and they are inclined to resent being interfered with and being preached at. The more the Abolitionists of the North thundered against slavery and inveighed against the the South, the more doggedly the South resolved to stand by its slavery system. The hot Southern pride was promptly roused by the lectures and the condemnations of the philanthropists of the North. Men of the slave States, who might possibly under other conditions have been readily alive to the evils of slavery, economical as well as ethical, were goaded by the reproaches and the denunciations of the Abolitionists into seeking in all directions for arguments with which to defend what they believed to be their right. Undoubtedly neither the North nor England could with any great consistency cast stones against the South. Their own fire-new brand of virtue was too patent. England had given slavery to America before she awoke to a sense of its iniquity. The North had been content with slavery for long enough. The South would not be lectured out of its custom, would not be menaced out of its custom, would not be persuaded out of its custom.

The slave-holding party were in the ascendant. The slave-holding principle directed the policy of the country. The slave-holding policy forced the States into their third war, the war with Mexico. In 1845, two slave States, Florida and Texas, were added to the Union, and in obedience to the law of compensation they were in time duly balanced by the admission of two non-slavery States, Iowa in 1846 and Wisconsin in 1848. Originally a portion of Mexico, Texas had been largely invaded since the second decade of the century by settlers from the States. These settlers in time revolted against Mexico, defeated the Mexican armies under Santa Anna, and established a republic larger than any European Empire, except Russia. They did not desire to retain their independence. What they did desire was to enter the Union as a slave State, and afford to the South the advantage of their vast territory for cotton and black labour. For a long time, owing to the energy of the anti-slavery party, their desire was not gratified, and Texas stood apart in picturesque isolation as the 'Lone Star State.' In the end the slavery party succeeded, and Texas became part of the Union. A dispute as to the boundaries of Texas involved the United States and Mexico in a quarrel which ended in war. The war ended in the complete defeat of Mexico, and in the addition to the United States of territory equal in size to about half Europe. Out of this vast dominion no slave State was ever made. Texas was the last slave State admitted to the Union. The war with Mexico is memorable as the training-school for a much greater war, as yet undreamed of.

Of course there had always been statesmen and thinkers in the South keen-witted enough to recognise the dangers and the disadvantages as well as the immorality of negro slavery. These would have been as glad as the most eloquent Abolitionists of the North to find some way out of a bad business. Many ways were proposed in the North. There were schemes to raise money for a gradual purchase and subsequent manumission of all the negroes in the South. But the South did not want to sell its negroes in that way, and could not be persuaded to sell them. There was a vague vision, cherished by a dreamy colonisation society, of a plan by which all the negroes in the South might be gradually removed back to the land from which they stemmed. But the idea of a colony at Liberia, composed of the negroes from the slave States, however flattering in theory to the promoters of the scheme, proved ineffective when they attempted to put it into practice. In the meantime two facts were gradually forcing themselves upon the convictions of the civilised world. The first was that negro slavery in the States must, sooner or later, come to an end. The second was that the South would never willingly consent to the abolition of negro slavery.

One of the strongest forces in directing and consolidating civilised thought against slavery was a novel by a woman, the *Uncle Tom's Cabin* of Mrs. Harriet Beecher Stowe. Mrs. Stowe studied the South in 1850. She wrote and published her book

and conquered the reading world. Seldom has any
book been accorded the circulation and the influence
of this famous political pamphlet which was also a
fascinating romance. It must have converted listless
into ardent champions of abolition by the thousand
and the ten thousand. It aroused the attention of
those who had never given the matter a thought and
made them thrill with a sense of the iniquity of such
a system of bondage. It was translated into every
language; it was read in every land, and wherever it
was read it made converts to the cause of human
freedom. It was recognised in the South as one
of the most formidable attacks upon slavery that
had yet been made. Lawyers and statesmen and
divines might argue and condemn and produce little
effect, but here was a book that went into every
household all over the world, was read with rapture
by children, women, and men, and wherever it was
read created some enemy to slavery. Well might
Southern writers, compelled to admit that everything
in *Uncle Tom's Cabin* had occurred in the South,
protest, and protest in vain, against undue importance
being given to 'that book of genius, true in all its
facts, false in all its impressions.'

The admission of California into the Union gave a
new heat to the slavery controversy. California was
an old Spanish settlement. It came under the rule
of Mexico in the first quarter of the century. A
bloodless revolution made it practically independent
in 1836. It passed to the United States after the
Mexican War. In 1848 the discovery of gold in the
Sacramento Valley, caused an army of people from
all parts of the world to pour into the country. It
soon had a population large enough to qualify it for

NEGRO SLAVERY

admission to the Union. It came in as a non-slavery State. This roused all the latent anger of the South, which clamoured for compensation for this disturbance of the balance. Clay of the Missouri compromise came to the front again with an armful of new compromises. To balance the admission of California, as a free State, and the abolition of slavery in the District of Columbia, a law was introduced and carried in spite of the opposition of all the anti-slavery orators, called the Fugitive Slave Law. By this law the owners of slaves were allowed to recapture their slaves in any part of the non-slavery States, and to carry them back without trial by jury. If the Missouri compromise was bad, the 1850 compromise was worse. It darkens Fillmore's administration with an ineradicable stain, but it served to bring the slavery question to the front as the most immediate and pressing of all possible public questions.

The grief of the abolitionists and the exultation of the slave-holders over the Fugitive Slave Law, which stained the administration of Fillmore, made the administration of his successor, the Democrat Franklin Pierce, a battle-ground for the two parties. It sometimes was in the literal sense of the term a battle-ground. The representatives of the people went to the seat of government armed and ready to use their weapons. The eloquent abolitionist, Charles Sumner, was taken unawares by a Southerner, Preston Brooks, while he was seated at his desk, and beaten so savagely with a stick that for a time his life was despaired of. The exultant slave-holders, flushed with one triumph, yearned for and obtained another. Clay's early compromise, the famous Missouri compromise, which had at least served to preserve a

P

semblance of peace for nearly a generation, was now to be sacrificed to the zeal of the South. Above that line where the Missouri compromise had decided that slavery should cease to be, it was now proposed to organise two new territories, Kansas and Nebraska, and to leave the inhabitants of the new territories to decide for themselves whether they should be free territories or slave territories.

This breach of faith was fought against strenuously but vainly by the abolitionists. The South carried the day. The new territories were to be slave or free as their inhabitants chose. Then came a scramble of the friends and foes of slavery to occupy the new territories and decide their course. From Missouri came bands of border ruffians to swamp elections, and to propagate the gospel of slavery with the pistol and the bowie knife. From the Free States came emigrants resolved to save Kansas for the cause of liberty. Both sides were prepared to fight for their principles. The most conspicuous of the anti-slavery men was John Brown, who met the border ruffians from Missouri with their own weapons, and beat them with the odds heavily against him.

While the struggle was going on, Pierce's administration came to an end and another Democrat, James Buchanan of Pennsylvania, was elected in his stead. The South felt confident that under such a President it could still go its own way unquestioned. It was supported in its belief by the famous decision of Chief-Justice Taney, of the Supreme Court, in the case of claim to liberty by the negro slave, Dred Scott. Taney ruled that a negro was not a man, but a thing; that he had no rights against the white, and that his master could take him from slave into free States, just as he could take his horse or his purse or his watch.

The abolitionist North was not going to let the slave South go its own way unquestioned. Its orators spoke as eloquently, its poets wrote as passionately as ever. Its men of action acted with daring and determination. John Brown, with his two sons and a small body of twenty men, boldly invaded Virginia at a place called Harper's Ferry, seized the arsenal there, and called upon the slaves to rise and rally round him. The slaves did not rise. A force of fifteen hundred militia marched against John Brown. He held his position gallantly until his little force was killed or disabled. One of his sons was killed, the other hurt. He himself, fighting to the last, was only captured when he was so badly wounded that he was believed to be dying. He did not die just then. He lived to be tried, to defend himself with intrepidity and ability, to be sentenced and to be hanged. Several of his companions were also executed. A few, with his surviving son, managed to make their escape.

John Brown's raid and John Brown's death at once roused the agitation to fever heat. Brown's deed might have been illegal, but it was done against the detested slave system. John Brown's death made him a martyr; his dead body seemed to cry aloud to heaven for vengeance. Brown was not long in his grave when Buchanan's term of office expired. Then a split in the Democratic party gave the Presidency into the hands of a Republican candidate, whose support came almost entirely from the North, and who would never have been elected if the South had voted solid for a single candidate. The victory of a Republican was bad enough, but worse remained behind. The Republican President was known as an earnest anti-slavery man, pledged to put slavery where the people would be satisfied that it was in course of ultimate extinction. The new President's name was Abraham Lincoln.

Abraham Lincoln is a remarkable figure in the history of the United States, and not merely in the history of the United States, but in the history of the world. Had he lived in the Athens of the Peloponnesian war, he would have afforded to Aristophanes an efficient substitute for Socrates as a butt for his divine malice. Had America of the fifties and the sixties been blessed with an Aristophanes, the satirist might have rejoiced to magnificent purpose in anatomising the ungainly giant from Kentucky, and immortalising in deathless verse his awkward presence, his taste for queer stories, his merits as a splitter of rails, his domestic affairs, his singularity of attire, his amazing physical strength, his rude, shrewd humour, his downright commonsense. If we had nothing but the Aristophanic caricature to go upon, we should know but little of the wisest of the Athenians. If some man of the stupendous genius of Aristophanes could have gathered together and concentrated in one majestic effort of spite all the petty scorns and sneers and flouts and gibes of which Lincoln was the indifferent victim, and if Lincoln had never found his Plato or his Xenophon, Lincoln would have suffered more than Socrates.

A great historian, not long dead, once drew—and afterwards suppressed—a very amazing and curiously far-fetched parallel between Julius Cæsar and the

Founder of the Christian Faith. If historical parallels of this kind were anything better than trifles, it would be easy to maintain a greater closeness of resemblance between the Socrates of Athenian yesterday and the Lincoln of American to-day. Both were extremely ill-favoured. Both were astonishingly strong. Both loved to address themselves to the 'plain people.' Both were persistently misunderstood while they lived. Both served their State beyond any State's power of gratitude. Both were brave beyond the common, straightforward beyond the common, truthful beyond the common. Both had like trials in private life. Both could work with the strength of ten men. Both were practised in the use of words. Both were victims, both were martyrs in their tragic deaths. The greatest of the Athenians was not greater in Athens than the greatest of the Americans—saving and only saving Washington—in his own country and among his own people.

Abraham Lincoln was a Kentucky man. He was born in Hardin county in 1809, of a pioneer family that was closely allied with the family of Daniel Boone. Lincoln's grandfather was killed by Indians. His father seems to have lacked the stubborn strength and earnestness that was characteristic of the family. He drifted from Kentucky to Indiana and from Indiana to Illinois, and from one home in Illinois to another, consistent only in ill-success. The strong qualities of the race reasserted themselves in Abraham Lincoln. He learned all that any teacher to be found in the backwoods could teach him. He read every book he could lay his hands on. He gained some knowledge of surveying and patiently pursued his study of Law. He kept a store which came to grief through the fault of a partner. He was for a time postmaster of New Salem. He was four times elected to the State legislature. He began to be known as a politician, as a speaker, and as a lawyer. In 1846 he was elected to Congress, and was recognised as the ablest mouthpiece of the Whig party in Illinois. His success at the bar was slowly but surely drawing him away from politics when the repeal of the Missouri compromise brought him back to the fight, and forced him into the front of the anti-slavery fight. A debate that he held with Senator Stephen Douglas, the most eminent member of the reactionary party, so added to his reputation that when the Republican convention met in Chicago in May 1860, to elect its candidate for the Presidency, its choice fell upon Lincoln. How fortunate that choice was the country was at first slow to learn.

The men of the South had so long had things their own way under Presidents of their own choice, and their own way of thinking, that they were in no temper patiently to accept even the nominal dominion of an anti-slavery Republican. They would not even wait for Lincoln's inauguration. While Buchanan was still holding the office that he was so soon to hand over to Abraham Lincoln, the leaders of the Southern States agreed together upon a course which resulted, as it was inevitable that it must result, in civil war.

CHAPTER XVI

SUMTER

RIGHTLY to understand the American civil war it is essential never to forget the diametrically antagonistic principles which animated the two disputants. Whatever the cause of quarrel—negro slavery or another—the attitude adopted by North and South with regard to that quarrel was not merely hostile to, but totally irreconcilable with, the attitude of its opponent. The Civil War is often called the War of Secession. It is perhaps still more often called the War of the Rebellion. The Southerner who would accept the first name would reject the other with energy and scorn. While the South insisted upon secession, upon its absolute right to secede if secession seemed good in its eyes, it steadily refused to admit that it ever was, or indeed ever could be, in rebellion, and it resented, may even still resent, being written of as rebellious. It was the Southern contention—a contention which the South was prepared to take up arms to defend—that the Union of States which the American Revolution had called into existence, and which had been growing and multiplying for three generations of citizens, did not constitute a nation in itself, but merely an assemblage of nations. This assemblage of nations had agreed for general convenience, for mutual advantage, to adopt a constitution. This constitution was merely in the nature of a treaty, and only bound those who accepted it so long as it was convenient, so long as it was advantageous. In the Southern view every State of the Union was a sovereign nation, inherently endowed with as free a right to withdraw from the Union as it had exercised in entering the Union.

This was a theory of national existence which the North would never consent to admit. The North maintained that it was the Union which constituted the American nation. It declined to admit the existence, even the possibility, of a Virginian nation, of a nation of South Carolina. A great Union had been agreed to, a great principle had been accepted. Inspired by that principle, and sustained by that Union, the American nation had come into being. To injure that Union, to abjure that principle, was to strike a blow at the life of the American nation, and to make those who aimed the blow mutineers, rebels, and traitors. The South believed itself to be defending its territories from unjustifiable invasion. The North was convinced that the action of the Southern States put them in a condition of flagrant insurrection, whose success would destroy the power, the grandeur, and the very life of the great American Republic that had been created by the War of Independence and the genius of George Washington.

Between two sets of men, holding irreconcilable opinions, and resolved to support their own opinions at any cost, war was a question of time. The North did not go to war to abolish slavery. The South did not go to war to defend slavery. But the question of slavery was the core of the whole business. If the South had not believed that the North aimed at the abolition of negro slavery, the South might never have dreamed of putting its theoretical right of secession into practice. Once resolved, however, it made its theory practical with a vengeance. The conditions of the national existence gave the Southern States certain advantages, and the Southern States in their eagerness hastened to make use of those advantages in a fashion which compelled because it initiated a conflict.

The Southern States seized upon the forts, arsenals, and stores of arms within their borders, and asserted their intention and their right to seize others which were still in the hands of the Federal government. The South maintained that these forts, arsenals, and stores of arms, although called into being by the general government, ceased to belong to that general government when the States in whose boundaries they lay withdrew from the alliance which acknowledged that general government. The South declared itself prepared to make good that portion of the cost of these public works which had not been defrayed by the States in which they stood. But the seizure of these strong places, the lowering of the flag of the Union, and the flying in its place of the flag of the seceding State were undoubtedly acts of war, and acts of war at a time when negotiations on a vital constitutional question were still unattempted. The South no doubt felt that in the end the North would never agree to secession, and that she had better secure all the advantages she could in view of the unavoidable struggle. The policy was technically illegal. It did not prove permanently to be wise.

In the Presidential message of December 1860,

Buchanan announced his intention of holding the forts in the Southern States. He was not, however, prepared to inflame Southern susceptibilities by reinforcing the forts in anticipation of any attempt upon their integrity. South Carolina was the first state to take action. It declared through its representative that pending negotiations the people of South Carolina would make no attack upon the United States forts in Charleston harbour, provided that no reinforcement should be sent into them, and that their relative military status should remain unchanged. The forts in question were three in number: Fort Moultrie on the north side of the harbour, Fort Sumter in the midst of the sea, more than a mile from Fort Moultrie, and Fort Castle Pinckney. Fort Sumter was not entirely completed; neither it nor Castle Pinckney, a small fort, was garrisoned. The garrisoned fort, Fort Moultrie, would be difficult to defend from a land attack. Fort Sumter was far stronger and better situated.

Fort Moultrie was garrisoned by Major Anderson with about one hundred men. His instructions were to avoid any provocation of aggression, but on any evidence of attack, or of occupation of either of the ungarrisoned forts, he was to place his command wherever it might be used to the best advantage. Anderson believed this critical situation to have arisen, and on the evening of December 26th, he very skilfully transferred his command from Fort Moultrie to Fort Sumter. It is probable that the authorities of South Carolina had not the intention of attacking any of the forts. South Carolina Commissioners were actually in Washington at the moment, treating with the Federal Government for the delivery of the forts and other public property in the State. The news of Anderson's occupation of Fort Sumter exasperated the Commissioners into the most intemperate language, the most unreasonable demands. They insisted that Anderson should be ordered back to Fort Moultrie, that his action should be apologised for, and that the United States troops should be removed from Charleston harbour. In the meantime, South Carolina troops had occupied Fort Moultrie and Castle Pinckney, and seized the arsenal. Buchanan refused to agree to the demands of the South Carolina Commissioners, who immediately returned to Charleston. The South had committed its first act of war. Anderson's action in transferring his command from one to another of the forts, of which he was lawfully in possession, was in no sense an act of war. The seizure of the two other forts was an act of war. But another and more flagrant was yet to come.

In the meantime a new power had formally asserted its right to rank with the civilised nations of the world. On the 8th of February 1861, at Montgomery in Alabama, the Confederate States of America declared their existence. They were composed of seven Cotton and Gulf States:—Georgia, Florida, Alabama, Mississippi, Louisiana, Texas, and South Carolina. All these states in seceding, with the exception of South Carolina, had seized upon all the strongholds in their territories, with the exception of Fort Pickens at Pensacola, of Fort Taylor at Key West, and of Fort Jefferson at the Dry Tortugas. They established at first a provisional government, and in March adopted a constitution that was very much the same as the constitution of the United

States. The new confederacy elected for its President Jefferson Davis of Mississippi, and for its Vice-President Alexander H. Stephens of Georgia.

Jefferson Davis was a remarkable man, a man well fitted in many ways to take the command of an insurgent nation. He was born in Kentucky in 1808. He had received a military training at Westpoint. He had made the rough experiences of war in the Black Hawk campaign of 1831, in the Pawnee campaign of 1833, and in the Mexican War of 1846. He had represented Mississippi in Congress in 1845. He entered the Senate 1847. His first speech in the Senate was applauded by John Quincy Adams. 'That young man, gentlemen, is no ordinary man; he will make his mark.' He was secretary for War during Pierce's administration. When the secession movement began he was once again a senator of the United States, but he resigned his seat as soon as the secession had taken its definite shape. The rebel States could scarcely have chosen a better leader for their desperate adventure. Something of a statesman, something of a soldier, something of an orator, Jefferson Davis was many-sided enough to appeal to a people proud of its soldiers, its statesmen, and its orators. His was not the most heroic, not the most commanding figure of an insurrection which had the glory of being generalled by Robert Lee, and by Stonewall Jackson, but he was strong enough and resolute enough to hold his difficult post with distinction, and to make as much of the Southern chances of success as perhaps it was possible for any man of the South to do.

Jefferson Davis professed reluctance to accept the Presidency. The summons came to him while he was at work on his plantation at Brierfield, very much as the summons came to Diocletian in the midst of his cabbages. It is possible, it is even probable, that, as has been suggested, he would have preferred to take high rank in the army. He was a good fighting-man, and might well have believed that his genius lay in the direction of guiding armies. But he accepted the Presidency, and took advantage of his inauguration at Montgomery on the 18th of February to formulate his policy, and the policy of the Confederacy, in a careful speech which made no allusion to slavery, and which represented the South as suffering 'wanton aggression on the part of others.' The speech was received with rapture throughout the South. There had been a time when Davis was looked upon by many of his associates as of too conservative a temper to lead the advanced secessionists. The inaugural address may well have answered all misgivings. It was an uncompromising advocacy of the extremest form of States-rights, a justification of that remedy of separation which, as Davis said, had been resorted to as a necessity, not as a choice. There was no hesitation about his interpretation of the resolution of the South to support its claims by the sword, 'if passion or lust of dominion should cloud the judgment or influence the ambition of the North.'

Words like these were well calculated to spur the turbulent chivalry of the South. Through all the seceding States the address of President Davis went as a message of comfort, of encouragement, of determination, of defiance, and as such was received with rapture. Vehement Southern politicians proclaimed that the United States were dissolved for ever.

Vehement Southern journalists wept ironic tears over the 'poor Yorick' of the North, and dismissed him contemptuously as 'a sad rogue.' Davis's proclamation may well have delighted those of his colleagues who had most misdoubted him, amongst whom perhaps the most conspicuous was the man who was now his second in command.

Alexander H. Stephens, the Vice-President of the new power, was an able man, of a lower order of ability than Jefferson Davis. A Georgian man, four years younger than his chief, he began in 1843 a public life that was starred with honourable successes. He was one of the first to advocate the annexation of Texas. He was one of the most zealous in aiding the passage of the Kansas and Nebraska Act of 1854. Up to this point he had belonged to the Whig party; later he became a Democrat, and a supporter of President Buchanan. He was destined to make an even more remarkable change of political opinion, for he was at first opposed to those principles of secession, which, when he had adopted them, made him the second citizen of the new commonwealth, and came near to making him the first. Stephens had seemed to many the most fitting choice for the Presidency of the new power. The members of the new government were able men. The name of Leroy Pope Walker of Alabama, the Secretary for War, lives in the list of false prophets. He publicly declared in the April of the year of secession that before the 1st of May the Confederate Flag would float over Washington. Another memorable man, Judah P. Benjamin, the St. Domingo Jew, the successful New Orleans lawyer, Senator for Louisiana, was Attorney General. He had yet before him in an undreamed-of future a career of honour and distinction at the English bar.

The cabinet was, like most cabinets, a compromise. Davis in many instances would have liked other men, or the same men in other places. Many of the members desired other offices than the offices they consented to hold. But they formed a good working government, and they set about their work in earnest. The Provisional Congress rapidly passed acts providing military means for the war that now seemed more than possible. Three commissioners were appointed to go to Washington to negotiate a treaty of amity with the Federal government. The new nation faced its old associates with proffers of peace and menaces of war. Yet the great division did not destroy the sanctity of national memories. It is touching to read that on Washington's birthday, the 22nd February, in Charleston harbour, Castle Pinckney under the rebel flag, and Fort Sumter under the Stars and Stripes, fired each its salute in honour of the Father of the country that was about to be torn in two.

When the new Confederacy was two months old it struck its first stroke of war. It ordered the bombardment of Fort Sumter. Anderson sustained very gallantly a hopeless defence through two days for the honour of the Union flag, while the quays of Charleston were thronged with fashionable women watching in a rapture of enthusiasm the dawn of war. Then Anderson honourably surrendered, and Sumter was a Southern fort. It is hard to understand why the Confederates delayed this deed so long. It was urged upon President Davis by cool and wary advisers that it would be well to secure Fort Sumter before the conclusion of President Buchanan's term of office, before the accession of the new President, Abraham Lincoln. It was more than probable that Buchanan would not have replied to the capture of Fort Sumter by a call to arms. It was at least probable that his successor would not feel compelled to resent to the extreme of war an event that was already ancient history as far as his own administration was concerned. But President Davis insisted on delay. He professed himself prepared for 'the criticism which the rash often bestow upon unnecessary caution.' So it happened that Buchanan was once more an ordinary American citizen, and Abraham Lincoln was some six weeks President when the cannon of Beauregard beat down the defence of Anderson, and added Fort Sumter to the strongholds of the South.

If the Southern President had been determined that the act of secession should not pass unaccompanied by civil war he could not have acted in a manner better calculated to carry out his purpose. There were no small number of people in the North who were secretly, who were even openly willing to let the South go its own wild way unchallenged, or at least unopposed. To be free from the stain of slavery in the Union, to end without blows the long hostility between the South and the North, such men would perhaps have consented to oppose nothing more potent than a protest, nothing more forcible than a regret to the secession of the Gulf and Cotton States. There were many, too, whose disapproval of secession took a far stronger form, but who yet were reluctant to resort to arms to coerce their mutinous compatriots. Even those most ready to fight were only ready to fight as a last resource, and clung as long as might be to hopes of conference, of conciliation, of compromise. On both sides there was a general desire to avoid war, if war could in honour, by any exertion of statesmanship, be avoided. It is one of the might-have-beens, which are for the most part a vanity, that if Governor Pickens had acted as he had wished to act and captured Fort Sumter early in February, the Confederate States might have flourished for a time at least in peace.

But the delay of Davis, and the bombardment of Beauregard settled the matter. The shots that were fired on those two April days inaugurated a fierce, bloody, and famous war. They roused in a moment the passionate indignation of the North. They ended all doubts, answered all hesitations. They fused contending parties, principles, opinions in one common determination to give back blow for blow. If the statesmen of the South had fancied that it would be hard to stir the sluggish pulses of the North, they learnt, and that instantly, their mistake. The Southern Confederacy had made its act of war, and by that act had ended in a moment the patience, the forbearance, the toleration of the North. It had been made against a people divided, uncertain, unused in arms, reluctant to engage in hostilities, busy with their own businesses, anxious for their trade, their commerce, their industries, their agriculture, a people well-to-do, appreciating the advantages of peace. It converted them into a nation of soldiers, and of soldiers animated with one resolve, to preserve the Union at any cost of life and money. 'In your hands, my dissatisfied fellow-countrymen,' Lincoln had said at the close of his inaugural address, 'and not in mine, is the momentous issue of civil war. You can have no conflict without being yourselves the aggressors.' The dissatisfied fellow-countrymen had made themselves the aggressors, and the men of the North were unanimous in their acceptance of the momentous issue.

Lincoln issued a call to arms. The proclamation was curious in its form. It ignored the fact that the Union was opposed by an organised and formally proclaimed Confederacy of seceding States. It spoke of illegal combinations too powerful to be dealt with in the ordinary course of law, and it summoned the militia of all the states of the Union 'to suppress said combinations.' It dealt with a belligerent power as if it were dealing with a parish riot. In its quiet, dry technicality, in its formal phraseology, in its legal calm, it was in strange contrast to the passions that were tearing a great and seemingly stable republic into two opposed irreconcilable sovereignties. If the proclamation appeared parochial in the heady temper of the time, the response to it was imperial. The Northern States gave all the men, gave more than all the men, that were demanded of them. A flame of national devotion blazed over the North. It has been said that no one who did not witness the patriotic enthusiasm of that moment can form any conception of its magnificence.

While the crowded churches of Charleston returned thanks to Heaven for the fall of Sumter, while the taverns of Charleston rang with triumphant toasts and patriotic sentiments, while the streets of Charleston were tramped by bands of armed men singing war songs, in the North the heather was indeed on fire. In the fine phrase of Emerson, the attack on Fort Sumter crystallised the North into a unit, and the hope of mankind was saved. But if the North sprang to arms with an eagerness that amazed the world, it did so with none of the joyousness, none of the reckless exultation that characterised the South. A sterner and graver people were prepared to make every sacrifice in defence of the nation and the national honour, but they reckoned the cost of the sacrifice, and they looked ahead with a sombre unrest to the dark days that were coming. Men have confessed to an ever-present weight at the heart as they thought of the shame, the folly, and the outrage of civil war in the land. Their anger and their gloom only animated their purpose to deserve well of their country.

The first steps to be taken were for the preservation of the Capitol. People remembered Leroy Walker's prophecy. Massachusetts poured troops into Washington as fast as it could. These troops were attacked in Baltimore, and had to fight their way from one railway station to another, killing and being killed. So furiously secessional was the spirit of the capital of Maryland, that to avoid needless bloodshed for a time, further troops taken to Washington were carried around instead of through Baltimore. In all parts of the North men were enlisting, arming, drilling, eager to be sent to Washington, eager to be led to the South. In answer to this general arming, Jefferson Davis made a proclamation authorising letters of marque to privateers prepared to prey upon the merchant marine of the United States. Lincoln retaliated by a declaration that Confederate privateers would be treated as pirates. This menace he never could have maintained, and he made it impossible to maintain by declaring the blockade of the Southern ports. A State cannot blockade its own ports. By declaring the Southern ports blockaded, it recognised the existence of a belligerent enemy, it recognised the fact of war, and in doing so had to recognise privateers as belligerents. It may be said here, once for all, that while the North was able to make its blockade of the Southern ports effective, the South by its privateers succeeded in ruining the merchant marine of its enemy.

CHAPTER XVII

BULL RUN

AT the time when the American Civil War began America and American affairs did not hold the place they now hold in the public mind of other nations. It would scarcely be exaggeration to say that the political life of the United States in those days was as unfamiliar to the average Englishman as are to-day the politics of the fantastic Republics of South America. The length of time that it took for news to travel from the States was the chief cause of an ignorance, an indifference, that have now dwindled, if they have not disappeared. Before the Civil War began Cyrus Field had made his splendid attempt to link the old world with the new by means of the Atlantic cable; but the great enterprise failed at first, and was not carried to success until the war was a thing of the past. All through the war, news came to Europe only as swiftly as steam would carry it. The events that thrilled London and Paris, the two European capitals most interested in the progress of the war, were already ancient history: The victory that one mail announced might have been turned into a defeat, the defeat into a victory. All was hidden in clouds, all was done in darkness, all was speculation, prophecy, and waiting for the next mail.

To England and to France the war was especially

interesting. France had owed the liberties of which in that hour she was deprived to the example of the American Republic. England had twice pitted herself in arms against the American States, and twice been unsuccessful. In England the common tongue and the common blood compelled a sympathy with one side or the other in the great struggle. In France the wearer of the Napoleonic name, the bearer of the Napoleonic tradition, had aims of his own on the North American continent, which might be furthered by the fortunes of the war. In France the genius of de Tocqueville had done much to familiarise the more intellectual of his countrymen with the institutions, the people, and the purposes of the Western Republic. In England, two generations of writers and travellers had worked to place pictures of varying accuracy of life and manners in America before the eyes of the untravelled. In these two countries, therefore, the progress of the Civil War was followed with at least a degree of the attention that it deserved.

It can hardly be questioned that the general feeling of England and of France, so far as it was manifest, was in favour of the South. In France the emperor, dazzled by the hope of establishing a Europeanised empire in 'Mexico dim as dreams,' was eager to recognise formally the Confederate States. In England, on the whole, the voice of public opinion expressed itself in favour of the South. Even so shrewd a man, even so great a statesman as Gladstone was so far misled as to declare later, that the South had made an army, had made a navy, and had made a nation. A large number of Englishmen were annoyed with the North for making a war which interfered with England's commerce and with

England's comfort. In their eyes the most sensible way out of the whole difficulty would have been to let the South go about its business, and play at being a nation in its own way. This would have caused no interference with the English cotton trade, and so would have been eminently satisfactory for England.

It must be admitted that the Northern government did something on its side to cause unfriendly feeling in England. It seems to have assumed from the first that England actively disliked, and was prepared secretly to injure the North. The Northern government was unreasonably offended by England's recognition of the Southern Confederacy as a belligerent power. This very recognition was urged by the best friends of the North in England, and was an act essential to the welfare of the North. Without a recognition of the South as a belligerent power, England could not have recognised the right of the North to blockade the Southern ports. The Northern government did resent the recognition, did show itself extremely susceptible to imaginary grievances from England, and did soon have very real grievances to complain of. The diplomatic relationships between the two countries began to suffer from a tension that slowly tightened. In recognising the Southern States as a belligerent power—though not of course as an established government—England proclaimed its neutrality, and warned all its subjects against affording any kind of assistance to either combatant. It would have been well for the North, and it would have been better still for England, if the principle so properly proclaimed had been properly maintained.

It is a little difficult now to understand why people

in England and people in France were so confident in the success of the Southern arms. Alone of European powers, the English and the French governments showed signs of favour to the cause of slavery and the cause of Secession. A kind of misty impression prevailed that the South was a nation of gentlemen and the North a nation of hypocritical and poor-spirited tradesmen. The Southerners were known to be men trained in arms, skilled in manly exercises, daring horsemen, lovers of the country life. The Northerners were comprehensively nick-named Yankees, and were considered to be for the most part traders and shopkeepers, acute enough in their own way, but not the men to fight or win battles. Yet it would seem now, when the Civil War lies a generation away, hard to understand how any reasoning man could believe positively in the ultimate triumph of the South. In the long run, as should have been obvious, all the odds were against it. If at the outset the Southern States were better prepared for war than their antagonists, they had not the resources to fall back upon which made the enmity of the North so formidable, the superiority of numbers from which to recruit armies, the superiority of wealth with which to maintain armies, the superiority of resources for producing the material of war. Population against population, purse against purse, the South was outmanned and outbidden from the first.

What the South did not appreciate, what the foreign admirers of the South did not appreciate, was the perseverance and the passion with which the North took up the quarrel and fought it out doggedly to the end. There were of course lookers-on acute enough to see most of the game. Prince

Napoleon, the ablest and the least successful wearer of the name since the First Empire, studied the North and the South during the progress of the war, and warned the Emperor that in his belief the cause of the South was doomed to failure. It would have been well for the Emperor if he had accepted his cousin's judgment. There were politicians in England as far-sighted as Prince Napoleon. Cobden, whose own impression was that it might be better to let the mutinous States secede, wrote of them to Sumner that 'they have gone about the work of dissolving the Union with less gravity or forethought than a firm of intelligent drapers or grocers would think necessary in case of a dissolution of partnership.'

It so happened, however, that the earlier events of the Civil War did much to justify those who pinned their faith to the fortunes of the South. The North lost more than many battles in losing the services of Robert Lee. Friend and foe alike have nothing but words of admiration for Lee. He came of a distinguished and honourable family, with whom statesmanship and soldiership were a tradition. His father was Henry Lee of Virginia, a gallant soldier, dear to his world as 'Light Horse Harry,' a glowing orator, always to be remembered as the author of the famous eulogy of Washington, 'first in war, first in peace, and first in the hearts of his countrymen.' His first cousin, Richard Henry Lee, was one of the signers of the Declaration of Independence. Robert Edmund Lee inherited a name thus doubly illustrious only to increase its fame. He was fifty-five years of age when the Civil War broke out. He was married to a daughter of

Washington's adopted son, George Washington Parke Custis. He was a noble specimen of a Christian soldier and gentleman. Of splendid physique, with hair ungrizzled, he had all the qualities that become a soldier, tempered by all the virtues that become a devout and pure-minded man. He was of ascetic habit. He did not use tobacco; he seldom tasted wine. He believed, and he acted up to his belief, that 'duty is the sublimest word in our language.'

Lee had done splendid service in the Mexican War. He was devoted to the Union, and the Northern statesmen hoped that he would consent to take command of the Northern army. The command was unofficially offered to him. He declared that if he owned all the negroes in the South, he would sacrifice the value of every one of them to save the Union. But he added that he could not draw his sword upon his native State. It became a question of Union as against State with Lee as with so many other men of the South, and with him as with so many the State carried the day. Virginia withdrew from the Union. Lee was like Randolph, first of all things a Virginian. He sacrificed his political opinions, and followed the fortunes of his State. He resigned his commission in the United States army. He was summoned to Virginia. He was offered, and he accepted, the position of Commander of its Forces. The cause of the South had gained a great gain. The cause of the North had suffered a great loss.

The cause of the North was destined for some time to suffer losses. At first things looked very gloomy. There was every fear that the South, flushed by its bloodless victory over Fort Sumter, might make a rapid raid into the District of Columbia, and capture the capital and the Capitol. We have a grim picture of Lincoln pacing up and down his room, and waiting with the patience of despair for the coming of the troops that were to save the State. The strongest man might well despair in such a moment. Washington was practically defenceless. General Scott's assurances that under certain conditions he might be able to hold the public buildings were not reassuring. The neighbour State was in rebellion. Any hour might bring news of the approaching march of a rebel army. If the South succeeded in capturing Washington, the whole conditions of the desperate game would be altered. The seat of the Federal Government would be in the seceder's hands. It would be hardly possible under such conditions for foreign governments to deny recognition to the Southern Confederacy. When the Massachusetts Regiment, bloody from its fight in Baltimore, entered Washington, it came to Lincoln like a message of salvation. Yet the Massachusetts Regiment was but a handful. Where, Lincoln asked, were the levies promised by the North, where was the 7th Regiment from New York? With a humour that was more bitter than mirthful he told the Massachusetts Regiment that he believed there was no North, that the 7th Regiment was a myth. Lincoln despaired, or professed to despair, too soon. On the 19th of April the 7th Regiment marched down Broadway 'through a tempest of cheers two miles long.' On the 25th of April it halted in front of the White House in Washington, and proved to Lincoln that the 7th Regiment was not a myth. Its soldiers had crossed

Maryland, but they had avoided Baltimore. They were the pioneers of a new route from the North. More regiments were on the march at their heels. In a few days there were ten thousand troops in Washington, and the capital was considered to be safe.

If the leader of the Northern people had trembled for his capital city, the Southern leaders had been no less alarmed for theirs. Beauregard feared for Richmond as Lincoln had feared for Washington. Two days after the 7th Regiment had started on its memorable march Richmond was thrown into a panic by the unfounded rumour that a United States war-vessel was steaming up the James River. Each side felt naturally enough that the capture of the adversary's seat of government would be a great move in the game. The newspapers of the South were clamorous that Washington could and should be taken out of hand. A little later the Northern papers were crying the cry of ' Forward to Richmond,' and insisting that the National army must be within its walls by the middle of July. The Southerners might perhaps have succeeded in capturing Washington if they had made a bold stroke at once. The Northerners found that it took years and not days for any soldiers of the National army to pass within the lines of Richmond except as prisoners or as spies. It is not easy to understand why the South did not strike its bold stroke. Possibly the men who were going to war to defend the sanctity of their own States-rights felt that they could not, with any show of consistency or logical statesmanship, violate or even infringe upon the States-rights of others. North Carolina had not yet seceded, and Washington was not to be reached except across North Carolina.

Virginia had not yet seceded, and, though her secession was well-nigh certain, her tardiness served to delay any dreamed-of dash upon Washington. Further, Washington was in a sense upon the soil of Maryland, and Maryland, that had been so hostile to the march of Northern troops to the South through her territory, might by the law of nations be assumed to be no less reluctant to welcome the invasion of a Southern army. Whatever the reason, any chance the South had of a sudden surprise was gone now, and proved to be gone for ever.

The Southern exultations over the fall of Sumter were dashed by that rage of New York which was its direct consequence. Southern statesmen hoped for the aid of New York; had been confident of the neutrality of New York. New York was essentially democratic. The South could not believe that it would consent to follow what it called in contempt the Black Republican party. It never seems to have dreamed that the insult to the national flag could have fired all hearts in New York to a common purpose, and overwhelmed the spirit of party with the spirit of patriotism. It believed that New York would actively, and certainly passively, assist the cause. It believed New York to be well affected towards slavery, to be well affected towards Secession. It does, indeed, seem as if there had been a conspiracy in New York City of a fairly widespread kind to rise in insurrection, seize all the arms in the arsenals, all the war shipping in the navy docks, and declare New York a Free City, independent of either of the two warring races. Any such vision vanished into space when the Stars and Stripes were hauled down from Fort Sumter. There was no more talk of Democrat or

Black Republican, no more dream of Free City. New York was for the Union ; New York was for the flag.

The first few tosses of the war were favourable to the North. The Federal army entered Virginia. In Missouri a Federal army was raised and a Federal victory won. A defeat at Big Bethell, Virginia, was compensated for by the evacuation of Harper's Ferry and the surrender of a Confederate force at Beverley. Up to this point the war had been little more than a series of desultory skirmishes hardly justifying the title of 'the series of brilliant and decisive victories' accorded to them by Congress. They served to free upper Western Virginia from Confederate forces. They cheered and animated the North with a cheer and enthusiasm that was destined to be short-lived. The first serious battle of the War was the battle fought on the 21st of July, which the South calls the Battle of Manassas, and which the North calls the Battle of Bull Run.

By this time the Northern army numbered about two hundred thousand men and the Southern army about half that number. Neither force was an army in the Continental sense of the term. Each lacked training, experience, skilled and practised leadership. All that is essential for the carrying on of a great campaign, all except the bookish theorick, had yet to be learned by the commanders on both sides. The Southerners' inferiority in numbers was partially compensated for by their better training as militia, by their greater familiarity with and dexterity in the use of arms. The North was impatient for some decisive battle. The Union government, pressed by the impatience of the North, put pressure on its military leaders. General M'Dowell was reluctantly compelled to move a Federal army of some thirty thousand men against General Beauregard who headed a somewhat smaller force. Beauregard withdrew behind Bull Run. Each general relied for success upon the action of another. As M'Dowell and Beauregard faced each other at Bull Run, so Patterson and Johnston faced each other in the Shenandoah Valley. It was Beauregard's hope that Johnston might be able to reinforce him. It was M'Dowell's hope that Patterson would be able to hold Johnston in the Shenandoah Valley and prevent him from reinforcing Beauregard, or, failing this, would speedily reinforce M'Dowell. M'Dowell's small numerical superiority over Beauregard would be of no avail if Beauregard's army was swelled by the army of Johnston. Fate granted the wish of the Southern soldier. Patterson was an old man. He does not seem to have known very clearly what he was expected to do. He certainly allowed Johnston to slip away from him.

The winding stream of Bull Run had wooded banks capable of serving as a formidable defence against troops more experienced than those under M'Dowell even if held by troops less experienced than those of Beauregard. M'Dowell had harder work to do and to demand of his troops in attack than Beauregard had in defence. Each opponent tried to turn the other's left. M'Dowell nearly succeeded in his purpose. Suddenly the battle was decided by the arrival of Johnston's reinforcements. This ended all chance of victory for the exhausted soldiers of the North. What was left of M'Dowell's army broke into a retreat which soon became a desperate rout. The North had received a crushing and terrible defeat. Luckily no pursuit was attempted; indeed, the Confederates had suffered so much that pursuit was practically impossible.

The first news that came to Washington, the first news that came to the North, was of victory for the Federal arms. When the grim truth was known at Washington, Lincoln faced it with fortitude, and set to work at once to frame fresh plans and to cheer his soldiers. When the grim truth was known in the North, grief for the defeat was swallowed up in shame at the panic. The enemies of the North exulted. Bull Run had proved the truth of the Southern charge that the Northerners were cowards who would not, who could not fight. In England the news increased the public feeling of sympathy and enthusiasm for the South. But there were Englishmen who read the lesson of Bull Run with clearer eyes. Anthony Trollope, the novelist, was in New York at the time of the disaster. He was impressed by the way in which those who deplored the disaster made no weak ignoble attempt to minimise it. There were no excuses, no half-hearted explanations. People frankly admitted that they had been well whipped. Anthony Trollope argued rightly, that a people who could face defeat in this frank spirit were destined for something better than defeat. The temper in which a race accepts defeat is a surer sign of their moral greatness than the temper in which they accept a victory. To the South Manassas appeared not merely the beginning of the end, but the very end. The South acted and spoke and wrote as if this one victory over the Federals was enough to end the war.

The battle of Bull Run gave for the first time one very famous name to the world. In the beginning of the battle when fortune seemed to favour the Federals, the Union troops drove the Confederates back up the slope of a plateau, on the summit of which a brigade of men stood in line calmly awaiting the Northern onset. This brigade was under the command of Thomas J. Jackson. General Bee called out to his retreating troops to encourage them: 'Look at Jackson! There he stands like a stone wall.' The story has been affirmed again and again. It has also been denied. It is at least certain that the nickname 'Stonewall' was given to Thomas Jackson, and that he carried it all through his splendid career to the end. At the time of the battle of Bull Run Jackson was only thirty-seven years old. Like most of the generals on either side who distinguished themselves during the war, he was a West Point man. He was considered at West Point to be a dull and slow student. While he was at West Point he followed the example of George Washington, and drew up a little code of maxims for the government of his life. We are told, however, that nothing in this volume shows that his thoughts had any turn towards religion. It is as free from all reference to the teachings of Christianity as the maxims of Marcus Aurelius. He earned distinction in the Mexican campaign. He seems to have lived in a romance while in Mexico, some romance powerful enough to make him learn dancing and Spanish, and the memory of this romance seems to have lingered with him throughout his life. After Mexico he left the army, and became a professor in the Military Institution at Lexington, Virginia. Here he married twice. Here his nature underwent a great change. He had passed his early youth in a community where the pleasures of life were highly appreciated, and where morality and religion were treated, if not with irreverence, at least with indifference. He had been a boon companion, a lover of horse-racing; he seemed to share in all the enjoyments that life could offer to a spirited young soldier. Now the spirited young soldier became an austere, devout, earnest Puritan. He grew into a likeness of some figure from the old Colonial days, with his passionate habit of almost ceaseless prayer, with his rigid observance of the Sabbath, with his ascetic domination of a body whose inclinations were by no means ascetic. He lived the religious life with the zeal of an early Christian. He trained his body to strength and his mind to knowledge with infinite pains and infinite patience. He found consolation for sorrow in this thought, 'We know that all things work together for good to them that love God.' In his devotion to, and knowledge of the Bible, he resembled some of the ironside lieutenants of Cromwell.

If the war had never taken place, Jackson would have been remembered in Lexington as an austere Professor of artillery, who read much, who never smoked, or played cards, or drank, or danced, who would walk a mile in the rain to set right some trifling mistake, and interrupt people who used the familiar phrase 'you know,' with the emphatic assertion that he did not know. To the outer world he was a formal precisian, a rigid Sabbatarian. He was no favourite with his pupils. He was not appreciated by the little public of Lexington. But in his own home he was bright and happy, with a boyish brightness and a boyish sense of fun that would have surprised some of those who believed that they knew and understood him.

When he left the teaching for the practice of war, he governed his men with the stern discipline of obedience which was the ruling principle of his life, but he was more loved by his men than any other general with the exception of Lee. It is certainly significant to remember that the two ablest generals of the South were also the noblest, that the two most eminent in arms were the two most devout in soul. A cause had much to commend it which commanded the services of such soldier-saints as these.

CHAPTER XVIII

ARMS AND THE MEN

SOUTH and North had alike believed that the war could be ended in a very short time, and perhaps by a single decisive battle. Indeed many of the Southerners believed that the battle of Manassas was that decisive battle. In that belief, a great number of the Confederate soldiers disbanded and returned to their homes, thus making the very victory something of a disaster for the South. To the Northerners, on the other hand, Bull Run proved in the end a salutary lesson. It taught them that the hope of reducing rapidly the Southern rebellion to ruin was baseless; that much had to be learned and much unlearned before the voice of secession could be silenced, and the hand of secession disarmed.

The great Civil War lasted for four years. It made and unmade many reputations. When it began, the people of the North were convinced that in George Brinton M'Clellan they possessed a general admirably qualified to beat rebellion to its knees. M'Clellan did not realise the high hopes that had been formed of him. Like so many of the soldiers of the war he was a West Point man; like so many he had served his apprenticeship to arms in the Mexican campaign. He had left the army, and was chief engineer of the Illinois Central Railway when the Civil War broke out. As commander of the army at Washington he proved to be admirable at re-organisation and discipline, and the conversion of green recruits into sterling soldiers. But he was dilatory; he was vain; he was quarrelsome. His head was full of schemes which he could express in sonorous sentences, but which left behind them an uncomfortable sense of vagueness. He was always going to do great things, and never accomplishing them. He was always wrangling with his government, and attributing all his ill-success to their interference. When General Scott retired in the November of 1861, M'Clellan was appointed Commander-in-Chief, but four months later he was relieved from the command of all the departments except that of the Potomac. At last, just a year after he had been made Commander-in-Chief, he was removed from all command, as the result of his failure to follow up a victory, and his delay, so long as to amount to disobedience, to obey orders given him to cross the Potomac and drive the enemy south.

M'Clellan's appointment was an unfortunate thing for the North. His removal from command would have been more fortunate if it had happened sooner. He was a brave man; he was, with many limitations, an able man; but he was wholly unconscious of his own limitations; he was consumed with self-conceit. His behaviour to Lincoln, whom he was unwise enough to despise, was insolent, even insulting; but it had its value in bringing into relief the patience of Lincoln, that proud patience which the gods are said to love. To those who remonstrated with the President on his submission to the ill-manners of M'Clellan, he replied with an admirable humour, ' I will hold M'Clellan's horse if he will only bring us success.' The answer was as characteristic of the genius of Lincoln as the insolence which provoked it was characteristic of the incapacity of M'Clellan. What Lincoln was working for was the success of the great cause, and he was willing to put up with any boorishness on M'Clellan's part, any affronts, either to his personal dignity or his official position, so long as M'Clellan 'will only bring us success.'

M'Clellan did not, could not, bring success, and then M'Clellan had to go. He had been tried and found wanting. He had been given a splendid chance and had miserably squandered his opportunity. In the phrase of Lowell, 'our chicken was no eagle after all.' He had great personal charm. We are told that he was sensible and genial, that he was kindly, and that his bearing was modest. Lincoln's private secretaries, Nicolay and Hay, have put it on record that his unusually winning personal characteristics succeeded in inspiring a remarkable affection and regard in every one, from the President to the humblest orderly at his door. But all these qualities, however admirable in a man, were not the qualities essential for a soldier. To have these too, with the other qualities, is great; and other soldiers had that greatness. His personality gained him the love of his men in a most remarkable degree, and his moral character commanded the respect of all who knew him. But when admiration allowed itself to offer him the epithet of 'the young Napoleon,' admiration blundered lamentably and grotesquely.

It is not pleasant to think of what might have happened to the war if M'Clellan had been permitted to remain in command. His removal happily placed the destinies of the armies of the North in the hands of greater men, of men whose names will be remembered for ever in the history, not merely of their own country, but of all military enterprises. With the disappearance of M'Clellan from the saga, the story of the war took a new meaning, and the fortune of the cause began to wear an unfamiliar brightness.

There came a moment when the United States found itself within an ace of a war with England, and possibly of a war with France. The relationships between the United States and Great Britain, which had been strained since the beginning of the war, seemed as if they must snap at last over the affair of the *Trent*. Jefferson Davis, very anxious to secure the recognition of the Southern Confederacy, and well aware that a large proportion of the public in England and in France were well-inclined for recognition, resolved to send envoys to Europe to help in bringing recognition about. He chose from among his following two men. John Slidell was an eminent lawyer, who had been a successful politician. Born in New York sixty-eight years earlier, he had settled in the South, and had served the United States as Minister-Plenipotentiary to Mexico. Davis selected Slidell to represent the interests of the South at the Court of Louis Napoleon, if he could persuade the Emperor to receive him. The envoy chosen for England was James Murray Mason, a Virginian politician, some five years younger than Slidell, and chiefly known to fame as the framer of the Fugitive Slave Law of 1850. Both men had belonged, in the days when they still served the Union, to the strongly anti-English party in America.

The two envoys succeeding in running the blockade of Charleston harbour in a small steamer in the October of 1861, and got to Havana, where they embarked for Southampton on the English mail-steamer *Trent*. The day after she left Havana, the *Trent* was brought to in the Bahama Channel by the United States war-sloop, *San Jacinto*, under the command of Captain Charles Wilkes. Wilkes had rendered a better service to his country's science by his discovery of the Antarctic Continent in 1838 than he was destined to render to his country's politics by this exploit. He had learned at Havana that the Southern envoys were there on their way to Europe, and it entered into his hot head that it would be a fine thing to intercept them. He boarded the *Trent* after firing a shell across her bows, and took the two envoys and their secretaries prisoners, in spite of their appeal to the British flag for protection, and in spite of the angry protest of Captain Williams of the *Trent*. The captive envoys were immediately carried back to Fort Warren in Boston Harbour, there to await the trial which might possibly end in their death.

It would be hard to say whether this action aroused greater delight in the Northern States or greater indignation in England. It is not now questioned, it was really scarcely questioned then, that Captain Wilkes had acted illegally. The United States had gone to war, and rightly gone to war, half a century earlier to prevent England from exercising that very right of search which Wilkes had now exercised, and which the first unreasoning impulse of the nation appeared to approve. That first impulsive approval is easy to understand. To prevent the arrival of two hostile envoys in Europe, to secure the persons of two of the men in the Southern service most hated by the North, to hold two such important hostages as security for the lives of the Northern prisoners— here was a series of advantages won at a single blow, and not easy to forego. But the blow was illegal, and the advantages had to be foregone.

Lincoln at once recognised the illegality and the necessity to give way. But Lincoln was appreciably unpopular just then. His sane, sound judgment was in collision with fiery impatience all over the North. He was found too cautious and too yielding by men who did not see when caution was essential, and when it was inevitable to yield. The temper of the North was neither for caution or surrender in the cause of the *Trent* and the captive envoys. Public meetings, public banquets, public prints, had applauded the deed of Wilkes. The Secretary of the Navy had commended it. The House of Representatives had passed him a vote of thanks 'for his arrest of the traitors Slidell and Mason.' There was a fairly general feeling that 'the traitors Slidell and Mason' ought to be hanged; there was a very general determination that they should be hanged if Jefferson Davis hanged any Federal officers who were prisoners in his hands. This Davis had threatened to do in case the pirate's punishment had been given to any of the rebel privateersmen captive in the North. There was too much talk of hanging on both sides of the quarrel. But passions were hot and men said wild things.

The passion and the heat were not diminished by the international controversy between the States and Great Britain. On neither side was the controversy

conducted with even a decent degree of calm. The
long growing exasperation of each country with the
other seemed to have come to a head. On both
sides of the Atlantic the noisy multitude seemed to
be agog for war. Every effort was made by excitable
extremists in America to vamp up some specious
show of legality which might seem to justify them
in refusing to surrender their prize. Pretty women
parodied bearded men in poring over the pages of
International Law, and in citing Vattel and Puffendorf
and Stowell and Phillimore and Wheaton in defence
of the retention of the envoys. The ingenuity of
the lawyers was more seriously taxed to find a workable defence.

All this was a waste of time. The act of capture
was an error, was indefensible, would have to be
atoned for. But atonement was asked for in England
and considered in America in an ungracious,
quarrelsome mood. Lord Palmerston's Government, prompted by Lord Russell, acted as if the
United States were only to be approached with the
menace of instant war. Lord Lyons at Washington
was instructed to make peremptory demand for the
liberation of the envoys, for an apology, and to insist
on an answer in seven days. Troops were sent out
to Canada, eight thousand in number, and a royal
proclamation forbade the export of arms and munitions of war. In the States a vast number of the
public were no less eager to meet defiance with
defiance. Heady enthusiasm was as ready in 1861
as in 1812 to meet the world in arms, and beat it
backward home. Some desperate dreamers actually
seem to have believed that a war with England
would at once induce the South to abandon its own

quarrel and rally to the old flag against the old enemy with the happy result of soldering the Union close again.

A clamant press on both sides fanned the flame. The majority of English journals were fiercely anti-Northern. Of daily papers only the *Daily News* and the *Morning Star* enthusiastically and consistently supported the North. All the friends of the North deplored the possibility of a war between the two countries. Some friends of the North, however, admitted that England not only might, but ought to go to war over so flagrant a violation of international law. Others, like John Bright, urged the United States, 'even if you are right,' to give way for the sake of saving the Union, to make a great concession rather than give another nation a pretext for assisting in the breaking up of the country. America had no better friends in England than the Queen and her husband, the Prince Consort. Both used all their influence to bring about a peaceful settlement of the dispute. Happily for the world, the good sense of the United States was greater than its sense of irritation. It recognised that it had made a mistake. Seward replied to Russell with tact and urbanity. He declared that Wilkes had acted without authority from the American Government; that the American Government recognised being asked to do to the British nation what it had always insisted that other nations ought to do to her, and that therefore the prisoners would be cheerfully liberated.

If Lincoln had to suffer much from impetuous naval officers, he had to suffer a good deal more from unruly generals. His patience was sorely tried by subordinates, who did not share his conviction of the necessity for going slowly and for going surely in the process of amalgamating the cause of preservation of the Union with the cause of abolition of negro slavery. To Lincoln, the first, the immediate business in hand, was the preservation of the Union. There were men about him and below him who regarded the war as, if not mainly an abolition war, at least as much that as anything else. These were anxious as rapidly as possible to associate the progress of the Northern armies and the triumphs of the Northern arms with the progress of Emancipation and the triumphs of Abolition. Lincoln's own point of view was that the Union came first. If the Union were to be saved by setting the slaves free, then he was for that; if the Union could be saved without setting the slaves free, he was for that. It was the Union with him, first and last. Besides this he had all the legal respect for vested rights. One of his generals, Benjamin Butler, solved the question for himself by describing all negroes who came within his lines as fugitives from rebel states as 'contraband of war,' and by retaining them as such. The whole question of negro slavery was unexpectedly raised in a much more vehement fashion by another general of Lincoln's, John Charles Fremont, whose action for a time perilously injured Lincoln's popularity.

Fremont was a Savannah man with an extraordinary record. He had abandoned a professorship of mathematics in the navy to become an explorer, and had made himself famous by his exploration of the Upper Mississippi, the Des Moines river, the Rocky Mountains, and the Great Salt Lake Region.

His adventures among savages, and in the savage places of nature read more like the dreams of romance than the sober record of human enterprise. Made Governor of California in 1846, he refused to recognise the authority of a superior officer, was arrested, court-martialled, found guilty of mutiny, and pardoned by the President. He refused to accept the pardon, resigned his commission, and devoted himself again for years to exploration and travel. In 1856 he ran unsuccessfully for President against James Buchanan. When the war broke out he was appointed commander of the department of Missouri. He was a brave, daring, reckless man, but without administrative qualities. He had a great belief in himself, in which he was encouraged by his wife, Jessie Benton Fremont, who seems to have believed that if he pitted himself against Lincoln, he could overthrow Lincoln. Fremont did not distinguish himself in his new command. He was as dilatory as M'Clellan without M'Clellan's gifts of organisation. He allowed brave soldiers to go to death and defeat at the battle of Wilson's Creek by delaying or denying the reinforcements that might have saved the day and the brave soldiers.

It soon became plain that Fremont was not the man for a high and important post, that he was surrounded by unscrupulous adventurers and advisers. It began to look as if the department he controlled was being used mainly for the purpose of putting money into the pockets of military contractors. Fremont seems to have carried himself more like the sovereign of some petty state than the officer of a republican army. It has been suggested that Fremont got some idea of the disapproval with which he was beginning to be regarded, and that he resolved upon a desperate course to commend himself to the extreme anti-slavery party, and to cover with a cloak of philanthropy his shortcomings as a soldier and an administrator. He suddenly issued a proclamation pronouncing the freedom of all slaves of rebels and friends of rebels in Missouri. This stroke was done, to use Palmerston's famous phrase, 'off his own bat.' Lincoln and the Government were not consulted. News of it reached Lincoln, as it reached any private citizen, through the newspapers. Lincoln, busy with the delicate task of persuading a dubious Kentucky to stand by the Union, was alarmed at Fremont's unauthorised manumission of slaves, and called upon him to withdraw it. But Fremont's act had set loose a flood of popular enthusiasm. Lincoln's action turned the flood into popular resentment against the President. Even men of the high standing of Sumner were inclined to applaud Fremont, and to condemn Lincoln. The friends and admirers of Fremont declared and believed that any attempt to interfere with him might provoke a military insurrection in Missouri, and must prove a public calamity.

The result proved that the orderly spirit of the North was maligned by these too zealous advocates. Lincoln sent Secretary Cameron and Adjutant-General Lorenzo Thomas to investigate and report on Fremont's administration. The report declared that Fremont was unfit for his command. An order for his removal was immediately despatched, and was unhesitatingly obeyed without the slightest disturbance in the army or in Missouri. But Fremont had done much mischief. In many parts of the

North, by many people, he was regarded as a martyr, and Lincoln as an enemy to the cause of Abolition. That the feeling was neither widespread nor enduring was made plain later when Fremont put himself forward as a candidate for the Presidency in opposition to Lincoln's re-election, and failed signally. Lincoln's cautious action with regard to the slave question undoubtedly held many factions together for Union, which would otherwise have held aloof, or even have drifted into secession. The cause of the Union first was Lincoln's policy, and its wisdom was justified by its success.

The retirement of M'Clellan seemed to end the era of inaction and incapacity in the Civil War. With his disappearance from the scene came the opportunity of the three soldiers whose parts stand out most conspicuously in the great drama—Grant, Sherman, and Sheridan. The cause of the Union was blessed with many brave and able soldiers, but time has decided that these names are the names of the three men most eminent in the military service of the North. Of the three, Grant undoubtedly was the greatest man. His career was exceptionally remarkable. It is not very much that he rose from humble life to eminence. Other men have done that elsewhere than in the Great Republic whose proud boast it is that all men are born to an equal chance of success. The strangeness of Grant's career lay in this. He rose from poverty and obscurity to a position of distinction. He lost this position through his own fault, and dropped back into obscurity, into poverty, and into worse than obscurity and poverty. He lifted himself again out of the Slough of Despond to a position far higher

than he had ever attained before, and ended by
enjoying in unusual measure the highest honours
that his country could offer him.

Grant's youth was passed in the severe simplicity
of the hard and healthy life on his father's farm
in Clermont County, Ohio. Grant's father was a
tanner as well as a farmer, but Grant seems much
to have preferred the life on the farm to the life at
the tannery. Indeed it would seem that young Hiram
Ulysses Grant—for this was the boy's name—would
have been content to live out his life as a farmer.
The father was more ambitious than the son. Hiram
Ulysses was sent to West Point, where, by an error,
his name was entered as Ulysses Simpson Grant,
Simpson being his mother's name. The mistake
was stronger than the truth, and he remains Ulysses
S. Grant to his countrymen. He cared little for his
military studies, but he proved himself to be a good
mathematician, and an extremely good horseman.
He entered the army, and served with great credit
in the Mexican war, distinguishing himself at the
storming of Chapultepec, and in the assault on the
city of Mexico. He married; he remained in the
army four years; then he was ordered to the Pacific
coast, where what threatened to be the tragedy of his
life began. He fell into intemperance. He left the
army and made an effort to gain a livelihood on his
wife's farm at St. Louis. He seemed like a broken
man. At thirty-eight he had to appeal to his father
for help. The father referred him to his second son,
Ulysses's brother, Simpson, who took him into his
hardware and leather store at Galena. Grant still was
intemperate, and intemperance had brought with it
its attendant vices of idleness and impecuniosity.

We are told that acquaintances in St. Louis and Galena used to cross the street to avoid meeting Grant and being solicited for the loan of small sums of money. It might well have seemed to those who knew him that a man who had fallen to this depth could scarcely be expected to rise again.

But Grant did rise again. The first shot that was fired at Fort Sumter was the signal for his regeneration. A public meeting was called at Galena, and as Grant held rank in the army he was called upon to preside. He spoke vigorously for the Union, and for fighting in its defence. He drilled a company of volunteers, and accompanied them to Springfield. He offered his services to the Union government, but no notice was taken of his letter. He tried twice to see M'Clellan at Cincinnati, but failed both times. In June he was appointed Colonel of the 21st Illinois Infantry, and from that moment his new life and his memorable military career began.

On the 7th of August Grant was appointed a Brigadier-General of volunteers. His first great success was the conquest of Fort Donelson, a victory almost as valuable for the North as the victory at Bull Run had been for the South. The glory of Donelson was dimmed by the gloom of Shiloh. The Confederates indeed lost the day. They lost a fine soldier by the death of General Johnston. But the Union losses were heavy; and they were loudly attributed to Grant's carelessness. A strong force of public opinion was exerted against him. Great pressure was put upon Lincoln to order his removal. There is a touching story told of how Lincoln sat and listened in silence for two hours while one of Grant's opponents reiterated the charges of recklessness against him. When Grant's antagonist had said his say, Lincoln still remained silent for a long while, absorbed in thought; then he suddenly and decisively said, 'I can't spare this man. He fights!' This settled the matter. The saying showed as profound a view of the situation and the thing to do, as Lincoln's former declaration of willingness to hold M'Clellan's horse so long as M'Clellan brought success. Grant was allowed to go forward on his victorious way. The cause of the Union would have suffered an irreparable loss if it had been deprived in that hour of Grant's services. Lincoln happily was a wise judge of men. He appreciated the greatness of Grant as clearly as he had appreciated the littleness of Fremont for those purposes for which in that hour greatness was essential and littleness fatal.

The battle of Shiloh, which came so near to staying Grant's career and wrecking his fame, brought prominently before the world the name of another friend, Grant's dearest comrade and lifelong friend, William Tecumseh Sherman. Sherman too was a West Point man. He was still a young man, only forty-one years of age, when the war broke out. He had joined the artillery after leaving West Point, but he had never seen service, and in 1853, with a captain's rank, he had left the army and devoted himself to the business of a banker in San Francisco. The war which had called Grant from his hardware shop and M'Clellan from his railway called Sherman from the superintendence of a military academy founded by the State of Louisiana. His ability was so highly esteemed by the chief men of the State that every inducement was made to persuade Sherman to throw his sword into the scale of the South. But Sherman, a Unionist to the core and an Ohio man by birth, could serve at the same time his belief and his State. He offered his services and his advice to the Government at Washington. The Government at Washington accepted his services and ignored his advice. Sherman insisted in vain on the necessity for preparing for war on a large scale. He had against him the dominant impression on both sides that the war was going to be the affair of a battle or two.

Sherman fought at Bull Run. In the October of 1861, in consequence of the illness of his superior, he assumed the chief command of the army in the department of Kentucky. Once again Sherman gave advice to his Government, but this time it was asked for and this time it was acted upon, though not exactly in the way that Sherman expected. When he was asked by the Secretary of War how many men he should require, he answered that he would want sixty thousand men to drive the enemy out of Kentucky and two hundred thousand to finish the war in that section. His answer was considered absurdly extravagant, and in consequence he was removed from his command in Kentucky. It must be admitted that a cause singularly blessed with able generals did not always know how to make the best use of them. When the battle of Shiloh was fought Sherman was serving with Grant in Tennessee. Grant paid Sherman the highest tribute for his courage and military skill on that day. 'To his individual efforts,' Grant wrote, 'I am indebted for the success of that battle.' From the hour of Shiloh Sherman's star rose. His policy was formulated in his fine saying, 'The people of the

North must conquer or be conquered. There can be no middle course.'

Sheridan, the third of the three great war generals, was the youngest of the three. Born in 1831, he was only thirty years old when the war began. He was educated at West Point like his comrades, but unlike his comrades he never knew any other than the soldier's life. Like Grant and like Sherman he was born in Ohio; like Sherman he knew no active service until the Civil War. But he had all the aptitude and all the training for his career. From the very first he distinguished himself. Again and again Sheridan showed himself to be the soldier of promise who was also the soldier of fulfilment. His fame belongs to the latter part of the war, but his fame began while the war was still in its dreary and often disastrous dawn.

Among the many brave and able soldiers who were not of the first rank one deserves some special mention for the romantic picturesqueness of his too brief career. The story of Philip Kearney's life reads like some fable from the magic pages of Dumas. He might have been of the brotherhood of the immortal guardsmen; he might have stemmed from the splendid adventurers whose bright swords glitter in the hilarious, chivalrous atmosphere of Lever's fiction. He was born in New York in the Waterloo year, in the Waterloo month. While he was still almost a boy he was sent to Europe by his Government to study the tactics of the French cavalry. He served valiantly in Mexico, where he lost his left arm. He resigned his commission and spent several years in Europe. The loss of his arm did not make him any the less a soldier. He entered the French service. He fought under the French flag against the Austrians. He distinguished himself by his daring, and was accorded the Cross of the Legion of Honour on the battlefield of Solferino. When the Civil War began he served the Union as brigadier-general. Sixteen months more of a soldier's life ended at the battle of Chantilly on the first of September in 1862. By the irony of fate Philip Kearney was killed by a shot in the back after a desperate charge that had carried him into the midst of the enemy. Handsome, brilliant, dashing, reckless, he was a splendid type of the adventurous man-at-arms, the man who is a soldier not from necessity of circumstances, but from necessity of temperament. He was a man born to be a fighter, and if not under his own flag then under the next best that flew. The United States had greater and wiser soldiers; it had none more courageous, more high-spirited and high-hearted, more honourable or more true. The cause is fortunate for which such men fight.

CHAPTER XIX

THE WAR AT SEA

SATURDAY, the 8th of March 1862, opened a new era in naval warfare. On that day a battle was fought which revolutionised the navies of the world. When the Norfolk navy yard had been abandoned by the Union forces, they set on fire and sunk the frigate *Merrimac*. The Confederates succeeded in floating the vessel, and proceeded to reconstruct her after a plan new in naval warfare. In 1858 France had made a curious experiment in ship-building. She had built an armour-plated frigate, and England, not to be behind-hand, had built another. The new experiment had not yet been put to any practical test. The time for the test had now come. The Confederates built on the deck of the *Merrimac* a structure of five-inch iron that sloped down her sides like the roof of a house, fitted her with an enormous ram, and sent her forth on her mission to destroy the wooden navy of the North.

The idea of armour-plating was not confined to the engineers of the South. In the North John Ericsson, the great engineer who invented the screw propeller, was hard at work upon an armour-plated ship of his own devising. Time was short; time was precious; the *Merrimac*, rechristened the *Virginia*, was fast building. The *Monitor* ought to be

THE WAR AT SEA

ready as soon as she. In one hundred days Ericsson had his vessel ready for action. She was a turret ship; she was a singular looking vessel; those who first saw her likened her to a cheese-box on a raft. Her low armour deck rose less than two feet above the water; a revolving iron turret on the deck carried two eleven-inch Dahlgren guns. She was only built just in time. Indeed she was not built quite in time.

On Saturday, March 8th, the *Merrimac*, as history must continue to call her, steamed into Hampton Roads, where the United States had a fleet of five wooden ships as fine as any five ships then afloat on any sea. As the *Merrimac* came along, looking like a huge half-submerged crocodile, the five ships, the *Minnesota, St. Lawrence, Roanoke, Congress*, and *Cumberland*, advanced to attack her. The first three ran aground, as the water was low. The *Congress* and the *Cumberland* opened fire upon their strange enemy without the slightest effect. Their shells rebounded from her iron sides as if they had been tennis balls. In a few minutes the fight was over. The *Merrimac* rammed the *Cumberland* with her great beak, knocking a huge hole in her side. The *Cumberland* went down with colours flying, and scarcely a man escaped. The *Congress* was driven aground under a hail of shot, which finally set her on fire. Content with the work for that evening the *Merrimac* returned to her mooring, her officers looking forward to the morning for the destruction of the remaining vessels.

It would be impossible to exaggerate the terror which the telegraph carried to every state and city of the North. What was there that this new marine monster, this death-dealing Leviathan, might not be expected to accomplish? Before the armoured sides and the deadly beak of this terrible prodigy the stately wooden frigates, the splendid ships of which the North was so justly proud, were as worthless as the paper boats that a child floats on a pond. Ministers trembled in Washington, expecting at any moment to see the black horror hurrying along the Potomac, expecting at any moment a shell from one of her guns to shatter the White House. New York feared for her harbour, for her shipping, for the pride of the Empire City at the mercy of this invulnerable engine of destruction. What hope, men asked each other, could there now be of maintaining the great blockade when the *Merrimac*, unscathed herself, could sink every vessel that was unfortunate enough to cross her path?

In the consternation of men's minds, it seemed as if the war was ended. The enemy had conjured up this unconquerable steel devil, and all hope was gone. But while men talked in despair of the danger, the little flat-decked boat with the round revolving turret and the two guns was beating its way from New York through stormy seas to pit the strength of the iron pigmy against the iron giant. Twice it barely escaped shipwreck on its voyage. At ten o'clock on Saturday, the 8th, the *Monitor* arrived at Hampton Roads, and took up its station hard by where the apparently doomed *Minnesota* lay aground waiting like a new Andromeda the coming of the monster.

Early on the morning of Sunday, the 9th, the *Merrimac* quitted her moorings, and steered with the confidence of invincibility for the *Minnesota*. As it began to attack, the *Monitor* made for the *Merrimac* and opened fire upon her. While those on board the mighty *Merrimac* were looking, it may well be believed with amazement, upon the queer sea-creature that was steaming towards her, the *Monitor* hurled against her plated side the heaviest ball that had ever yet been thrown in war. As the *Merrimac* shook with the stroke, the turret of the *Monitor* revolved, and another, and another, and another ball came thumping upon the ringing steel. The blows bruised, but did not break. The giantess made for the pigmy, blazing away with all her might, but her lighter balls glanced off the revolving turret as surely as the heavier shot of the *Monitor* glanced off her own sloping sides.

Again and again the *Merrimac* tried to ram the *Monitor*, but the *Monitor*, with maddening agility, eluded her unwieldy efforts, never receiving more than a glancing blow from her cruel beak, which did no mischief. At one moment of the astonishing fight, the commander of the *Merrimac*, noticing that his guns were silent, asked why they were not being fired. 'Because,' was the answer, 'our powder is very precious, and after two hours' incessant firing I find I can do her about as much damage by snapping my thumb at her every two minutes and a half.'

About noon the fight came to an end. Worden, the Commander of the *Monitor*, was injured and temporarily blinded by a shell which struck the iron pilot-house directly in the sight-hole. The *Monitor* ceased firing, and the *Merrimac*, sorely battered though not disabled, and leaking badly, staggered back to Norfolk. The battle was technically a drawn battle, nominally indecisive. But as it practically ended the *Merrimac* and its course of death and destruction, it must be regarded as very decisive indeed.

Surely there was never a more wonderful battle fought at sea since the world began; never a swifter, more amazing sequence of prodigious events. Holmes might well ask, 'Is it not the age of fables and of heroes and demigods over again?' On one day a sea monster makes its appearance, apparently invincible, apparently invulnerable, a thing that can break blockades like pack-thread, and annihilate navies with irresistible ease; the scourge of every port it chooses to threaten, the doom of every ship it chooses to assail. For four-and-twenty tremendous hours the terror of this awful thing, this sea-dragon whose scales no stroke could pierce, dominates the minds of men. Then, as in a breath, the terror ends, the horror dissipates; the great sea-shaking beast of yesterday is a disdained memory to-day.

That sea-fight was the last of the *Merrimac*; it was also almost the last of the *Monitor*. When in the June of 1862 the Confederates evacuated Norfolk, they destroyed the creature they had themselves re-created. What they had rescued from destruction they gave again to destruction. The *Monitor*, never a good sea-going vessel, foundered in December off Cape Hatteras. Its name remains honoured for ever in the story of the sea. The name of John Ericsson stands high among the highest in the roll of noble citizens who helped to save the Union.

The immediate consequence of this great fight was the doom of the wooden ship. The wooden walls of Old England, the wooden walls of New

THE WAR AT SEA 283

America were of no more avail. In a single day they had been made as antiquated as a Viking's long ship, or a Triumvir's galley. The nations of the world had to set to work to build their fleets anew, and to accept for the sea that armour which had long been abandoned on land.

The April that followed the adventure of the *Merrimac* and the *Monitor* preserved the naval supremacy of the North, in giving another great victory to the war-ships of the Union. A Federal fleet of men-of-war under the command of Admiral Farragut, and of mortar-boats under David D. Porter, captured New Orleans in a very daring and audacious manner. New Orleans, which lies about one hundred miles from the mouth of the Mississippi, was believed by the South to be practically impregnable, defended as it was by the shallowness of the water at the river mouth, and by the strength of the great forts of St. Philip and Jackson seventy-five miles below the city.

After bombarding these forts unsuccessfully for some time, Farragut resolved to try the desperate hazard of running his fleet past the forts. It was one of those daring, rash, and seemingly impracticable and unwise feats which are justified by success and wholly damned by failure. Farragut actually succeeded in getting the greater part of his fleet across the bar, and made straight for New Orleans. A force of Confederate gunboats, hurriedly gathered together to oppose his progress, was soon defeated and destroyed. Nothing was left to New Orleans but surrender. Before it surrendered, its citizens carried all the cotton in the city to the levee and set fire to it. New Orleans was in so far the Moscow of the South. The enemy might hold the city; it should not gain the advantage of its wealth.

The forts that had been so successfully eluded surrendered on the 28th of April. On the 1st of May General Butler occupied New Orleans with two thousand five hundred troops. The capture of New Orleans was of the greatest service to the North. It afforded a basis of operations up the Mississippi. The control of the river as far as Baton Rouge, not far from Vicksburg, was in the hands of the Union government. At the same time the river fleet operating down the river gained two serious victories. Aided by a land force under General Pope, it captured Island Number Ten, an important fortress commanding the Mississippi river. Then the river fleet went on down stream and destroyed the Confederate fleet at Memphis.

Much has been written for and against the behaviour of General Butler during his occupation of New Orleans. It has been said truly of him that whatever his defects as a general, he made an admirable Provost Marshal, and that New Orleans was never healthier than under his rule. But he was not the kind of man to administer a conquered city with a graciousness that might at all soften the sense of defeat in the conquered. He made it plain that he was determined to stand no trifling with his authority, no disrespect to his army or his cause. A man who had the folly to tear down the flag of the Union from the Mint Butler ordered to be shot. He compelled Secessionists to pay money for the support of the poor. The Mayor of New Orleans, Monroe, ventured to be insolent to Butler. Butler showed that he would stand no nonsense by promptly imprisoning the Mayor in Fort Jackson. He armed free coloured men and recruited his army from them.

Of all his actions in New Orleans that which most infuriated the South was the famous order 'that any female who should insult an officer or soldier should be regarded and held liable to be treated as a woman of the town, plying her avocation.' It must be remembered, however, that the Southern women did not at all times restrain their show of hatred and contempt for the Northern soldiers within the bounds of discretion and decorum. Butler believed that men wearing the Federal uniform were spat upon and otherwise insulted in the streets by excitable women, on whom it was impossible for a soldier to retaliate, and he framed the order in the hope of restraining such excitability from overt acts of offence. It is said that the order did produce a restraining effect. It is impossible to justify the acts alleged to have been committed by the women of New Orleans. If they did commit them it was in their own interests that they should be kept from deeds which might in the end provoke rough soldiers beyond their patience. But the order earned Butler the ceaseless hatred of the South. Jefferson Davis went so far as to issue a proclamation in which he branded him as a felon and declared him to be an outlaw, quite in the spirit of the *hors la loi* decrees of the French Terrorists.

In the November of 1862 Butler was relieved from his command and succeeded by General Banks. It is curious to note that when Butler entered New Orleans he was a democrat and an advocate of negro slavery. He came away from New Orleans a radical and a convert to the anti-slavery cause.

Many wild charges of maladministration were brought against him. He was accused of embezzlement, even of theft. For years and years after the war it was a standing joke among Butler's political opponents to associate his name with the word 'spoons,' the implication being that during his occupation of New Orleans he had condescended even to so humble a means of enriching his exchequer. The charge was of a kin with that which during the Franco-German war maintained that every German Uhlan rode on his way with stolen French clocks ticking at his saddle-bow.

The irritation in the United States caused by the affair of the *Trent* was in a large measure calmed even before its settlement by the news of the death of the Prince Consort. The Prince Consort was generally believed then to act, as he is generally known now to have acted, as the sincere advocate of a policy of friendship and good understanding between Great Britain and the United States. His death was undoubtedly a grave loss to all those in England who were supporters of that policy. The indirect influence which the Prince Consort exercised upon the government and the thought of England was never more needed, would never have been better employed, than in the new quarrel between the two countries which sprang up almost immediately after the quarrel over the *Trent* had been allowed to die and be buried.

The quarrel over the *Trent* was trivial in its results compared with the longer and more bitter and more memorable quarrel over the Confederate privateers. Jefferson Davis's announcement of his intention to issue letters of marque had an especially exasperating effect upon the people of the North. It was at one time rumoured that many of the applications for letters of marque came from New York and from people of standing and repute. This has been emphatically denied by those who have searched the actual Confederate records of their privateersmen. If aid and succour for the South had come in this way the matter would have been bad enough. It was much worse that such aid and succour came from a European power, and from that very European power which in the beginning had been suspected by the United States of scarcely-veiled hostility. It is an unfortunate fact that no less than five of the formidable privateers which did so much to destroy the merchant marine of the United States were built in British dockyards. Of these the first was the *Florida*, built at Birkenhead ostensibly for Italy. The American Minister was aware of her true purpose and called the attention of the English Government to her aim, but she was suffered to sail unhindered on her mission of destruction.

The most famous of the English-built privateers was the *Alabama*. The story of the *Alabama* is one of the grimmest stories of the war. Her commander was Raphael Semmes, who entered the United States Navy as a midshipman in 1826, and remained in the service till 1861, when he resigned and joined the Confederate Navy. Her career was the career of a bird of prey, and her quarry were defenceless merchant vessels flying the Federal flag. By the trick of hoisting the Union Jack the *Alabama* was able to get within easy reach of her intended victim ; then the Confederate colours went to the masthead, and the prize was secured. Some seventy vessels were captured and destroyed by the *Alabama* during her two years of piracy. Against all this, of course, the States had no redress except such as they could give themselves. Privateering existed, and if they could not defeat the privateer they must put up with his depredations as best they might. But behind the *Alabama* America saw the hostile strength of England. There was indeed an ironical appropriateness in the fact that its captain, Semmes, when he was to lure some merchant ship to its doom, flew the British flag. The *Alabama* was in point of fact a British ship. She was built by the house of Laird, one of the greatest shipbuilding houses in Great Britain. She was launched from an English dockyard on the Mersey. Her guns and her gunners were English. She was largely manned by Englishmen, and, as has been happily said, she never was in nor even saw a Confederate port.

Nothing of course could be more unfriendly, more opposed to the usage of international law, than for a neutral power to permit such flagrant violations of neutrality. Mr. Adams, the American Minister, while the *Alabama* was building, called the attention of the English Government, and called it in vain, to the fact and to the purpose for which the vessel was intended. While the English Government hesitated, delayed, and, it must be said, equivocated, the *Alabama* was finished and put to sea and steamed on her career of destruction. It must also be said unhappily that her career was followed with admiration and applause by a large portion of the press and the public of England. It is scarcely surprising that with the tacit connivance of the Government to encourage them, and the noisy raptures of certain papers to cheer them, the Confederate Government went on briskly placing orders for privateers with British shipbuilders. It is difficult now to understand how the English Government could have permitted themselves to act with such disastrous folly. Only the assumption that the United States was a bankrupt power, never again likely to hold up its head among the nations of the earth, could—not indeed justify, for the thing was utterly unjustifiable —but even excuse such wanton disregard of the duty of a neutral power.

Once again the American Minister had to call the attention of the English Government to the fact that Confederate privateers were being built in English dockyards. This time the vessels were powerful iron rams made for the express purpose of destroying the blockade. Again and again Mr. Adams brought the matter to the notice of Lord Russell. Again and again Lord Russell put Mr. Adams off with meaningless expressions of incapacity to act. At last the United States made up its mind that this state of things could go on no longer. Its hands were full enough. The seemingly endless struggle with the South dragged on. To risk bringing a new and powerful enemy on its hands was a great risk. But it had to be run. No country of brave men, no country with any respect for its dignity and its place among the nations of the earth could stand tamely by and allow a neutral power to violate neutrality for the benefit of its enemy. Mr. Adams wrote one final despatch to Lord Russell on the matter, a despatch for ever memorable in the history of international diplomacy. In this despatch Mr. Adams informed Lord Russell

T

that one of these iron rams was on the point of departure from Liverpool to harass the United States. 'It would be superfluous in me to point out to your Lordship that this is war.' Mr. Adam's superfluous point ended the matter, and saved the situation. Lord Russell immediately wrote to Mr. Adams that the departure of the two ironclads would be prevented. The departure of the two ironclads was prevented. That ended the building of privateers in British ports for the Confederate service. But it did not end the whole matter as far as England and America were concerned.

The career of the *Alabama* came to an end in time. She fought her one stand-up fight with an equal foe when she fell foul of the Federal warship *Kearsage* off Cherbourg in France. In an hour the Confederate privateer was knocked to pieces, and went to the bottom. Captain Semmes was saved, appropriately enough, by an English steam yacht, the *Deerhound*, belonging to an Englishman. Semmes served the South till the close of the war, and ended his career as a lawyer at Mobile.

If the *Alabama* had run its course, the mischief it had done had yet to be atoned for. Years afterwards, when the States were themselves again, and all danger of that ruin so confidently predicted by false prophets had disappeared, America reminded England that the *Alabama* was to all intents and purposes an English vessel, and that by the law of nations England was responsible for the damage she had done. The English sense of justice was strong enough to show that England had erred, and must make an honourable amend. There was some fear—there need have been no fear—that a war might break out between the two countries over the *Alabama* claims. The claims were referred to international arbitration. A heavy award was made against England. England paid up cheerfully enough, and so the *Alabama* question came to an end.

CHAPTER XX

APPOMATTOX

ON the 22nd of September 1862 Lincoln took a memorable step. He issued a proclamation stating that on the first day of the new year 1863, he would declare free all slaves in any part of the country which should at that time be in rebellion against the United States. It had taken a long time to bring Lincoln to this point. He had clung steadfastly to the statement in his inaugural address that an essential part of the American system was the right of each State to regulate its own domestic institutions according to its own judgment. He had squashed Fremont when Fremont attempted his little experiment in manumission. He had over-ruled General Hunter when Hunter had proclaimed the freedom of the slaves in South Carolina, Florida, and Georgia. He had accepted Butler's 'contraband of war' policy, but this was the furthest he would go for long enough. To him the war was a war to preserve the Union, not a war to liberate the slave. Pressed hard, however, by the strong force of the Abolition movement, and perceiving the opportunity of harassing the rebellious South through its peculiar institution, Lincoln began to move slowly on the road towards emancipation.

In March Lincoln recommended Congress to grant

pecuniary aid to any State which should undertake the gradual abolition of slavery, with compensation to the slave owners. In June of the same year Congress went much further by abolishing slavery in the Territories without compensation, and in July Congress authorised the seizure of slaves of persons then in rebellion. The Emancipation Proclamation of 1863 did not abolish slavery as an institution. It liberated slaves in any portions of the States in insurrection occupied by the Union armies. Missouri in June 1863, and Maryland in October 1864 abolished slavery. The total abolition of slavery was rejected by Congress in 1864, but after Lincoln's re-election to the Presidency, the measure was carried by the necessary two-thirds majority. In December 1865 slavery was legally abolished throughout the Union. If that was not the aim for which the Union went to war, it was the aim for which many persons wished it to pursue the war. Indirectly the cause of secession and of strife, emancipation was the inevitable end of the struggle. Lincoln postponed it, not out of hostility, but because, with his usual sagacity, he chose to wait until the time had arrived when it would do as little harm to the cause of Union and as much harm to the cause of secession as possible.

The war, which in the confident belief of both belligerents was to have ended in a few weeks, lasted exactly four years. At first the fortunes of the Confederates seemed to be in the ascendant. Then victory seemed to alternate, giving and taking with equal hands. Finally the North, through success upon success, established its supremacy. For those four years Virginia was the battle-ground of the

Northern army of the Potomac, defending Washington and seeking to capture Richmond, and of the Southern army of Northern Virginia endeavouring to defend Richmond and to attack Washington. There were battles in the West; there were battles in Tennessee; but Virginia was the great theatre of the war, and in Virginia the drama was played out to the end. While M'Clellan was in command the Confederates roughly speaking had it all their own way, as far as holding Virginia and defending Richmond were concerned. Again and again Stonewall Jackson defeated the Federal forces. Again and again Lee drove back the invading army of the Union. Flushed with victory, Lee carried the war into Carthage. There was a second battle of Bull Run, on the 29th of August 1862, which ended in a second Federal defeat. Then Lee crossed the Potomac near Harper's Ferry. He declared that he was coming to release Maryland from the foreign yoke, but to his disappointment he found that the majority in Maryland had no desire to join the South. M'Clellan met Lee at Antietam, one of the bloodiest battles in the war. The Northern army was double that of the South, but M'Clellan with his usual want of luck or want of tact, wasted his advantage. Lee indeed was driven across the Potomac, but at the cost of terrible loss on the Union side.

M'Clellan was superseded by Burnside, who tried to capture Fredricksburg and failed, again with terrible Union loss. He in his turn was superseded, and the command of the army of the Potomac given to Hooker, known to the army and the public as 'Fighting Joe.' In the June of 1863 Hooker was transferred to Tennessee, and the command of the army of the Potomac given to another West Point general, George G. Meade. Meade, whom Grant called 'the right man in the right place,' was the hero of the battle of Gettysburg, a battle fought on the 1st July. It lasted for three days, it ended in the defeat of Lee, and it contributed very greatly to the final triumph of the Union cause. On the 4th of July, the day after the end of the battle of Gettysburg, the Federal army under Grant captured Vicksburg, the most important Southern post on the Mississippi on account of its batteries, which commanded the river for miles.

Lee, persistently hard pressed by Grant, was resolved to make a desperate attempt to divert him from his steadfast purpose. He ordered one of his ablest lieutenants, Jubal Early, to penetrate the Shenandoah valley in order to attack, and if possible capture, Washington. Once again there was wild alarm in Washington; once again the capital was saved, and largely as before through Confederate delay. Grant sent Sheridan with forty thousand men against Early. Sheridan's orders were to devastate the Shenandoah valley so that no Confederate force could live on it. Sheridan carried out his instructions very thoroughly, though there was a moment when the North came near to suffering a disaster which was only averted by the personal courage and the personal popularity of the Federal general.

Sheridan was at Winchester. He was retiring from the Shenandoah valley, having done his work of devastation, and expecting no further immediate fighting. His army was some twenty miles south of him at Cedar Run. This army was unexpectedly attacked by Early, routed and driven into ignominious flight. Sheridan, all unconscious of disaster, was riding slowly back to join his army when he was met by a messenger with the bad news. He immediately dashed forward at full speed on his famous black horse, met the first of the fugitives, rallied them with fiery, forcible words; bore them back with him as eager to fight again as they had been ready to fly. Defeat was redeemed, the tide of battle turned. Sheridan by his presence and by his words changed a rout into a charge, and led the charge to victory. Early was completely beaten, and put to flight, losing all his prisoners, all the guns he had taken, and nearly all his own guns. A large number of his men were taken prisoners. This battle of the Shenandoah is the most famous of all Sheridan's victories.

The latest day, the not-to-be-avoided hour, was drawing near. The end ought to have come sooner than it came. With the defeat at Gettysburg, with the capture of Vicksburg, the last hope of Southern success was gone. Still the desperate South fought on. Perhaps she hoped against hope that something still would happen to save her independence. Perhaps she knew that there were many in the North who were weary of the war, who were opposed to the war, who were eager that the war should come to an end. There were people in the North who thought that States-rights and the liberty of the citizen were being interfered with for merely military purposes. An angry controversy raged around Lincoln's action in suspending the operation of the writ of Habeas Corpus. The Constitution had made the necessary proviso for the possible suspension of the writ of Habeas Corpus 'in cases of rebellion or invasion,' but it did not expressly state whether the

APPOMATTOX 297

exercise of this suspending power was confined to Congress or was in the hands of the Executive. Lincoln, brought face to face with the need for arresting persons suspected of hostility to the Union, but hard to convict of crimes recognised by the law, acted as if the power of suspension was vested in the Executive. He ordered the suspension of the writ of Habeas Corpus when Congress was not in session.

Like every act of all his administration this met with almost as much censure in the North as in the South. Many honourable, admirable citizens believed that Lincoln had exceeded his constitutional rights, and were not prepared to accept the success of the Union at such a price. It was urged by those who defended Lincoln's action that unless the Executive exercised this function of suspension of the writ of Habeas Corpus it could not be exercised at all in very critical moments. The matter was settled temporarily in 1863, when Congress formally conferred on the President the right to suspend the operation of the writ. Much later the Supreme Court decided that the final decision as to the suspension of the writ in a particular case belongs to the Courts.

There was another element of dissatisfaction in the North, which was made full use of by the friends of the South in the North, and which did much to give the South cheer. This was caused by the Act which Congress passed in 1863 authorising the general Government to have recourse to a draft or conscription to swell the ranks of the armies. Conscription is always and inevitably unpopular in a country where conscription is not part of the established law of the land. The Copperhead Democrats, who were named after the satellite of the rattlesnake, the emblem of the South, made themselves busy in a crusade against the draft. Their efforts resulted in riots in New York which lasted for days, and left the city at the mercy of the rioters. The municipality were of Copperhead inclining, and little was done to stay the rioting, which was culminating in arson and in murder. At last the 7th Regiment came from Pennsylvania to New York and made short sharp work of the rioters. There was rioting in Boston too against the draft, which was severely suppressed by the 11th Massachusetts. The worst of these unpatriotic protests against the necessity and duty of the Government was the encouragement they gave to the defeated South. They led Secession to believe that it had powerful friends in the enemy's camp, that the traitors in the North were more influential than as a matter of fact they were.

These ceaseless dissensions in the North did much to encourage the South in its protracted resistance. Undaunted by Vicksburg, unconvinced by Gettysburg, they still fought on. It would have been better for them if they had been less valiant; but, had they been less valiant, history would have lost what is perhaps the most interesting, as it is the least tragic, episode in the whole war—the episode of which Sherman is the hero, the episode of the March to the Sea.

The city of Atlanta, one of the last hopes of the South, long threatened by Sherman, was, in September, abandoned by the Confederates. Sherman immediately divided his army. He sent rather less than half his force to deal with the Confederate army retiring from Atlanta, while with rather more than half, all picked men and hardened veterans in light marching order, he prepared to carry out a long cherished scheme. This was the March to the Sea. It was a dangerous experiment, but it might be and it proved to be worth the risk. It would be hard indeed for opinion in the North, for any opinion in Europe, to believe in the enduring power of the Confederacy if a Federal army could march at its pleasure through the heart of the country. If successful it would further result in the evacuation of the seaports still remaining in the hands of the Confederates. So long as Grant could keep Lee employed, and Federal Thomas hold Confederate Hood in hand, the enterprise had every prospect of success. After due consideration Grant gave his consent to the attempt, and Sherman went on his eventful way. Sherman regarded his march as a shift of base, as the transfer of a strong army which had no opponent, and had then finished its work, from the interior to a point on the sea-coast, from which it could achieve other important results. He was not decided as to the special point on the seaboard he should arrive at, but he made his calculations to meet the Union fleet in the neighbourhood of Ossabaw Sound.

Sherman and his men set off, absolutely in high spirits, as if they were schoolboys on a holiday, to march through Georgia, cutting, as has been effectively said, a swathe sixty miles wide as they went. Many of Sherman's men were skilled railway mechanics. The skill that could be used to build railways could also be used to destroy railways. The whole of the railroad system along Sherman's line of march was so completely destroyed that it could not be repaired again until after the war. The adventure was completely successful, and was carried out with exceptional humanity. The soldiers lived in the country they marched through, but they behaved well, and the rights of private property were on the whole respected. The march was, as Colonel Dodge says, the one thoroughly enjoyable operation of the war. 'The weather was bright, and everything tended to give the whole affair the aspect of a frolic.' Sherman compelled the evacuation of Savannah and of Charleston. He entered in turn Columbia in South Carolina and Goldsboro' in North Carolina. In the meantime Thomas had annihilated Hood's army. The South was at its last gasp.

The capture of Charleston was followed in the next month by Grant's final movement against Richmond. Between Grant and Sheridan, Lee's army was hopelessly pressed. Lee recognised the impossibility of saving the capital. He sent a message to Jefferson Davis, who made his escape, only to be captured a little later in Georgia. Richmond was swiftly evacuated, and was occupied by the Unionist troops. The Confederacy was without a capital; it was soon without an army. Lee in full retreat, hotly pursued by Sheridan, surrendered to Grant at Appomattox on the 9th of April 1865. The great Civil War was at an end. It had cost a vast amount of lives. It had cost a vast amount of money. It had carried mourning into every family in the Union and in the Confederacy. It had left behind it bitter feelings that it took a generation to soften. But it had two great results.

It decided once for all that the United States constituted a nation, and not a confederacy of sovereign States. It cleansed the American continent from the stain of negro slavery. So many brave lives on both sides of the struggle had not been given in vain.

Four years of war had come and gone since Lincoln had been elected President of the United States. The time had come when the States must choose a new President or re-elect the old one. The old President was not, unfortunately, to be re-elected without protest. There were all along many men of Lincoln's own party who were discontented with him. They had grumbled at his slowness in urging emancipation. They had grumbled at his audacity in dealing with States' rights and citizens' rights. They had grumbled at every act and every word of his since he had come into office, and since the war had begun. These men and their kind were resolved to make a try to get a President more after their own heart. Their choice was appropriate; it had the curious felicity commended by the poet. The factious Republican party nominated for their President John C. Fremont, the brave, vain, foolish, showy man of the Missouri fiasco, the man whose wife had assured Lincoln that if ever Fremont were to pit himself against Lincoln, it was Lincoln who would have to go down. The hour had come, but the man was not equal to the hour. Fremont did pit himself against Lincoln—for a short time—and Lincoln did not go down.

The Democratic party not unnaturally made haste to oppose Lincoln's re-election. They insisted that the war had been a failure—an argument that should have sounded coldly in ears still dizzy with the noise of Vicksburg and Gettysburg—and with an unconscious irony they selected for their candidate General M'Clellan. Even M'Clellan could not fail to see that there was something preposterous in his candidature being supported by statements that the war was a failure. At least he had the grace to say that for his part he did not think that the war was a failure. He went on with his candidature however. Fremont, finding that he had not the slightest chance, did one wise thing. He withdrew from the contest. The battle therefore was between Lincoln and M'Clellan, and Lincoln won the day, and swept the country by a splendid majority. When he first took office, four years earlier, he was the representative of a minority, he was in one of the most uncomfortable positions that a statesman can occupy. He resumed his office as the representative of every State in the Union with the exception of his native State, Kentucky, of Delaware, and of New Jersey. In the fulness of time the American Republic had learned to understand and to appreciate the genius, the patience, the far-seeing wisdom, the wise, the strong, the gentle statesmanship of Abraham Lincoln. It chose him with a glad heart to rule it for four years more. *Si qua fata aspera rumpat.*

CHAPTER XXI

AMERICA VICTRIX

THERE is a legend that Lincoln was a dreamer and a believer in dreams. It is said that on the 14th of April 1865 he told his Cabinet that he had a dream which seemed to him in some way significant of imminent danger. On the evening of the same day Lincoln with his wife and some friends went to Ford's Theatre in Washington to see a performance of 'Our American Cousin.' The audience was startled by the sound of a shot in the President's box. The next moment a man leapt on to the stage holding a dagger, shouted 'Sic Semper Tyrannis,' and disappeared. The man was a crazed actor named Wilkes Booth. He had just killed Lincoln. The heroic life was rounded by the martyr's death.

The assassin escaped from the theatre. Lamed by his leap to the stage he was still able to mount a horse and ride into the country. He was tracked and pursued by troops. He took refuge in a barn. The barn was set on fire, and Wilkes Booth was shot down by the light of the flames. Booth's crime was part of a conspiracy. On the same night that Lincoln was murdered Secretary Seward was attacked in his own house and badly wounded, but not killed.

Lincoln was buried with a nation's lamentations.

The joy for the great peace was overshadowed by grief for the great dead. At least it was consolation to remember that the end had not come too soon. Lincoln's life had been threatened many times; many times his assassination had been elaborately planned. Lincoln was a wise man, and he took, or allowed to be taken for him, all precautions to preserve his life. He had work to do and he was eager to do it, and he was not willing to offer his life lightly to the assassin. At one time his life was in as much jeopardy as if he had been a Czar of Russia and not an American President. But he was a brave man, and the danger once guarded against did not prey upon his mind as it preyed upon the mind of Cromwell. He did his great work in his great way, and when violent death at last took him unawares, it found him ready for his rest. He had saved the Union. He had freed the slave. What was there left for him to do which could add a glory to that record? He died the death of Cæsar, of William the Silent, of Henri Quatre, of Gustavus the Third. He ceased to live, but he had lived. His death no less than his life linked him with the leaders of the world.

For fourteen days America mourned for Lincoln, while the nations of the earth mourned for America. The loss was not to be made good. Lincoln was one of those rare spirits that Fate sometimes accords to a country in that country's hour of greatest need. The elements were well mixed in him. The strength and gentleness, the kindness of heart and firmness of will, the simple dignity of nature, the lofty intellect, the fine balance of judgment, the wide reach of intelligence, the unfailing knowledge of human character, the generous refreshing sense of humour, the wisdom, the humanity, had united to make Lincoln great among great men. Now he lay buried at Oakridge, near Springfield in Illinois, and the saddened country turned to the work it had to do. There was much to do.

In accordance with the law, the Vice-President Andrew Johnson became President. A vehement, pugnacious man, he proved a vehement pugnacious President. Johnson began life as an illiterate tailor's apprentice. He learned to read when he was ten. He could not write at all until his marriage, nor with ease until he had been in Congress. He was a self-made man, whose dogged determination to succeed had brought with it its measure of success. He had been the bitter enemy of secession. He had been hated and threatened in the South. He had held off a hostile mob in Liberty, Virginia, with his pistol. He was undoubtedly a strong man, but he was certainly not a discreet man. He was called upon to fill a most difficult position, and the demand was too much for him. It had been feared from the fury of his old assaults upon secession that he would be relentless in his punishment of the conquered South. To all men's wonder he was found too prompt to err in the other way.

The question what was to be done with the conquered South agitated all minds. Had the rebel States unstated themselves by secession? Were they so many subjugated appanages of the Federal government? As a Territory becomes a State when it enters the Union, so some men argued that a State by leaving the Union becomes a Territory again. The Congressional theory was that the mutinous States were outside the Federal law and could only be privileged to come within its pale again at the pleasure of the sovereign Congress. To the surprise of every one Johnson took a view more lenient to the South. The man who had been burnt in effigy so many times in the cities of the South was ready to let the Southern States return to the Union at once on their acceptation of abolition and their promise of obedience to the Constitution.

The result of this difference of opinion was a long and bitter struggle between the President and the Congress. The world was offered the unseemly sight of a President stumping the States to denounce his own Congress; of a Congress impeaching its President for flagrant crimes against the State. In the end Johnson was acquitted for want of the necessary two-thirds majority, but Congress was successful in enforcing its plan for the reorganisation of the South. The Southern legislatures that had been recognised by Johnson were ignored by Congress. The Southern States were grouped in five military districts, under military commanders empowered to conduct the process of reconstruction. Reconstruction was revolutionary, but it was not rapid. While it altered the whole conditions of life in the South, it was not until the January of 1871, five years after the war had ended, that all the States were once more represented in Congress, and that the Union was again complete. Three new amendments had been added to the Consitution in this time. The thirteenth amendment abolished slavery. The fourteenth amendment made all persons born or naturalised in the United States citizens of the United States. The fifteenth amendment laid it down that the right of citizens to vote should not be denied or abridged on account of race, colour, or previous servitude.

It was inevitable that the South should feel bitterly its defeat. It was inevitable that it should resent the consequences of its defeat. It was inevitable that it should chafe at the altered circumstances which converted a race of slaves into a body of free men able to vote against, and often to outvote, their former masters. But the South had played a game and lost it, and had to pay the stakes. Unsuccessful secession meant military occupation. The vicious system of slavery brought its own punishment with the emancipation of the slave. To the onlooker it is plain that the North proved a generous victor. It was confidently expected in Europe that the conqueror would deal sharply with the conquered. It was believed that the leaders at least of the secessional movement might be condemned to death. There were plenty of people in Europe who would not have been in the least surprised if the North had redeemed the pledge given in the old marching song of 'John Brown's Body,' to 'hang Jeff Davis on a sour apple-tree.' European expectation was not justified. The rebel leaders' lives were never in danger from their magnanimous foe. Jefferson Davis suffered only a term of imprisonment, and lived long years after to write the story of his brief, amazing rule. Only imprisonment, only deprivation of the rights of citizenship, were the punishments meted out by the Union to the men who had tried to destroy the Union.

It took of course a long time for the South to settle down into the new conditions of prosperity and peace that were awaiting her. It took a long time for her to discover that free labour was better than servile labour, that her possibilities of wealth were not limited to cotton plantations, that her resources in coal and iron were magnificent, that she might hope to compete with the North in her manufactures. It took a long time for all feeling of anger against secession to die away in the North. The South for a time was a chaos of aggressive blacks, assertive carpet-baggers, and mysterious secret associations like the Ku-Klux Klan, formed to fight the one and to frustrate the other. In the North the tardiness of the South to accept the new order with submission prompted fiery orators like Wendell Phillips to express the wish that the South might once again raise her mailed hand in rebellion in order that the rebellious spirit might be again and finally stamped out. Time the Consoler, as in Voltaire's tender, melancholy story, soothed all these sorrows and angers. More than a generation has passed since the war spent its fever, and the men of to-day have forgotten the enmities and forgiven the errors of their sires.

When the Civil War was scarcely over, before the words North and South represented again only two geographical distinctions and not two hostile powers, when the term United States was scarcely yet a truth and not a mockery, the victorious North had to address itself to a foreign power that had allowed itself to become involved, unwisely and unjustly, in the affairs of America. At a time when the fortunes of the North seemed at their ebb, France and England had united with Spain to compel Mexico to pay her national debt. England and Spain withdrew from the alliance very soon, and Louis

Napoleon was left to work out his own destruction in his own way. Full of his insane conviction that the days of the United States were numbered, and that the Monroe Doctrine was the deadest of dead letters, Napoleon proceeded to execute the craziest scheme ever entertained by an amateur empire maker.

He regretted the old days when the Lilies of France floated over so wide an area of the American continent. He believed that the Napoleonic Bees might at least swarm upon the shores of the Gulf of Mexico. He took advantage of certain French claims upon Mexico to land a French army in Mexico, and to conquer the country for the time being. Of course the American Government protested, but their hands were overfull; they could do no more than protest, and Louis Napoleon paid no heed. The hour seemed to him propitious for the foundation of a Mexican Empire. He declared Mexico to be an Empire. He induced the Archduke Maximilian, brother of the Emperor of Austria, to wear the newly-fashioned imperial crown. He ringed the new Emperor about with French troops to ensure the solidity of his throne. He assured his friends that he regarded the Mexican Empire as the greatest creation of his reign.

Yet in a little while the Mexican Empire was in the dust, and its unhappy Emperor in his grave. When the tide turned in the cause of the Union, when the Confederate general had surrendered his sword at Appomattox, when the Confederate President was a prisoner, the American Government was free to remember Mexico and the Monroe Doctrine. The French Minister at Washington was informed by Seward that the United States desired the withdrawal of the French troops from Mexico. At the same time a significant movement of United States troops, under the command of Sheridan, was made in the direction of the Mexican frontier. France instantly and absolutely gave way. The French troops were promptly withdrawn from Mexico. The poor puppet Emperor was left unguarded to his fate.

His fate soon came. The Mexicans rose against him the moment the French troops had gone. He was as chivalrous as he was misled. He tried to raise an army for himself. He made a vain fight for his throne. When he first came to Mexico, acting under the bad advice of the French General Bazaine, he had decreed that all who resisted his authority in arms should be shot. Under this shameful decree Mexican officers, rightfully resisting the invasion of a foreign prince, were treated like traitors. When the Mexicans won the day they remembered this unpardonable offence. Maximilian suffered, as Murat suffered, by his own decree. He was tried by court-martial and shot. That was the end of the Mexican Empire, and of an Emperor who deserved a better fate.

When Johnson's turbulent, grotesque Presidency came to a close the unanimous Republican party chose the victorious captain of the war for their candidate. Grant was elected to the Presidency. He held the office for two terms from 1869 to 1877. His administration was one of recuperation and reconstruction. The solidified Union laboured to repair the losses of the war, and to qualify itself for the great career that it desired and deserved. In the celebration of the centenary of 1777 the United

States renewed their glorious youth. On the whole Grant's was a successful administration. Its efforts to promote peace may well be permitted to atone for some unhappy scandals of executive and legislative corruption.

While Grant was in office the world was reminded that the great Republic had still to deal with a difficulty and to face a danger that taxed and threatened the companions of John Smith and the companions of Miles Standish. The red man still remained. As American civilisation moved ever further and further west, it drove the red man before it, absorbing his hunting-grounds, setting up noisy cities in his ancient solitudes, cooping him ever closer and closer in special reservations. In the long struggle between the white man and the red it would be vain to say that the red man has always been treated well or justly. It was Grant's wish that the ever-present Indian question should be dealt with and answered by kindness and by justice. The Indians were hard to deal with. A quarrel with the Sioux Indians in 1876 over a reservation ended in a calamity as great as any in the days of Philip, or the days of Pontiac. At the battle of the Little Big Horn, General George Custer and all who were with him were cut off and massacred by Sitting Bull's Sioux. Two hundred and sixty-two men rode with Custer into the multitude of their enemies. Not one man came out alive. Custer was one of the bravest of soldiers, a famous Indian fighter, feared and revered by his red enemies, loved by his soldiers and his friends. The Indians called him 'Long Yellow Hair.' He died a soldier and brave, facing fearful odds in one of the most terrible fights of the few against the many that the world records. His brother died with him, and Rain-in-the-Face, revenging an old grudge, cut out Tom Custer's heart from his warm body and ate it. The memory of that day is one of the darkest of all the stories of the Indian wars.

Grant's successor was another republican, Rutherford Birchard Hayes, an Ohio lawyer, who had served well as a soldier during the Civil War, and served well as a politician in Congress. There was a very bitter quarrel over the legality of his election, which at one time seemed to rise to the height of threatening civil war. The quarrel left a very angry feeling behind it, which even the wisely conciliatory policy of Hayes could not assuage. Hayes deserves great credit for completing Grant's policy of withdrawing the United States troops from the States that had seceded, a policy that was justified by the result. Hayes, who had announced from the first that he would not seek re-election, was succeeded by another republican, who was like him an Ohio man, a lawyer, and a soldier of the war, James Abram Garfield.

Garfield's story offers one of the most extreme illustrations of the opportunity offered to ability by the American Republic. He was born in the Ohio wilderness in 1831. He had lived from his boyhood the rough frontier life. He had been schooled in a log hut, inured to labour on a farm, tempered to fortitude by varied experiences as a canal-boat hand, as a carpenter, as a harvester, as a labourer at any kind of manual labour that would bring him the money necessary for the education of his mind. Few men have ever worked harder than Garfield, or worked with better result. Doggedly, persistently, and cheerfully he taught himself, slowly and patiently he earned and put by enough money to pay others to teach him. In 1854 he entered Williams College, and graduated with the highest honours in 1856. His toil bore its fruit in successive advance. He became President of Hiram College in Ohio. He was elected to the Senate of his State. When the Civil War broke out he volunteered, greatly distinguished himself, and earned the rank of Brigadier-General. He left the army in 1863 to enter the House of Representatives, where he soon became a prominent man. Seventeen years of active public life brought him to the Presidency, with every prospect of an honourable and useful career before him. He had not been four months in office when he was shot and mortally wounded by a disappointed office-seeker, whose disappointment seems to have turned his brain. The fine life ended untimely by a madman's hand.

Garfield was succeeded by the Vice-President, Chester Allan Arthur. One great event of Arthur's administration was the passage of an Act for the reformation of the Civil Service. Another was the completion of the great Brooklyn Bridge, one of the engineering wonders of the world. It spans the wide East River, and links the millions of New York City with the millions of Brooklyn City in one gigantic metropolis.

A reaction against long dominant republicanism gave a democratic successor to Arthur in Grover Cleveland of Buffalo. He was forty-eight years old. He had been a clerk in a country store. He had been a teacher in the New York Institution for the blind. He had been a clerk in a Buffalo law firm.

He was admitted to the bar in 1859. He played no part in the war. Two of his brothers were in the army. He had a mother and sisters dependent upon him. With great difficulty he raised a loan and bought himself a substitute. For many years he followed his career of growing success as a lawyer. In 1881 he was elected Mayor of Buffalo. He was elected Governor of New York in 1883. His earnestness in promoting measures of administrative reform earned him the approval not merely of his own party, but of a number of the Republicans who were more earnest in that direction than their own party candidate. The alliance of these Republicans with the Democratic party exalted Cleveland to the Presidency.

Cleveland's administration was not very eventful. It was chiefly devoted to the discussion of the tariff question. It was followed by a returning wave of Republicanism, which defeated Cleveland and returned Benjamin Harrison, a grandson of Tippecanoe Harrison, the President for a month. When Harrison's calm administration came to an end, Cleveland was nominated again and elected. This was the first time in the history of the United States that any President had been elected for a second term with the administration of another President intervening between the first and second term. It was also the first time since the Civil War that a Democratic President could count upon a Democratic majority in the House of Representatives and a Democratic majority in the Senate.

Cleveland's new administration was as vexed and turbulent as his former administration had been calm. He was confronted on his entry into office with the question of Hawaii. Harrison had concluded a treaty for the annexation of Hawaii, with a provisional goverment that had been established in the island. Cleveland found that this provisional government had been bolstered into existence by the unjust action of the United States. He was resolute to repair the injustice. He refused to submit the treaty of annexation to the Senate, and he advocated the restoration of the Hawaiian queen and the status before the establishment of the provisional government. He had to deal with a grave financial crisis. He had to deal with a grave question of tariff. He had to deal with a difficulty more directly dangerous than either of these, the labour war of 1894.

There was a strike of the persons employed by the Pullman Palace Car Company, one of those vast organisations incidental to the vastness of America, whose administration is as important and as difficult as the administration of many a European State. The strike spread over a wide area, covering many of the railroads entering Chicago. Whatever the rights of the strikers, their action threatened to jeopardise the peace and the order of the whole State of Illinois. Travel, commerce, the distribution of the mails, were partially paralysed or brought altogether to a standstill. For a while, what seemed like a state of revolution ruled in Illinois. President Cleveland faced the difficulty boldly. He despatched a large force of Federal troops to Chicago to remove obstructions to the mails and inter-state commerce, to enforce the law, and to disperse unlawful assemblages. The Governor of Illinois and the Mayor of Chicago were both in sympathy with the strikers. They protested against the presence of the Federal troops. Cleveland justified his action by a reference to the constitution, declined to argue the matter further with the Governor and put down the disturbances.

At one period of Cleveland's administration the relations between England and the United States were strained as they had not been strained since the time of the *Alabama* trouble. The dispute arose over Venezuela and her boundary. For more than half a century there had been difficulties between Great Britain and Venezuela as to the boundary line between the South American State and British Guiana. Rich gold mines had been discovered in the debatable land which England claimed, and gave it an increased value to both claimants. The American Government had for a long time been trying to induce the English Government to submit the whole question to arbitration. The English contention was that the matter concerned England and Venezuela alone, and that America had no right to interfere in the matter. The United States reminded England that the forcible increase of territory of any European power in the New World was a violation of the Monroe Doctrine. The argument grew keen, even acrimonious. President Cleveland issued a famous message which did something more than hint that the United States would go to war in defence of the Monroe Doctrine. Happily the quarrel did not pass beyond the stage of words. Arbitration was agreed to, and a stormy episode ended, as it was right that it should end, in amity between the English-speaking nations.

The Presidential contest of 1896 was fought in the main on the great question of gold and silver. The question was whether a gold standard of coinage should be maintained, or whether there should be a free and unlimited coinage of silver. The question divided the Republican party. It divided the Democratic party. It practically created two new parties, the Gold party and the Silver party. The Gold party chose for their candidate William M'Kinley. M'Kinley was an Ohio man. He had served well in the war. He was, one might almost say of course, a lawyer. He had been in public life since 1877. He was famous as the author of the M'Kinley Bill, which revised in a spirit of protection the duties on imports. He had once and again made a very successful Governor of Ohio. He was a powerful and impressive public speaker. The Silver party took for its champion William J. Bryan, known as the Boy Orator of Nebraska from his youthful appearance and his remarkable eloquence. If a skilful phrase could have settled the matter the struggle would have ended when Bryan declared that his opponents should not be allowed to crucify humanity upon a cross of gold. The contest was perhaps the most serious and the most strenuous in the story of the Republic. It ended with the triumph of the Gold party and the election of M'Kinley.

At the moment in which this brief record must close, the United States of America have successfully ended their third war with a European power. The island of Cuba, which Columbus discovered on his first voyage, and in whose great cathedral his bones were laid to rest, had been for more than half a century a thorn in the side of the American Government. Under the dominion of Spain the island suffered, as Spain's colonies always suffered. Stupid mismanagement was accompanied by brutal oppression. Incapacity for administration provoked a discontent that was only met by merciless severity. Again and again the unhappy people of Cuba rose against their tyrants. Again and again their insurrections were beaten bloodily down. The condition of Cuba was a disgrace to civilisation. America naturally felt most keenly its shame and horror. Cuba lies at America's Southern gate. A few brief miles of water divide it from Florida. Havannah faces New Orleans across the Gulf of Mexico. No wonder if Cuba turned again and again to her great neighbour, imploring succour, imploring at least the recognition of her belligerency in her ceaseless insurrections against Spanish rule. No wonder if again and again filibustering expeditions were secretly fitted out in America. No wonder if again and again American sympathy urged its governments to do something, anything for the relief of the unfortunate country.

In 1854 America proposed to buy the island from Spain, and Spain made answer that the sale of Cuba would be the sale of Spanish honour itself. The years went on and the story of Cuba grew grimmer. Filibuster after filibuster swooped down upon the coast, fought his brief fight, and flung away his life in the cause of Cuban freedom. Insurrection after insurrection kept the torch of war burning like a sacred fire. Spanish governor after Spanish governor sought by intensifying the ferocity of his predecessor's rule, and sought in vain, to stamp out the last spark of rebellion in the land, the last hope of freedom in the land's children. America looked on and was patient, faithful to a policy of non-intervention. In 1873 an American schooner, the

Virginius, conveying arms to the Cuban insurgents was captured. Its American captain and many American sailors were shot by the Spanish authorities in spite of American protests. For a moment war seemed imminent. Then Spain expressed her regret for what had happened, and agreed to pay an indemnity which she never did pay. The matter passed into a memory in the minds of American people, a memory with the burden of 'Remember the *Virginius*,' a burden hereafter to be changed from one ship's name to another.

For yet a quarter of a century the bloodshed and the cruelty persisted. The insurgents maintained unceasingly their guerilla war, their straggling revolution. The Spanish governors made new essays in the art of oppression. With the end of that quarter of a century came the end of oppression. America's attention was forcibly called to some fresh horrors of Spanish administration. America might not have intervened even then if something ominous had not happened. The American warship the *Maine* was mysteriously blown up in the harbour of Havannah. Careful inquiry made it plain that she had been so blown up by the springing of a submarine mine fired by some unknown hand. A great wave of anger swept over the States. It was no longer 'Remember the *Virginius*' now but 'Remember the *Maine*.' The destruction of the *Maine*, like the firing on Fort Sumter, made war inevitable. Spain would do nothing, promise nothing, perform nothing for the better treatment of Cuba. All she would do was to declare war upon the United States.

The war lasted three months. It left Spain with

a few ruined hulks of what had been a navy; with the remnants of what had been an army of occupation. It took from her the colonies for which she had sinned, and suffered, and struggled. It gave the United States their third triumph over one of the great powers of Europe. It gave her the control of Cuba. It gave her the control of the fate of the Philippines. It gave her a renewed confidence in her army, her navy, and her resources. She had added new names and new lustre to her roll-call of brave men. She had struck her stroke in the cause of freedom, in the cause of humanity, remembering that whenever any form of government becomes destructive of a people's rights to life, liberty, and the pursuit of happiness, it is not merely the right of the people to alter or abolish it, but the right of the strong to help the weak.

FOOTNOTE

To attempt to record my gratitude for help of books and writers would be to draw up a catalogue from Bancroft to Sterne. But I must speak with a personal affection of the monumental labours of Justin Winsor, the living pages of Fiske, the pure and luminous prose of Wentworth Higginson, the vigour and earnestness of Roosevelt, the lucidity and learning of Draper and Rhodes and Ropes and Eggleston and Channing. America is rich in admirable single volume histories of the country. Every student must have a thankful regard for the volumes of *American History told by Contemporaries*, edited by Albert Bushnell Hart.

www.ingramcontent.com/pod-product-compliance
Lightning Source LLC
Chambersburg PA
CBHW021204230426
43667CB00006B/557